The Undying Greek

Greek magic is the foundation and cornerstone of almost every form of ceremonial magic being practiced today. As if that were not enough, elements of Greek philosophy summarize the bulk of modern esoteric thought and occult teachings. Even the ubiquitous cabala—Christianized by Renaissance admirers of Plato and Plotinus—contains many features that appear to be Greek in origin.

This book explains in plain, informal language the grand sweep of Greek magic and Greek philosophical and religious concepts from the archaic period of Homer's *Iliad* right down to the present. From the plains of Troy to the streets of Los Angeles, Greek magic is alive and well.

For the practicing magician, rituals are given that incorporate the elements from each historical period that is discussed. These ceremonies may be easily adapted for Pagan or Wiccan practice or otherwise altered to suit the individual operator.

Our story begins with the magic and mythology of the days of classical Athens and its antecedent cultures, with an examination of the question of matriarchy versus patriarchy allotted a chapter of its own. We then pass to the Hellenistic age of Alexander's conquests and the later Roman domination. This leads directly into detailed considerations of Gnosticism, early Christianity, and Neoplatonism—all phenomena with a Greek foundation and a literature that is chiefly in the Greek language. The Renaissance revival of Neoplatonism and mythology is discussed, and at last we come to modern times—the Greek elements of the magic of the Golden Dawn, Aleister Crowley, and groups that are operating at the present moment.

An appendix presents the fascinating study of *isopsephos*—Greek "gematria" or letter-number mysticism. It includes an abbreviated dictionary of Greek words and names that are important in classical mythology, Gnosticism, the Greek New Testament, and Neoplatonism.

No one who has any interest in magic, occultism, or hermetic thought and who is also a citizen of Western civilization can afford to ignore this heritage.

About the Author

David Godwin, born in 1939 in Dallas, Texas, and a one-time resident of Houston, Atlanta, Miami, and New York, is a student of esoteric lore, magic, and the cabala. He holds a Bachelor of Journalism degree from the University of Texas at Austin.

The author of *Godwin's Cabalistic Encyclopedia* and compiler of the index to the current edition of Israel Regardie's *The Golden Dawn*, Godwin's articles have appeared in *Gnostica, Llewellyn's Magickal Almanac,* and elsewhere.

Godwin has worked as a manual laborer, a newspaper reporter, an editor for a petrochemical magazine, a technical editor for two NASA contractors during the Apollo missions, a typesetter, and a free-lance writer. He is currently senior editor at Llewellyn Publications.

To Write to the Author

We cannot guarantee that every letter written to the author can be answered, but all will be forwarded. Both the author and the publisher appreciate hearing from readers, learning of your enjoyment and benefit from this book. Llewellyn also publishes a bi-monthly news magazine with news and reviews of practical esoteric studies and articles helpful to the student, and some readers' questions and comments to the author may be answered through this magazine's columns if permission to do so is included in the original letter. The author sometimes participates in seminars and workshops, and dates and places are announced in *The Llewellyn New Times.* To write to the author, or to ask a question, write to:

David Godwin
c/o THE LLEWELLYN NEW TIMES
P.O. Box 64383-285, St. Paul, MN 55164-0383, U.S.A.

Please enclose a self–addressed, stamped envelope for reply, or $1.00 to cover costs.

Llewellyn's Western Magick Historical Series

#
LIGHT IN EXTENSION

Greek Magic from Homer to Modern Times

David Godwin

1992
Llewellyn Publications
St. Paul, Minnesota 55164-0383, U.S.A.

FIRST EDITION

Cover design by Christopher Wells
Map by Lisa Peschel

Library of Congress Cataloging-in-Publication Data
Godwin, David.
    Light in extension: Greek magic from Homer to modern times /
David Godwin
      p. cm. — (Llewellyn's western magick historical series)
     ISBN 0-87542-285-3
     1. Magic, Greek—History. I. Title. II. Series.
    BF1622.G8G63 1991
    133.4'3'0938—dc20   91-867
                                               CIP

Llewellyn Publications
A Division of Llewellyn Worldwide, Ltd.
P.O. Box 64383, St. Paul, MN 55164-0383

Llewellyn's Western Magick Historical Series

Weird shadows flicker over the figure of the Cro-Magnon shaman as he dances around the primitive campfire clad in deerskin and antlers. Sumerian magi study the sky and wonder. Greek nobles sacrifice sheep in attempts to speak with the wise who are no longer living, while their philosophers formulate ideas of mysticism that will dominate Western thought for two thousand years. In the Renaissance, an alchemist works his spiritual advancement through chemical analogs; a magus studies navigation and mechanics along with angelic communication; a member of the old religion, still called "witch" and thought to be evil by the established church, tends her healing herbs. Later, secret fraternities plot the overthrow of oppressive monarchies—and succeed in the French and American revolutions. Men and women band together in societies to practice magick or study unknown philosophies. The Age of Aquarius dawns as attention is focused on the deeper realities.

In an unbroken stream from that primordial campfire to the modern magickal awakening, a deeper reality continues to assert itself. Historians have tended to ignore magick and the occult as unworthy of serious study, yet how much of world history has been molded by the beliefs and practices of shamans, wise men, magi, astrologers, witches, alchemists, and adepts? From its roots in tribal practices, through the stargazing of the Chaldeans and the esoteric mathematics of Pythagoras, the mysteries of the *I Ching,* and the secrets of yogis and tantrists, magick became one of the noblest of the arts and sciences. Occult thought and philosophy were one and the same. The mystic ideas of the Greek philosophers, mixed with the qabala and other secret traditions, fed the Renaissance revival and led directly to modern scientific thought as well as New Age occultism. Only within the last two centuries has science become the religion of rationalism and sought vainly to divorce itself from its roots — roots that continually appear in new guises such as quantum physics and cosmology.

Llewellyn's Western Magick Historical Series will attempt to trace the myriad pathways that began with shamans and seers before recorded history and that lead in branching but continuous trails to the occult revival of the last decade of the our own century. The roots and the realities will not go unrecorded nor be forgotten.

Also by David Godwin

Godwin's Cabalistic Encyclopedia

Acknowledgments

Despite having my name on the title page, this book does not represent the isolated efforts of one person. I would like to extend special thanks to Osborne Phillips for his kind and extremely helpful advice, not only on the Aurum Solis, but also concerning several of the topics covered in this book. His counsel proved to be invaluable. Special thanks are due to G. M. Kelly for performing the onerous job of meticulously proofreading the section on *isopsephos*. Much thanks also to Donald Tyson and to Phyllis Galde for pointing out some of my errors and oversights. Thanks are likewise due to Thorsons Ltd. for their generous permission to reprint portions of rituals from Dolores Ashcroft-Nowicki's *The Ritual Magic Workbook* and to Spring Publications for permission to quote a stanza from the excellent Charles Boer translation of *The Homeric Hymns*. Naturally, Nancy Mostad deserves more than a nod for her encouragement and help, and I owe much thanks to my perceptive editor, Emily Nedell, for encouraging me to do things properly when I was inclined to be hurried and slipshod. And most special, special thanks to Thea Glaukopis Athene for Her most indispensable aid and support throughout.

Contents

---

*From *The Ritual Magic Workbook* by Dolores Ashcroft-Nowicki (Aquarian Press, Wellingborough, Northamptonshire, England, copyright 1986 by Dolores Ashcroft-Nowicki). Selected portions reprinted with permission of the publisher.

Preface

For reasons not at once obvious modern magic has largely by-passed the occultism of ancient Greece, preferring instead the system of the Jewish Kabbalah, practices drawn from the hieroglyphics of Egypt, and indigenous European expressions such as the Tarot cards and the Teutonic rune symbols. Even when Greek magic is used it is seldom explicitly designated as Greek.

This is a curious lapse since Western ceremonial magic is a direct descendant of the magic worked by Pythagoras, Plato and Plotinus. Perhaps the explanation lies in the scarcity of books on the subject and the difficulty of obtaining original Greek magical texts in English. Modern magicians have never been made aware of the legacy of Greek theurgy, or been exposed to the subtlety of its esoteric concepts which once threatened to overthrow Christianity, or experienced the undiluted power of its practical methods.

This book sets forth the complete evolution of Greek magic from earliest times through the Renaissance and down to the present in the forms and beliefs of current occult practices. Beginning with the Greek pantheon, Godwin examines the earliest written records of classical magic, setting it in the context of Greek philosophical thought, then moves on to the Mysteries, the Hellenistic period, gnosticism, the magic hidden in the Greek New Testament, and Neoplatonism. The revival of Greek magic during the Renaissance by such courageous and original thinkers as Ficino and Agrippa is examined, leading to a look at some of its modern expressions in the Golden Dawn and its offshoots, particularly in the occult system of Aleister Crowley.

Interspaced with the historical chapters are magic rituals based on Greek techniques that enable the reader to experience the effects of ancient theurgy firsthand. The extensive list of Greek words with their corresponding number values will be of use to serious ritualists seeking to integrate this form of magic numerologically with more conventional Western practices.

At the present time there is a strong surge of interest in the occult philosophy of the Renaissance. Since this is Greek at the core it is inevitable that the beliefs and methods of the Neoplatonists, the gnostics and the Mystery religions will exert an ever greater influence over modern magic. It is vital to know where these Greek ideas come from. *Light in Extension* is a guiding lamp into an unjustly overlooked region of our common Western occult heritage.

—Donald Tyson

Introduction

Greek magic goes back to the roots of Western civilization. There are older forms of magic—much older, going back into neolithic times—but none of these speaks to the modern soul in the Western world with the same degree of profundity as do the systems formulated by the direct progenitors of Western culture.

The influence exerted by such figures as Pythagoras and Plato upon all subsequent magical development is simply immense. There is some question as to whether either Neoplatonism or Gnosticism could have come into being without them, and these religious/philosophical systems had considerable influence upon cabalism and upon magi such as Albertus Magnus and Cornelius Agrippa, and they upon such figures as Cagliostro, St. Germaine, and at last Eliphas Levi. The lineage is unbroken from Homer to Aleister Crowley and beyond.

With all too few exceptions, this fascinating and ubiquitous field of magic has been too much neglected. Books abound on Tarot, channeling, Enochian magic, cabalistic magic, Celtic magic, Egyptian magic, Rosicrucian magic, Arthurian magic, Golden Dawn magic—you name it. But the books in print that are concerned with Greek magic or even the influence of Greek and Hellenistic philosophy and religion on modern hermetic philosophy—and on almost all of the types of magic named above—will not even fill a one-foot shelf.

It has been said in more than one place that Americans should not concern themselves with European traditions but should instead concentrate upon the Native American heritage. The theory is that these "Indian" religions are closer to the land in which we live. I have even read that we should make this choice rather than the Greek tradition specifically because Americans do not know any-

thing about Greek mythology unless they have had a classical education—as if they had somehow become informed about Native
American traditions simply by virtue of living on this continent.

But, for Americans of extra-American ancestry, the myths and
philosophies of Greek antiquity are the foundation stone of our cultural heritage. It is my opinion that they should not be abandoned in
favor of a spiritual tradition which, although we can and should
learn much from it, must remain for the most part a tradition in
which we are not qualified to partake by reason of our alien culture.
We cannot truly know what it was like to be a Native American before the European invasion. All too often, an attempt to follow these
native paths results in a demeaning, hollow co-option and pollution
of the beautiful and exalted faith of the conquered—along with their
land.

The book that follows is an attempt to present to readers who
might be interested in such an account the great panorama of magic,
magical ideas, and occult philosophy in the Greek language over a
period of more than two millennia, and to examine their influence
on present-day ideas and practices. Beginning with a few thoughts
on the religion and philosophy of classical Greece, we follow its development and metamorphosis in the Hellenistic Age, including
Gnosticism, Christianity as presented in the canonical scriptures,
and Neoplatonism. Thus we are led directly into a brief review of
the manifestations of Greek thought in the Renaissance and on into
the 19th and 20th centuries right up to the present day. Along the
way, various simple, representative rituals are presented to allow
the reader to get a feel for the approaches taken in the various periods. These rituals are in the nature of an experiment for those interested in the Greek heritage: They all work to some extent. The ones
that work best for you will point out the orientation most suitable
for you personally. For those of greater experience, they can probably be used indiscriminately to suit the occasion, but they are not
meant for simple-minded dabbling or to inject variety into a path to
which you are already committed—not unless you are ready to
make a new commitment which you will not drop when the next ex-
citing approach comes into view. That is not how progress is made
in these matters.

This book is intended for the general reader interested in magic
and occult philosophy and not necessarily for academics. A great
deal of material is covered. Accordingly, this account may seem

brief and even superficial to those well versed in these matters; I ask their indulgence. Those interested in digging deeper should find the appended bibliography somewhat helpful, and I hope that the readers of this volume will be moved to make use of it. The whole point of this book is to provide an introduction without the necessity of acquiring a library to find out what really interests you.

In matters of fact, I have tried to be careful, but the scope of the information presented would seem to maximize the possibility of a few errors—minor errors, I hope. For these I apologize, and I welcome corrections.

As to my opinions on this subject or that, I have tried to identify them as such. Anyone whatever is perfectly welcome to disagree. One often makes a closer approach to truth by the fundamentally Greek process of thesis-antithesis-synthesis.

I have assumed that the readers of this book will possess some degree of intelligence and initiative. Therefore I have not seen fit to lead them by the hand every step of the way, telling them to wear a Greek tunic in their rituals, showing them what names to inscribe upon their impedimenta, instructing them in the meanings or pronunciations of words that are to be found in any dictionary, and so on. At the same time, I have tried not to assume that they are already practicing magi looking for a new wrinkle. Anyone with average intelligence should be able to work from the materials presented here.

A word about certain styles of spelling and capitalization: I have used the spelling "cabala" throughout (rather than qabalah, kabbalah, or something else) for two reasons. First, it is the spelling to be found in most dictionaries. Second, current usage tends to associate it with the Christian cabala, and that is the sort of cabala that will for the most part be discussed in these pages. I have everywhere capitalized Gnostic/Gnosticism and Pagan/Paganism—contrary to the prevailing mainstream practice—because I often talk about Christianity at the same time. I do not wish to imply, by failing to capitalize the names of these other faiths, that they are somehow inferior. I have no excuse for capitalizing Tarot except that it "just doesn't look right" when it's not.

—David Godwin

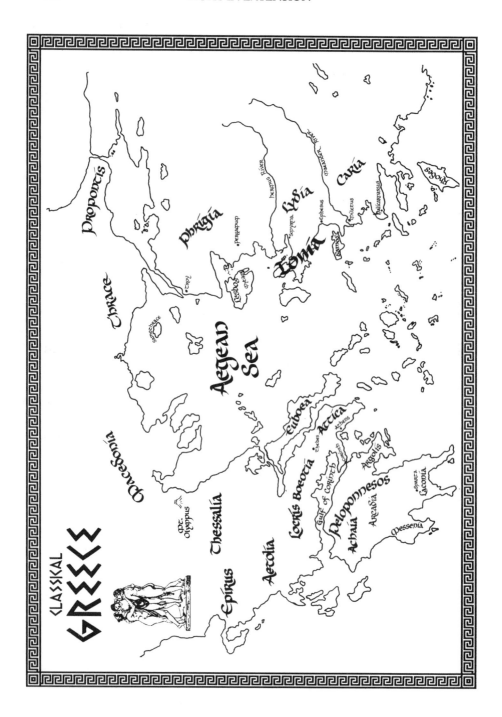

A Helpful Geography Lesson

Classical Greek civilization occupied not only Greece but also the west coast of Asia Minor, the huge peninsula now better known as Turkey. From north to south, the important cities on or near the coast of Asia Minor were Pergamum (inland from the island of Lesbos with its major city, Mytilene), Smyrna, Ephesus, the island and city of Samos, Miletus, and Halicarnassus. Phrygia included just about everything north of the Hermus (modern "Manisa") River, Lydia was between the Hermus and the Maeander (Menderes) Rivers, and Caria included everything south of the Maeander. The term Ionia was applied to the whole coast south of the Hermus.

Over in Greece itself, the northeastern part was and is known as Thessalia, the large island along the east coast which runs northwest-southeast is Euboea, and the peninsula running parallel to Euboea was Boeotia. Thebes was right in the middle of Boeotia. Attica was the southernmost peninsula, south of Boeotia, with Athens on the southwest coast just south of the narrow neck of land, or isthmus. This isthmus connects the mainland to a huge southern "island," technically a peninsula, known as Peloponnesos or "the Pelopennese," which gave its name to the Peloponnesian War. Corinth was at the southwest end of this isthmus, on the north side of it. Back on the mainland, Aetolia was south of Thessalia and west of Boeotia, with Locris between Aetolia and Boeotia. Epirus is west of Thessalia.

On the other side of the Gulf of Corinth, on Peloponnesos, was Achaia. South of that was Arcadia, and east of that was Argolis, which included the northeastern peninsula of Peloponnesos. Messenia was on the southwestern part of the island and Laconia on the southeastern part. Sparta was in Laconia. Mount Olympus was in northern Thessalia, and north of that was Macedonia, along the northern coast of the Aegean Sea separating Greece from Asia Minor. Thrace was also on this coast, but east of Macedonia, and included the part of modern-day Turkey north of the Sea of Marmara, then known as Propontis.

It helps if you look at the map.

I

The Greek Gods

There is something about the gods and myths and legends of ancient Greece that has an irresistible fascination for many people today. With me, I suppose the seeds were planted by the Walt Disney motion picture, *Fantasia*, and the animated sequence that accompanied Beethoven's Pastoral Symphony. I didn't know what it was all about, then. I was just a kid. Why was God hurling thunderbolts? Who were these beautiful beings who were half horse, half human? Certainly the vision of this part of the movie, trivial and distorted as it seems from an adult perspective, formed a tranquil and even uplifting experience compared with the extinction of the dinosaurs (Stravinsky's "Rite of Spring"), the devil playing with damned souls (Moussorgsky's "Night on Bald Mountain"), or even the washed-out pastels and dull visuals of a very dull rendition—for a child, at any rate—of Franz Schubert's "Ave Maria" at the film's conclusion. All I'd really wanted to see in the first place was Mickey Mouse! To this day, I still prefer Beethoven to Stravinsky or Moussorgsky.

When I got into high school, part of the prescribed curriculum in an English class was a study of Greek and Roman mythology. The idea was that the romantic poets made so many allusions to it. I didn't much care for Keats or Shelley, but I found the mythology fascinating. It spoke to something in me, some hidden longing, that I

1

cannot define. Most of the other kids thought it was "dumb," but I was enthralled. I even found myself praying to Zeus to improve my miniature golf game. He considered it beneath him.

Then a world literature class in college, because of the instructor's preferences, spent at least half the semester on the Greek drama, and I learned the terrible and stirring story of the house of Atreus. This "whole Greek thing" just had a way of popping up all the time. Many years later, I encountered a young lady on psilocybin who insisted she was the goddess Diana (that is, Artemis). Fortunately for me, I did not see her bathing. (In the myth, she sets her hounds on a man who did.) But the point is—why Diana? Why a Greco-Roman goddess? These gods are still very much with us.

I have seldom regained my teen-age state of enchantment with this ancient magic, but it's still there and will still occasionally surface. If all this were a unique experience, I would probably keep it to myself. But I have since found out that it is far from unique—very far. In her brilliant study of the Neo-Pagan movement, *Drawing Down the Moon,* Margot Adler describes a similar fascination in her own youth; she ended up wanting to identify herself with Artemis or Athene. Since then, she says, she has found that the experience is fairly widespread. (For publishers, dates, and other data concerning the authors and/or books referred to in this chapter, see the Bibliography at the end of this volume.)

In his youth, Howard Phillips Lovecraft, famous today for his weird tales that appeared in the magazine *Weird Tales* and for the half-dozen films that have been based on his work, was likewise fascinated. He wrote some pretty miserable juvenile poetry, made even more miserable by his labored imitation of Pope and Dryden, but most of it was dedicated to the Greek gods and beings of Greek mythology. He built altars to Apollo, Athene, and Pan. Once, he even saw Pan and a band of nymphs dancing in an oak grove. He said it was a religious experience just as meaningful and valid to him at the time as that of a Christian who feels the reality of Jesus. As an adult, he passed it off as illusion and became a strict materialist. Yet he still dreamed about supernatural experiences as a citizen of ancient Rome—dreams that were so real and detailed that most people today having a similar dream would feel sure it was the remembrance of a past life.

The Welsh writer Arthur Machen, who at one time was a member of the well-known Hermetic Order of the Golden Dawn, experienced something similar, but not quite the same. There were Roman ruins in the rural neighborhood of his youth. Partly due to their influence, he frequently sensed presences in the woods and fields. But these presences did not enchant him—they terrified him. As a good Victorian lad, he was appalled by what he thought of as their primeval, distinctly non-Christian sexuality and license. To him, they were evil, they were a threat—perhaps a projection of his own repressions. They haunted his fiction for the rest of his life, making perhaps their most memorable off-the-scenes appearance in his story, "The Great God Pan."

All this is no recent phenomenon. Many have been enthralled by the ancient myths and legends of the Greeks for more than 2,000 years now. In Europe, interest awakened in the Renaissance and has continued ever since. The first buildings and monuments of the United States were copies of Greek temples. A Greek goddess, "Freedom," stands atop the capitol dome in Washington. The new country may have represented, as the great seal proclaims, a "new order of the ages" *(novus ordo seclorum)*, but the architecture of the public buildings was Greek. So was the ideal of democracy.

Since this book is supposed to be at least partly about magic, you may be asking, "What does all this mythology stuff have to do with magic? Where's the spell to make everything I touch turn to gold?" But if you enter this world, and enter it far enough, everything will be gold already.

Just as the modern ceremonial magician calls upon the names of God, usually the Hebrew names, Greek magic called upon the Greek gods. It differed from ordinary prayers in that the deity was asked to empower the ritual. Aside from that, since a great deal of modern magic is theurgic—god-seeking—it behooves the magus to know the names of the gods. These—or, at the very least, the names of spirits—are also necessary for effective thaumaturgy; that is, "practical" magic (as if the goal of all human existence were impractical).

Incidentally, the pervasive influence of Greece in matters magical can be seen in the very terminology. "Theurgy" is from the Greek *theourgia*, "divine work," and "thaumaturgy" comes from *thaumatourgia*, meaning "conjuring" or "wonder-working."

Here, then, are the major Greek gods, the Olympian twelve, although I will make no attempt to describe them in any detail. That has already been done exhaustively a thousand times over. I have merely listed key words for each, describing their primary rulership or area of concern.

Zeus (chief)	Here (marriage)
Apollo (Sun, poetry)	Aphrodite (love)
Ares (war)	Artemis (Moon, hunting)
Hephaestos (smith)	Athene (wisdom, war)
Hermes (messenger)	Demeter (agriculture)
Poseidon (sea)	Hestia (home)

There are legitimate spelling variations in the names of some of these gods, depending on whether the Greek or Latin versions are used and whether you use Attic, Doric, Ionic, or Aeolic spelling. Thus Athene could also be spelled Athana (Doric) or Athenaa (Aeolic). Homer used the Ionic spellings, and I have followed his example. The "ae" in "Hephaestos" represents the Greek characters alpha iota (αι)—one of the several confusing conventions of Greek-English transliteration. The name can also be spelled "Hephaistos." Note that the final eta (long e, η) in Here and Athene is often rendered as "a," and you will frequently see these names as Hera and Athena. Just bear in mind that Here is not pronounced "hear."

You should be aware of the fact that it wasn't until such writers as Homer and Hesiod began to impose order on chaos that the concept of the "twelve Olympians" arose. A deity of the same name or type may have been worshiped in a dozen different forms in as many villages and towns, and there were more gods than you could shake a thyrsus at. Since any sort of pre-Homeric divine telephone directory does not exist, you will have to stick with the later, regrettably patriarchal concept of Zeus as CEO, the Olympian twelve as the Board of Directors, and all the rest as officers (gods, demigods, and heroes) and employees (nymphs, satyrs, centaurs, and so on). Of course, you may choose to revert to the earlier Pelasgian myths as described by Robert Graves, wherein the goddess Eurynome is the Creator and supreme deity—bearing in mind that the Pelasgians (the original inhabitants of Greece) are obscure, their mythology conjectural, and their matriarchy doubtful. But beyond the fact that you will then have a god/goddess pair for each of the planets, you are strictly on your own. We know next to nothing about these gods and/or Titans except the legends later attached to some of them by the (alas) patriarchal archaic Greeks. There is no rich body of myth surrounding Phoebe, the Moon goddess, for example, as there is for Artemis. There is also the fact, of course, that half of the the Titans were, just like the Olympians, male. Nevertheless, the male half of each pair can safely be considered a mere consort as opposed to an equal. Or not. Your choice.

Planet	Goddess	God
—	Eurynome	Ophion
Moon	Phoibe (Phoebe)	Atlas
Mercury	Metis	Koios (Coeos)
Venus	Tethys	Okeanos (Oceanus)
Sun	Theia	Hyperion
Mars	Dione	Krios (Crios)
Jupiter	Themis	Eurymedon
Saturn	Rheia (Rhea)	Kronos (Cronus)

Note that Ophion was a serpent, the equivalent of the worm Ouroboros who encircles the universe with his tail in his mouth. Nevertheless, despite this exalted status, he was created by Eurynome. Also note that many of these names were taken over by the Olympians. In the first place, Kronos and Rhea were said to be the parents of Zeus. Apollo is often called "Hyperion," and Artemis is also referred to as "Phoebe." Metis is the mother of Athene, swallowed by Zeus, and Dione (Dee-O-nay) is the mother of Aphrodite. And, yes, Atlas is that guy who holds up the world. However, all these were "post-invasion" developments.

Although there is nothing to keep you from using this system, be aware that it's highly unlikely that such a neatly worked-out scheme was universal to the pre-invasion Greeks. The term "Pelasgians" (or Pelasgi) was applied to the original inhabitants by the Greek historian Hecataeus (quoted by Herodotus) in the 6th century B.C. By that time, it had all been over for hundreds of years. The pre-Achaean Greeks were not likely to have been a monolithic, homogenous people all worshiping a Eurynomean double ogdoad; more likely they were an extremely mixed lot with differing beliefs and gods. In fact, Hecataeus himself used the term only to refer to the original residents of Athens. Homer referred to the Thessalian allies of the Trojans as Pelasgians. Only later was the term extended to cover the larger territory. We can see the same over-generalization at work in our own time in which cultures as diverse as the

Mohawks, Mound Builders, Cherokee, Hopi, Sioux, Aztecs, and Mayans are all lumped together and called "Indians." Well, didn't they all wear feathers on their heads and worship a Great Spirit named Masaw? No, not even if you discount the Aztecs and Mayans.

No doubt the archetypal myths of the Greeks have resonated with the psyches of their hearers in a powerful and timeless fashion, but our idea of ancient Greece and its gods is very much colored by and filtered through the notions of the romantic poets of the 19th century. It was romantic fancies such as these that led Heinrich Schliemann to recite the *Iliad* in Greek taverns and to re-discover Troy. But how close are they to the truth? The viewpoint of the Greeks was not romantic, but classical and rational, with the inevitable irrational elements explained away as the results of divine or daemonic intervention. Our concepts of gods change over time and are different at different times in different cultures. The archetypes they represent may remain unchangeable, but gods may shift about disconcertingly. The Artemis worshiped at Athens was not the same as the Artemis revered at Ephesus, and both of them varied from the Artemis previously worshiped in Crete, where She appears to have been a fertility goddess. This to say nothing of prehistoric periods of which we can know nothing. And all of these are different from Diana of the Romans, usually considered to be the equivalent of Artemis, and all these are yet again not the same as the Artemis/Diana depicted in neoclassic and romantic poetry. The late 20th-century version is different yet again, and in important ways. Yet there exists, in the human psyche and therefore in seemingly independent astral realms, an entity called "Artemis." A god who could not be different things to different people at different times would not be a god at all.

Incidentally, in order to avoid encumbering the language with "god/goddess" in addition to "he/she," and to avoid the constant use of the neutral term "deity," I have used the term "gods" in the generic sense to mean any deities, male and/or female. Two or three thousand years of constant reference to God as "He" should not necessitate the addition of a feminine suffix to distinguish a female deity. After all, we no longer refer to a woman pilot as an "aviatrix." Aphrodite is a goddess, to be sure, but She is also without doubt a god—a god with nothing whatsoever masculine about Her. This usage does, after all, have honorable precedent. In *The Odyssey*, the

Artemis Orthia

goddess Athene says in so many words, "I am a god" *(egō theos eimi)*, not distinguishing Her gender by saying "goddess" *(thea)*.

According to Robert Graves, Plato, in his *Timaeus*, identified Athene with the Lybian/Egyptian goddess Neith, who was at one time worshiped as "the One." Actually, Plato has Critias say that the citizens of Sais in Egypt told him that Athene was the same as Neith, and that they therefore had a high regard for Athens—which he also says was founded by Athene a thousand years before Sais. Not likely. Sais was thriving when Athens was a muddy spot in the road. But what this seems to amount to is that the people of Sais saw their own goddess reflected in Athene. This is very far from proving that the two goddesses were identical or that Neith was the origin of Athene. At a much later date, Julius Caesar said that the Germans worshiped Mercury as their chief god. He meant Odin. That does not mean that Odin was the original form of Mercury, or vice-versa.

In any event, Athene was also said in other myths to be the daughter of Poseidon or of the giant Pallas, whom She slew when he attempted incestuous rape. E. R. Dodds says nothing about a possible Lybian origin; he says Her probable origin was as "a Minoan house-goddess." Walter Burkert quotes M. P. Nilsson as saying that Athene was originally the great Snake Goddess of Crete, but he himself says She got Her name from the city of Athens rather than the other way around. Christine Downing (in Carl Olson's anthology, *The Book of the Goddess*) says that the origin of Athene was as the Attic version of Gaia, the great Earth goddess. (Attica is the region around Athens.) A related theory is that She was the original Great Goddess of pre-invasion Athens, who, with her foster-child Erechtheus (son of Gaia), mirrors Eurynome/Ophion. In the plays of Aeschylus in the 5th century B.C., She has been reduced to a "toady" of the patriarchs.

I have gone into all these conflicting ideas about the origin of Athene to illustrate the point that there is a lot more conjecture about Greek myths than there is factual knowledge. Let the reader beware.

Many people feel that Dionysos with His entourage of satyrs, nymphs, and maenads represents a traveling drunken orgy. Hence they say He is a god that man has made in his own extremely imperfect image. But this simplistic picture overlooks the fact that the maenads were in the habit of going into a frenzy and tearing people apart, not to mention animals, as they do in *The Bacchae* of Euripides. That doesn't sound like all the good old boys down at the Athens bar and grill getting soused and making a god in their own image. It sounds like the survival of a vegetation cult as described by Sir James George Frazer (*The Golden Bough*) or Robert Graves. In *The Bacchae*, you'll note, it's the king who gets torn apart.

At any rate, perhaps most people see Dionysos as an orgiastic god, a god of drunkenness, hedonism, and license—or as the drunken slob of *Fantasia* (who was actually supposed to be the Roman god Silenus). They may feel that anything having to do with religion is better exemplified by the calm, ascetic life of monks and nuns, involving prayer and self-denial and slow processions through a washed-out pastel landscape to a colorless rendition of "Ave Maria." If not that, they may at least find the musical, poetic gentility of Orpheus more to their liking. Yet one should not, I think, fail utterly to entertain the idea that "wine," "drunkenness," and so on may be understood symbolically, as they are meant in Omar Khayyam's *Rubaiyat* and other Sufi writings; that what is implied is not the false ideal of the American party animal—getting drunk, throwing beer cans at policemen, vomiting in the street, and causing havoc on the highway—but rather the ecstasy of divine union.

Admittedly, this ecstasy was achieved in certain times and places not only by drinking wine but also by wild dancing and an all-out effort to work yourself up into an often bloodthirsty frenzy. (This dancing, by the way, was just a trifle peculiar. It was not break dancing. It always involved an involuntarily throwing back of the head, wildly disheveled hair, and an inability to stop—or not to start, if you were in the vicinity.) Nevertheless, Dionysos did end up being the primal deity of the cosmos in the Orphic mysteries.

Thus we tend to make over the gods of antiquity in our own image, toning them down considerably when they begin to exhibit darker qualities or to favor ideals no longer held. Walter Burkert states that Artemis was a goddess of "cruel and bloody sacrifices." This image hardly accords with romantic ideas of the virgin huntress and Moon goddess, which are derived more from the efforts of 19th-century poets than from classical myth.

As another example, it has been said in more places than one that Athene is a goddess of war only when the war is truly just (as, for example, the war against Hitler) and feels that battle for its own sake is stupid; thus she is differentiated from the more savage Ares (or Roman Mars). In the words of Thomas Bulfinch, "She was a war-like divinity; but it was defensive war only that she patronized, and she had no sympathy with Mars's savage love of violence and bloodshed." Yet Hesiod says that she "delights in the clamorous cry of war and battle and slaughter." Still, I confess that I detect a certain anti-feminine bias in Hesiod.

Ares, on the other hand, is usually thought of as a brutal, bloody, battlehawk—the very personification of stupid, macho violence. Yet Gene Wolfe has one of his characters say (in *Soldier of Arete*) that Ares is just like the human warriors who follow him—all he really wants is to get home to Aphrodite! Hence, as a master of strategy, he seeks the most efficient means of winning a military conflict as soon as possible. In all this, I think we see a misguided attempt—in which both feminists and male supremicists have participated for different reasons—to tame, domesticate, and "emasculate" the goddesses—in short, to divest them of qualities now seen as "masculine"—while emphasizing the undesirable qualities of the male gods.

Ares and Aphrodite

In any event, it has been said that the gods of all pantheons have an independent existence. Our ideas of them, it is said, may be entirely false. This would certainly be so if they held to the images of the classical archetypes. In such a case, we might soon find that we had cause to regret our inquiries into the ways of the gods! When the notorious (and unfairly vilified) Aleister Crowley attempted the evocation of Hermes, the entity who manifested, whether Hermes or something else, ended up demanding human sacrifice—a demand which, despite his reputation, Crowley chose to ignore.

Back in that Pleistocene high school English class, we were taught that the Roman gods were the same as the Greek, but with different names. The Romans supposedly just took them over and renamed them. However, we now know that the Roman gods had quite different origins, usually Etruscan, and only gradually assumed the characteristics and myths of similar Greek gods. Magically, this is important. At the level of archetypes, on the astral, or elsewhere in the extramundane planes, the Greek and Roman gods are not the same. Minerva, originally one of the chief trinity of the Etruscans, is not the same as Pallas Athene—despite the fact that the Romans took over all the Greek stories about Athene and attached them to Minerva. Any attempt to magically regard the two as identical is liable to result at best in confusion, disorientation, and lack of results.

But gods and even archetypes may change over a long period of time. Only by the most strenuous efforts of theological doubletalk can the brainless, jealous god who caused children to be torn apart by bears for merely taunting his prophet be reconciled with the so-called loving father of the New Testament or the silent non-entity of today. (The Gnostic thinker Marcion went to some pains to show that they were in fact *not* the same.) But, for the most part, we are assured that it is the same god. Perhaps Carl Jung was correct in saying that God, or the gods, are evolving along with humanity. Therefore, there is no particular reason to deal with the deities of ancient Greece as if they still retained the savage and bloody qualities that the Greeks often seem to have seen in them. After all, their ideas may also have been misconceptions, projections of their own predilections. If you choose to see Artemis as a gentle virgin and protector of wildlife, then chances are that's just what She is, for you, and for all of us as we near the 21st century.

II

Greek Mythology:
The Battle Between the Sexes?

It is almost comical to observe the way in which Greek mythology has become modern mythology or allegory. As E. R. Dodds said (*The Greeks and the Irrational*), many of our modern notions about the Greeks represent "the unconscious projection upon the screen of antiquity" of our own ideas.

One modern myth, which I shall refer to as the "Graves scenario," originated in the last century with such scholars as F. W. H. Myers and Sir James George Frazer. Robert Graves more or less popularized this idea in his monumental *The Greek Myths* and *The White Goddess*, and it has been picked up and employed as received truth ever since by all manner of polemicists, dreamers, idealists, writers, Wiccans, historians, and scholars.

According to this idea, all the world once worshiped a great goddess and society was matriarchal. In these neolithic times, life was not "nasty, brutish, and short," but rather nonviolent, egalitarian, gentle, and earth-centered—a true Golden Age and a worthy ideal even now. This situation obtained in Greece until an invading patriarchal culture—worshipers of the sky god, Zeus—altered things by brute force. These invaders were somehow simultaneously savage and intellectual, at the same time rapacious and rationalistic to the point of being schizoid. (If this seems paradoxical, take a good look

13

at the Pentagon.)

In any event, this conquest and suppression of the native goddess-worship was then incorporated into the myths, in which male gods or heroes defeated female monsters and sorceresses and Zeus philandered with all the old goddesses and established his supremacy over them. Zeus is shamelessly depicted as some sort of rapist god, assuming the shapes of various fauna in order to have his way with the native goddesses—including his mother, Rhea—who are now for the most part mythologically reduced to mere mortal women, usually, like Ariadne, princesses and the daughters of kings.

"Oh, come on, now," you may be saying. "Zeus didn't rape all those women! He seduced them! They fell in love with him!" That may be the impression created by Victorian writers such as Bulfinch, but consider: Metis sought to avoid Zeus by shape changing until he finally caught her; Rhea turned into a serpent in a futile effort to avoid him; he turned into a bull to carry off Europa. These don't sound like normal love affairs.

But perhaps we are going too far in thinking of the gods as human characters in a human drama. This is myth, after all, not *General Hospital*. Leaving aside for the moment such considerations as the Goddess in Her lunar aspects (Artemis) or as the night sky (the Egyptian/Thelemite Nuit), if Zeus is considered in his role as Sky Father, then rain is necessary for the fertility of any Earth Goddess. Without this "seed of Zeus," She becomes withered, dry, and sterile. That may be all very well for the Wise Crone, but the Goddess has other aspects as well. By the same token, by whatever name He may be known, the Sky Father without the Earth Mother is nothing at all—just empty air. This is in fact one of the major criticisms now being leveled at contemporary monotheistic religions.

Nevertheless, it cannot be denied that a society less given over to ideas of male superiority and male violence would probably have found a less brutal set of myths to express this idea. It might also be said that the ideal nature of the primordial matriarchy was not a major feature of Graves' original presentation. In many respects, that part of it has been "added on" by later interpreters.

In any case, it's fairly plain that there is a grain of truth in this matriarchy vs. patriarchy legend, and it is unmistakably reflected in the myths of classical Greece. Still, I know of no law of nature that says a matriarchal religion and priesthood could not have existed alongside of and within an otherwise patriarchal culture. Indeed, there seems to be more evidence, at least in historical times, for the widespread and common occurrence of that state of affairs than for any other. Nevertheless, the need for a modern dualistic myth of the suppression of a feminine good by a masculine evil has caused the Graves scenario to be exaggerated and has in many cases—it is said—brought about a certain selectivity with regard to the archaeological evidence as well as interpretations that go beyond the evidence.

Unfortunately, in other words, the Graves scenario may not be strictly true in all its details. There can be little doubt that matriarchal cultures have existed from time to time, and the evidence is growing that the Amazons were not, as formerly supposed, a creation of myth. If they did not exist as a separate culture of their own, they may at least have been temple guardians, militant priestesses defending the sanctuary. Nevertheless, the idea of an ancient, universal, goddess-worshiping matriarchy is no longer academically fashionable (among male scholars, at least). It still has its adherents, but the majority seem to prefer to think that the evidence has been preferentially selected and arbitrarily interpreted. No doubt a goddess or goddesses were primary in Crete and the city of Catal Huyuk in what is now Turkey, and elsewhere as well, but the main deity at unequivocally patriarchal Athens was also a goddess, Athene—a much watered-down example of a goddess-worshiping patriarchy.

Greece, they say, appears to have been patriarchal even in neolithic times. Some statuary includes figures of a throned male figure attended by female servants. The myths of a sky god overcoming chthonic feminine forces seem to have been imported from Mesopotamian cultures long before the Indo-European invasion of Greece, although the Mycenean conquest of Crete undoubtedly conforms for the most part to the invading patriarchy theory—unless Minoan Crete was already in the hands of kings at the time, as it may well have been. The Minoan serpent goddess protected the house of the king, not the queen, in historical times. Be that as it may, the evidence for a widespread matriarchy among the "Pelasgians," at least, seems scant and contrived. In fact, Herodotus says that the Athenians drove out the Pelasgians because they had been raping and kidnapping Athenian women—hardly the behavior you'd expect from representatives of a Graves-scenario culture. Of course, even Herodotus says that this is only the Athenians' version of the story.

"Venus of Willendorf"—Goddess or Playmate?

And if Zeus overthrew the mother goddess, why does the principal myth have him overthrowing his father, Kronos, as well as later subjugating his mother, Rhea? According to Anne L. Barstow ("The Prehistoric Goddess," in Olson's anthology), the Graves scenario of a universal matriarchy is a doubtful myth. She says that, in fact, sex dominance may be an irrelevant consideration in preliterate cultures. The prehistoric "Venus" figurines found throughout Europe, although very similar to some early Sumerian images of Ishtar, may not, they say, represent a goddess. They may be no more than excellent examples of homeopathic magic. The "cavemen" did not have our population problems; there may have been instances of entire tribes simply dying out. Hence, fertility was desired. If it is highly desirable for the women of your tribe to be pregnant, what better solution than to make images of pregnant women?

It has been seriously proposed many times that they just didn't know any other way to go about it; they didn't make the connection. In fact, this rather startling ignorance is one of the arguments used to support the idea of ancient matriarchy. Women produced children; men weren't good for much of anything. However, even if the situation were otherwise and our remote ancestors were not so fuzzy minded and unobservant as we think, it would still be thought appropriate to help things along with a magical image. The surviving examples of cave painting may be another example, the magic being directed this time toward the abundance of animals to provide food and clothing. On the other hand, it has been suggested by German scholars that the figurines may have represented magical servants or may even have been the caveman's version of *Playboy!*

All this is not to say that matriarchies never existed, only that they were perhaps not, after all, the general condition of humanity in prehistoric times. There is no doubt that there were many cultures in which the primary deity was female, but to say that those cultures were therefore matriarchal and therefore kinder and gentler than the warlike patriarchal cultures may be an unwarranted inference. As for being egalitarian, consider that millions of Hindus worship the Mother Goddess as their chief or only deity yet adhere rigidly to the caste system. However, it would be unnecessarily bullheaded to deny the possibility that the older matriarchal/universal-goddess theories might be correct after all. The fact is, we just don't know.

What it all comes down to has little to do with the Greeks; either version of history is a modern myth imposed upon the unknown reality. Nevertheless, although it seems to me that we may have to acknowledge that mainland Greece itself may have been patriarchal from the earliest times, indigenous goddesses and the goddesses of surrounding cultures certainly seem to have been incorporated into the pattern of pre-exiting patriarchal myths.

The partly factual, partly theoretical, subjugation of neolithic matriarchies by invading patriarchs, and the subsequent attempted suppression of goddess worship in the name of Zeus or Yahweh, has become a feminist ideological weapon, a myth used to explain the inferior social and economic situation of women in today's world and a justification for the struggle for women's rights—as if any common-sense objective assessment of the situation along with any sort of sense of justice and fair play required any such mythological justification.

Whatever the truth may be, it is highly amusing to observe the other side of the coin—the almost frantic reaction of the classical academics, all male, mostly German, who hasten to point out the flaws in the feminist version while scraping the barrel for evidence to refute it. It is, they say, wishful thinking, a revisionist myth based on the outdated theories of Frazer and Myers and the most unscholarly poetic/romantic notions of Graves, a shameless attempt to press history and archaeology into the service of a political agenda. But hidden behind these attacks is obviously, though sometimes unconsciously, an effort to uphold another old myth—that of natural male superiority. From this viewpoint, patriarchy is the natural condition of mankind. (Never mind womankind.) Thus Greek mythology becomes an element in modern mythology and is pressed into service in the "battle between the sexes"—the most senseless war ever waged.

As for the myths themselves, it is undeniable that, like the Bible, you can find what you seek in them. The scene in Homer's *Iliad* in which the goddess Athene easily defeats the war god Ares is scarcely an example of the triumph of machismo. This particular lady, patron of Odysseus, also yanked Achilles around by his hair to dissuade him from killing Agamemnon. Yet, as Karl Kerenyi said (*Athene: Virgin and Mother in Greek Religion*), Athene may have represented the feminine in service to the masculine, the loyal female expression of the power of Her father, Zeus, whose favorite daughter She was, in a relationship reminiscent of that between Wotan and Brünnhilde in the operas of Richard Wagner. Nevertheless, She probably did not start out that way.

Athene almost certainly existed as a goddess long before Zeus ever came along; the macho-men of the Zeus cult denied both Her independence and the life-giving power of women by saying She was born from the head of Zeus. This same ultra-patriarchal appropriation of the one remaining power of women, to give birth, also appears in the book of Genesis. Adam is not born of woman; rather woman is created from his rib. Here we have a complete reversal of the hypothetical primitive idea that men play no role in procreation. The classical Greeks evidently seriously thought that all life-giving power is in the semen; a woman is merely an incubator, the plowed furrow that holds the seed. Apollo is made to say as much in the *Eumenides* of Aeschylus (5th century B.C.), wherein Athene has already sold out to patriarchal ideals. Thence arose, perhaps, later alchemical efforts to create a homonculus (a miniature human being) in a closed flask by adding semen to horse manure and certain other ingredients.

Of course, this "plowed field" analogy, besides being grossly in-accurate, overlooks the fact that a plant cannot grow without the life-giving nutrients contributed by the soil. At the same time, the Greeks affirmed wisdom as a male prerogative, for Zeus had be-come cerebrally pregnant by swallowing Metis, the Titan/goddess of wisdom. Hesiod seems to be responsible for this "head of Zeus" myth, although Homer did make Athene the daughter of Zeus with-out giving any details of Her birth.

So what's the choice for a man of the 1990s? Is the only alterna-tive either to follow one of the arrogant, repulsive, bloody, patriar-chal, rapist gods—Zeus, Jove, Odin, Jehovah, Allah—or to devote himself to a goddess via an emasculated and/or transvestite priest or consort doomed to die most horribly at the next solstice? If he chooses to revere a goddess, is the only choice between an authori-tarian matriarch such as Cybele (as She has been depicted by men) —who, most men may feel, demands entirely too much—or a sell-out such as the classical Athene of Aeschylus? Or between a danger-ous hag such as the Athenian Hecate or a Playmate goddess such as the classical Aphrodite? Is there no middle ground in all of this? Are there no co-equal gods and goddesses in Greek mythology, or are they all characters in a grand and horrid story of male vs. female?

The only workable solution, it seems to me, is to cease fretting about who really believed what in antiquity—something which we can never know with certainty—and consult the archetypes within your own psyche.

The whole sexual stereotyping involved in the conception of a gentle, environmentally sensitive, peaceful, intuitive, creative ma-triarchy (where the queen's consort was dismembered and eaten every six months, according to Graves) as opposed to a savage, ra-pacious, warlike, rationalistic, destructive patriarchy is, shall we say, a sexist oversimplification that reminds one of the verse about "What are little girls/boys made of?" The Amazons somehow fail to fit this stereotype very well. War goddesses abound in all cultures. Hunting, usually considered to be a typically insensitive and de-structive masculine activity, is the province of the goddess Artemis, described in the *Homeric Hymns* (Charles Boer translation) thus: "She has a strong heart,/she darts in and out/everywhere/in and out/killing/all kinds of animals." So much for Artemis as the god-dess of the Sierra Club.

Of course, this hymn can also be understood symbolically (for example, wild animals = ungoverned impulses in the individual psyche), but any such interpretation smacks of evasion. Incidentally, the Boer translation of *The Homeric Hymns* (2nd revised edition, Spring Publications, Inc., 1980, copyright 1970 by Charles Boer), here quoted with the generous permission of the publisher, is extremely effective and dynamic. It speaks to the modern mind and conveys the power of these hymns in a way that the stilted traditional versions cannot.

The classical Greek viewpoint, however, may help to explain why, in cabalism, "Severity" is seen as feminine and "Mercy" as masculine. If there is any connection in the history of ideas, the Tree of Life would seem to be rooted in classical Greek concepts.

Classical Greece was unquestionably a male-dominated society, perhaps more so than even ancient Palestine or modern Arabia. Greek culture seems to have gotten more extremely patriarchal as time went on, almost desperately and fanatically so at the time of classical Athens. Women were chattel, with no rights or privileges whatever. Love was a matter between men; women were a necessary evil for purposes of reproduction. If a man loved a woman, it was due to madness, a curse of Aphrodite.

This culture, which has for so long been looked upon as a golden age of enlightenment and learning, definitely had its dark side. For example, slavery was an accepted institution. So, before you climb in your time machine and go back to 450 B.C. to frolic in the groves of Arcadia, give these matters some thought. And before you begin the practice of magic with a classical Greek orientation, realize that you are dealing with archetypes that may not be quite what you think they are.

Yes, women were denigrated in classical Greece, despised, barely tolerated, and deprived of the most basic rights—but they were also feared and in many cases even respected and looked upon with awe. The major deity at Athens, as aforesaid, was Athene. Until Dionysos replaced Hestia, half of the twelve Olympian deities were goddesses. In this most patriarchal of all societies, there were highly respected priestesses—a situation not to be found in most Christian/Jewish/Islamic institutions in our present advanced, socially conscious times, when the "light" of monotheism has dispelled the "ignorance" of myth. The ordaining of a woman bishop not so long ago was almost enough to split the Episcopalian church. It would not have disturbed the Greeks, who otherwise regarded women as

Hera   Athene   Aphrodite

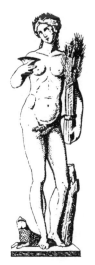

Artemis   Demeter   Hestia

less than cattle or slaves.

I confess that it is quite beyond my ability to deal with this contradiction, but some authors with greater expertise (and courage) than myself may have attempted to address the problem somewhere. Still, I have not seen anything that really attempts to deal with the larger question of why a patriarchal culture was so permeated by goddesses and priestesses. How could a man consult a priestess-oracle, offer sacrifice to Athene, and then go home and beat his wife? Was it a matter of the ruling class simply being unable to suppress the indigenous goddess-worship completely, just as the Christian church later made local deities into saints? Was it some sort of psychological compensation? This great paradox, however, is certainly no more baffling than some of our own customs and behavior. As one small example, consider warning labels and ad campaigns directed by the government against a product that they subsidize heavily.

As a possibly more realistic means of evaluating the male/female orientation of various ancient (and modern) cultures, I submit the following outline:

    I. Rulership
        A. Women only (e.g., Amazons)
        B. Men or women, as the occasion demands (e.g., ancient Egypt, modern England)
        C. Men and women jointly
           1. Co-equal king and queen
           2. King and high priestess
           3. Queen and high priest
        D. Men only (e.g., Saudi Arabia)
   II. Descent and inheritance
        A. Matrilineal
        B. Chaotic
        C. Neither patrilineal nor matrilineal, but ordered
        D. Patrilineal
 III. Society
        A. Men have no rights
        B. Equal rights (egalitarian)
        C. Men have more rights than women
        D. Women have no rights
  IV. Religion

A. Goddess(es) with no god(s)
B. Goddess(es) with subordinate god(s)
C. Co-equal god(s) and goddess(es)
D. God(s) with subordinate goddess(es)
E. God(s) with no goddess(es)
F. Nonhuman deities
    1 Subhuman (e.g., animal)
    2. Superhuman (e.g., The Unmanifest)
G. Universal atheism

Thus classical Greece was D-D-D-D whereas Yahwist Israel was D-D-D-E. Contemporary America is B-D-C-E, although it appears to be D-D-C-E with regard to the Presidency, or B-B-C-G with respect to the scientific community. A feminist utopia would theoretically be A-A-A-A. The ideal would probably be something like B-C-B-C. We still have a long way to go.

My own opinion for what it's worth is that we should cease attempting to stereotype civilizations and ideas as "masculine" or "feminine," realize that each individual contains some of the characteristics of both sexes regardless of physiological gender, and get on with the business of being human.

In evaluating Greek mythology or using it for magical purposes, we need not be tied to what this writer or that thinks the societies and beliefs were like among the Pelasgians or Athenians. We can make our own myths from the basic material. Why not? They did it.

A Modern Myth

Sing, O muse, of the fate of Thea Glaukopis Athene, the bright-eyed goddess, mother of Athens, victor over Poseidon and Ares, protector of cities, restrainer of Achilles, guide and mentor of the wily Odysseus, slayer of violators, wise beyond the wisdom of men. Is it true, what they say, that motherless She sprang from the head of the sky father and served his will as acolyte, affirming father right and mannish might, letting the matricide Orestes free because mothers count for naught? I tell you this tale that you may judge.

Bertram Hubris and Melanie Quarry were married in the church of his fathers. Melanie was a quiet woman, devoted to her husband, willing to help him in his career as an insurance agent and tolerant of his beer drinking, cigar smoking, and time-consuming devotion to the game of football as seen on television. She even shined his brown shoes, careful not to get polish on the bright white laces. As far as Bertram was concerned, Melanie and his VCR were of roughly equal importance, both being possessions that a man required for proper social adjustment. Her opinions and desires were of no interest, being merely the wanderings of the vacant mind of a typical female.

One Monday after drinking with his friends, Bertram came home to catch the fourth quarter while eating his dinner. Since he was late, the dinner, which had been ready on time, was rather cold and tasteless. In disgust, he hurled the dinner into the imitation fireplace and called for a beer.

Melanie gently pointed out that he was out of beer, having consumed the last of it the night before

"Goddam it!" Bertram yelled. "How much of your crap do I have to put up with, anyway? Are you crippled? Why couldn't you walk half a mile to the store and get me a six pack, at least?"

"You didn't leave me any money," Melanie gently pointed out.

"Always complaining!" Bertram bellowed. "Just get out and let me watch this game in peace!"

"Bertram, dear," she said, "the sink's stopped up." Bertram lost control. This was entirely too much. He sprang from his stuffed chair, grabbed Melanie—whom he outweighed by about 75 pounds—and shoved her into the wall. She screamed. He backhanded her, jerking her head to one side.

As he was reaching for her hair to haul her to the floor for further just punishment—such as a few good, swift kicks with his brown shoes with the white laces—he hesitated. A change seemed to be coming over Melanie. She was growing taller. Her drab blouse was taking on a hairy quality, like goatskin. Her head seemed to be encased in an open-faced helmet with a brush-like plume on top. The hem of her skirt now reached her feet, and, whereas before it had been a plain, faded blue fabric, it was now white and pleated. Instead of holding an offering of beer or food, her right hand grasped a long spear. She was beautiful more than a mortal might be, but, in horror, Bertram perceived that the goatskin she wore about her shoulders still had the grisly head attached, and the head was leering at him.

"By the law of the gods," spoke the awesome apparition, "thou shalt not strike an unarmed woman!"

"I—I—women need discipline!" Bertram stammered.

"And who art thou to discipline others?" She said. "A mighty warrior? Even if such thou wert, violence against a defenseless woman would be unworthy of thee. If thou needs must fight a woman, fight me!"

"Who are you, anyway?" said Bertram. "You're sure not Melanie!"

"There is no Melanie. For three months I have in her guise endured thy stupidity, thy cruelty, and thy smug superiority. Superior to what? Not to a slug, surely! But now thou hast transgressed. "Who am I?" She went on, eyes flashing, penetrating his soul with their accusing stare, boring into his inmost being like beacons revealing his shortcomings even to himself. "Know that I am Athene, a god."

"Athena?" Bertram gasped. "They drilled some of that into our heads in world lit. Aren't you supposed to be running errands for Big Daddy Zeus?"

"That pompous, goatish fool is no father of mine," She said. "My own father was no better. I slew him when he thought to violate me—and may all such incestuous vermin be slain where they stand! I was borne not in the brain of air-headed Zeus the sky patriarch, but in the womb of my mother, Metis, and they who say otherwise lie through their teeth. I never served Zeus. The strength of his followers was such that I found it wisest to work behind his back and not confront him openly. I helped Odysseus on my own initiative when the 'sky father' sat dreaming of more conquest. I did not judge Orestes guiltless as that liar proclaimed—I sentenced him not to death but to a deserved fate, pursued by Erinyes from one end of the earth to the other until he died at last from the bite of a serpent. And now it is time for another trial, in which thou already doth stand condemned by thy own deeds!"

"You sure talk a lot, Athena," Bertram said. "Why don't you sit down with me and watch the rest of the game?"

"A brave statement," She said, "but thy voice doth tremble and quake, as well it might. But thou art right. I have spoken too much. I have no need to explain myself to such as thee."

Bertram lunged forward to grab Her spear. After all, goddess or not, She was only a woman.

The Goddess calmly but swiftly, almost casually, raised Her spear. The butt end of the haft caught him in the chest. There was a blinding white light.

The front door of the suburban cottage opened. A quiet woman in a plain blouse and faded blue skirt tossed a brown football with bright white lacing to some children playing in the neighboring yard.

III

Archaic and Classical
Greek Magic

In plain fact, we know almost nothing about magic as it was practiced in archaic Greece before the time of Homer. Presumably, it was influenced to some extent by the magic of surrounding cultures—the Egyptian and the Sumerian, perhaps by way of Phoenicia and the Hittite empire—and an amalgam arose consisting of native magic that incorporated these influences. The oldest records that we have, however, would seem to indicate that the gods were called upon in a way that went farther than simple prayer, or even prayer and sacrifice. In addition, the oldest Greek magic seems already to have involved the simple principles stated by Sir James George Frazer in *The Golden Bough*—that is, sympathetic magic, categorized as either homeopathic (similarity) or contagious (contact). That is, two things which are in some way similar (homeopathy) or which have been in physical contact with each other (contagion) are magically connected, and one may be used to influence the other. "As I burn this hair from her head, so let her heart burn for me." Besides the employment of these principles—which seem to be so widespread that they must have some basis in the human psyche if not in fact—the use of herbs and roots was common, as in modern Wicca. We know that love philters were used in the 5th century B.C.

Beyond that, at least in fictional/historical accounts such as those of Homer, the use of a wand *(rhabdos)* as a magical implement seems to have been almost universal. Of all the modern paraphernalia of the magician—wands, chalices, swords, daggers, pentacles, and so on—the wand seems to be the oldest and most widespread. Its use seems to reach as far back as Egypt, at least, where the gods are ordinarily depicted as holding a wand or staff. The use of a wand as an expression of the will of the magician, as an object of command, may have its origin in the use of a staff to chastise slaves, servants, and employees. (The standard phallic explanation doesn't explain these attributes quite so well.) Nowadays, threatening spirits (or astral entities) are commonly held at bay with a magical dagger or sword, but historically the wand may have been used for this purpose—or, in a more authoritarian age, to chastise disobedient spirits.

There are hints here and there, and Homer describes a few magical operations in *The Odyssey*. The best known of these is the one in which Circe instructs Odysseus in the method of speaking with the deceased seer Teiresias—necromancy, pure and simple. However, this ritual yet retains a religious framework and involves animal sacrifice (a ram and a ewe). Furthermore, it follows hard on the heels of the account of Circe turning men into swine with a drug and a touch of her wand. Such being the case, we have to make some arbitrary decision about where fantastic fable leaves off and accurate reportage begins. I suspect that Homer may have used a little poetic license here and did not consult any magicians or witches.

The oldest written Greek magical ritual that I would consider very likely to be authentic and that does not seem directly related to public religious and divinatory rituals dates from a rather distressingly late date—the 3rd century B.C., in the Hellenistic period, and then in the form of a fictional (?) account in a poem. Nevertheless, the ceremony, presented in a form of a dramatic monologue enlivened by asides to a servant, apparently contains elements later borne out as authentic.

In this ceremony, presented in second *Idyll* of Theocritus, the goddesses Hecate, Artemis, and Selene are called upon to empower the operation (along with a nod to Aphrodite), and the incantation includes the refrain, *"Iunx, elke tu tenon emon poti doma ton andra."* This phrase has been variously translated (everything from J. M. Edmonds' "Wryneck, wryneck, draw him hither" [1912] to Georg Luck's "Draw to my house my lover, magic wheel" [1985]), but which seems to have something to do with a wryneck woodpecker bound to a revolving wheel. (It is not stated whether the unfortunate bird is dead or alive.) Purple thread is used in some way to bind the errant lover.

Besides the wheel, which is not described, the magical implements include a bull-roarer and a gong. Materials used include bay leaves, bran, wax, coltsfoot, pulverized lizard, and a piece of the lover's cloak (magic of contagion again). Besides the use of these materials and the above-quoted refrain, the history of the relationship is recited along with a second refrain imploring the Moon Goddess to "tell me" or "list" to the history: *"Phrazeo meu ton eroth' hothen hiketo, potna Selana."* This monologue is reproduced in Georg Luck's *Arcana Mundi*, a superb compilation of Greek and Roman magical writings.

However, given this relative paucity of material—there is certainly no such thing as a grimoire from classical (much less archaic) Greece—let us examine something extremely relevant that we do know something about—the Greek gods.

For traditional magical workings, you may feel that you need to know some sort of correspondence system for these gods with regard to the elements, the planets, and the signs of the Zodiac. Aleister Crowley listed the correspondences of various pantheons to the 32 Paths of Wisdom in *Liber 777*. Here are his Greek attributions:

Fire—Hades
Water—Poseidon
Air—Zeus
Earth—[Demeter], Gaia

By the use of the brackets around "Demeter," Crowley evidently means that the attribution is doubtful or that this represents a less important function of the goddess. The primary attribution for Demeter in his system is to the sephirah Binah.

For the planets, Crowley lists:

Moon—Artemis, Hecate
Mercury—Hermes
Venus—Aphrodite
Sun—Helios, Apollo

Mars—Ares
Jupiter—Zeus
Saturn—[Athena], Kronos as Saturn

Athene is listed for Saturn because She represents the Higher Wisdom, says Crowley. The connection is through the sephirah Binah (although he has Athene listed for Chokmah and other goddesses listed for Binah).

Except for certain refinements, however, the planetary attributions are obvious. Five of the seven planets bear the names of Roman gods that roughly correspond to analogous Greek gods. Without ambiguity, the most important and significant attributions can be said to be:

Moon—Artemis
Mercury—Hermes
Venus—Aphrodite
Sun—Apollo
Mars—Ares
Jupiter—Zeus
Saturn—Kronos

Crowley gives the astrological attributions as follows:

Aries—Athena
Taurus—[Here]
Gemini—Castor and Pollux, Apollo the Diviner
Cancer—Apollo the Charioteer
Leo—Demeter [borne by lions]
Virgo—[Attis]
Libra—Themis, Minos, Aeacus, and Rhadamanthus
Scorpio—Ares
Sagittarius—Apollo, Artemis (hunters)
Capricorn—Pan, Priapus, [Erect Hermes and Bacchus]
Aquarius—[Athena], Ganymede
Pisces—Poseidon

Athene is attributed to Aries because (in the official story) She emerged from the head of Zeus, and Aries (not to be confused with the god Ares) is the head of the Zodiac. There is also a connection through the Tarot trump, the Emperor, which combines the ideas of wisdom and military leadership. The goddess Here goes with Taurus primarily because Homer always described her as "cow-eyed" *(boōpis)*.

Crowley does not acknowledge any sources for these attributions, but it seems likely that he must have been familiar with those of Gaius Manilius, who lived at the beginning of the Christian era, particularly inasmuch as Manilius is quoted by Cornelius Agrippa. If so, he chose to ignore most of them. If not, there is the otherwise unexplained common attribution of Athene to Aries. Aside from the planetary rulership of Aries by Mars and the fact that Athene is a goddess of (among other things) war, this does not seem to me to be an obvious attribution. (But Kathleen Burt explains it very well and in greater depth in *Archetypes of the Zodiac*.) Manilius' attributions are for the Roman gods; the corresponding Greek gods are given in parentheses.

Aries—Pallas (Athene)
Taurus—Venus (Aphrodite)
Gemini—Apollo
Cancer—Mercury (Hermes)
Leo—Jove (Zeus)
Virgo—Ceres (Demeter)
Libra—Vulcan (Hephaestos)
Scorpio—Mars (Ares)
Sagittarius—Diana (Artemis)
Capricorn—Vesta (Hestia)
Aquarius—Juno (Here)
Pisces—Neptune (Poseidon)

This is the system quoted by Agrippa in Chapter 58 of Book II of *The Occult Philosophy*. Another translation indicates that Vesta rules the horse part of the centaur Sagittarius as well as all of Capricorn, leaving Diana with the human half of Sagittarius.

For the ten sephiroth of the cabalistic Tree of Life, Crowley listed the Greek deities as follows:

Kether—Zeus, Iacchus
Chokmah—Athena, Uranus
Binah—Cybele, Demeter, Rhea, Here

Chesed—Poseidon
Geburah—Ares, Hades
Tiphareth—Iacchus, Apollo, Adonis
Netzach—Aphrodite, Nike
Hod—Hermes
Yesod—Zeus (as Air), Diana of Ephesus (as phallic stone)
Malkuth—Persephone, [Adonis], Psyche

When more than one deity is listed, says Crowley, it is because they are needed to "complete the connotation" of the sephirah.

It should be borne in mind that scholarship has now uncovered considerably more information about the ancient pantheons (particularly those of Egypt) than was available to Crowley at the time he compiled his lists of correspondences. One system of attribution for the planets that takes these more recent findings into account is that given by Denning and Phillips in *Planetary Magick*:

Saturn—Here, Kronos, Aphrodite Ourania
Jupiter—Zeus, Athene, Poseidon
Mars—Ares, Hephaistos
Sun—Apollo, Dionysos, Helios
Venus—Aphrodite
Mercury—Hermes
Moon—Artemis, Selene, Hecate

Of course, all such attributions are more or less arbitrary and represent a somewhat artificial attempt to graft one system onto another. Unless you are working within a cabalistic framework, there is really no need to know the attributions to the Tree of Life. At any rate, in the final analysis, the attributions are correct only insofar as they feel right to you. You are certainly free to revise any of these lists in line with your own meditations and experiences.

So what about the use of the Greek gods in modern magical ritual? To begin with, you should familiarize yourself as much as possible with the gods as the Greeks saw them. There are a great many books available on the subject of Greek mythology, but it would be hard to beat *The Greek Myths* of Robert Graves for concise, accurate reporting that considers all the variations and alternate versions. Edith Hamilton *(Mythology)* and Thomas Bulfinch *(Bulfinch's Mythology)* provide even more basic grounding, while various mythological encyclopedias, notably that of Larousse, provide handy summary accounts. The Modern Library's *Great Classical Myths* quotes a vast amount of the original material in translation. I would advise staying away from the more technical approaches, however, until you have this basic background. Even motion pictures such as *Clash of the Titans* can give you some idea, but be advised that Athene did not have a mechanical owl that aided Perseus!

You may choose to form a magical link with one of these gods. Advice for so doing is given by Murry Hope in *Practical Greek Magic*, but it would be advisable to have some basic grounding in modern magical techniques—particularly "pathworking"—before undertaking such a venture. You should also be aware that, despite all your efforts at protection and testing, entities can slip through and claim to be one of the Greek gods, or a representative of one of them, while meanwhile having something in mind other than your welfare. There are astral beings (or, if you prefer, constellations of subconscious contents) who, by human standards at least, are evil and destructive. A good many others just seem to want attention. Iamblichus mentions a case in Roman times in which someone "channeled" the god Apollo only to find out that the entity was really the ghost of a gladiator!

There are various methods of testing any entity that presents itself—pentagrams, hexagrams, gematria, and so on—but no such system is 100 percent effective, and almost all of them aren't particularly Greek. One of the best tests, and one that was tacitly assumed in ancient Greece, is "signs hereafter"—a fairly precise prediction that comes true, or possibly a series of striking synchronicities. But the best test of all is common sense and a level head. If the entity asks for a human sacrifice, abandon and/or banish it as required. Even the "wickedest man alive" didn't fall for that one. If the "deity" tells you that you have been chosen as his/her priest/priestess and will soon (if you follow instructions) become rich and famous while bringing the Message to the world, I think you can discount it as the playfulness of an astral transient. Some will use flattery. Some of them may even try to win your favor with a little astral sex. Do as thou wilt, but don't be taken in by this ploy, either. Remember above all that no authentic god or guide will ever ask you to do anything criminal or exceptionally antisocial.

Also be aware that all such contacts will be astral—that is, in some respects imaginative—and do not expect a centaur/tutor wearing a mortarboard to show up on your front doorstep.

The question with such workings is always how much represents authentic subconscious contents—and therefore the astral plane, which at the deepest level is common to all of us and can thus be said to possess a reality of its own—and how much you are injecting into it yourself from your preconscious mind. Students are commonly concerned that they are controlling the scenario too much and doing nothing more than talking to themselves. There's no great harm if such is the case. One of the best techniques I know for getting invaluable advice is simply to imagine that you are talking to someone whose opinions you respect. This will help you to organize your thoughts and look at the matter objectively.

But, assuming that you seek an authentic astral contact with an authentic Greek deity, or a representative thereof, then all I can tell you is to trust nothing and no one until they have proven themselves unmistakably. Even then, do not take their advice if they suggest you do something altogether harebrained, such as walk naked down Main Street carrying a thyrsus and a bottle of Greek wine. The chief danger of this sort of working is self-delusion, and the chief defense against self-delusion is a good dose of level-headed common sense.

As for magical workings that employ Greek concepts, I do not suggest that you start trying to substitute Greek deity names for Hebrew names in, for example, the rituals of the Hermetic Order of the Golden Dawn, such as the Lesser Banishing Ritual of the Pentagram or the Middle Pillar. MacGregor Mathers may have been capable of working up a viable synthesis of this nature, but you and I are not. I can't say that it just flat does not work, but it doesn't work as well. The systems are not all that compatible.

Following, then, is a simple ritual of centering, sealing, and protection analogous to the Lesser Banishing Ritual of the Pentagram or the magical circle of other traditions. If the classical Greeks bothered with such things, we have no way of knowing, but I have tried not to depart too much from the classical Greek spirit or try to hammer Greek ideas into cabalistic or Rosicrucian molds.

For this ritual, you will need a good-sized wand. If you have been doing Golden Dawn magic, the Lotus Wand will do, but it would be better to have a wand used for nothing but Greek rituals. Greek wands, as nearly as I can determine, were nothing like the dainty little sticks used by stage magicians and fairy godmothers. They were more like a short staff than anything else. A sawed-off broomstick would do very well, although you may prefer a straight section of branch taken from a living tree.

The wand should be long enough so that it can be held in one hand with one end resting on the ground while you are standing. The wand may be decorated and consecrated "as the ingenium of the student may devise." It is better to do a lot of study and work to come up with something personally meaningful than to follow a set pattern devised by someone else. You may glue a pine cone on one end to form a thyrsus, a common form of the classical Greek wand, but this is not essential.

The wand represents the will of the magician and is used in this ceremony instead of the more usual dagger or athame because (1) the Greeks were not known to routinely use magical knives and (2) Greek magic (unlike Greek philosophy) is more concerned with Will than with Intellect and Discernment, represented by the dagger. This seems to be true despite the fact that the notion of will (*thelema*) seems to have been foreign to the Homeric Greeks. They never did anything out of the strictly ordinary without being prompted by a god or a daemon or by their *thumos* or *phanes*—perhaps best understood as the autonomic nervous system. "Sorry, Hector," Achilles might have said. "I can't do battle with you until I get the fight-or-flight reaction."

This apparent inability to make a decision without being told what to do by a god prompted Julian Jaynes to theorize (in *The Origin of Consciousness in the Breakdown of the Bicameral Mind*) that they were not, in fact, conscious at all. The "gods" who advised them, he says, were voices from the right half of the brain that were heard in the aural centers of the left brain—a mechanism that also accounts for the frequent stories about talking statues, a major feature of Hellenistic theurgy. But I digress.

Classical Greek Ritual of Centering and Protection

Centering:

Stand facing East in the center of the place of operation. Holding your wand in your right hand, lift it above your head, keeping the wand vertical. Say, in an authoritative voice, *"From the heavens above..."*

Bring the wand down in a straight line until the lower end rests on the ground or floor. Say, *"...to the Earth below..."*

Point the wand straight ahead of you, to the East. Say, *"...from the regions before me..."*

Bring the wand overhead, with your arm straight, pointing behind you to the West. Say, *"...to the regions behind me..."*

Bring your arm and the wand over to your right, pointing South at arm's length. Say, *"...from the regions on my right hand..."*

Bring the wand across your chest and point to to the left, toward the North. Say, *"...to the regions on my left hand..."*

Hold the wand vertically at arm's length above your head. Say, *"...may all find their center in me, chosen of N, as I stand in this place of holiness."*

"N" will be the name of a Greek deity you have selected as being appropriate to the main ceremony. For general purposes, or as a daily ritual performed in its own right, you may use the name of a deity you have selected as patron. Otherwise, "Zeus" will be adequate. Since Athene is the traditional protector of cities, the use of her name would be equally appropriate if the centering is immediately followed by the protection phase given below.

This simple little ceremony is not so simple as it sounds. To be effective, it must be accompanied by strong visualizations involving vertical and horizontal shafts of brilliant white light.

Protection:

Go to the East of the place of working. No, you are not going to trace a pentagram in the air. You will never find a pentagram used in any classical Greek art; therefore, we may assume that it was not a common religious symbol for them as it is for us. (We have 50 of them in our national flag.) Instead, simply lift the wand on high pointing slightly forward and say, *"By the authority of Zeus, Sky-Father, I seal the Eastern Quarter against the evil and the profane!"* This is to be spoken in an authoritative voice, and the name "Zeus" should be "vibrated"—that is, it should, above all, be deeply resonated so that it can be felt vibrating in your chest or, better yet, throughout your whole body. It should be visualized as likewise vibrating the entire Eastern quarter of the Earth and the Heavens. In my opinion—and there are practicing adepts who disagree with me on this point—it is not necessary to bellow the name at the top of your lungs. It seems to me that this technique tends to sacrifice vibration for volume—but the name should ideally be vibrated loudly enough to be heard by a hoplite in the rear ranks. Of course, even this much volume is not always practical in a small apartment. The name should burst forth in a crescendo of energy, and you should give it all you've got—but that doesn't necessarily mean going for decibels. The important thing is that the name be spoken authoritatively and with vibration. Do not let the spirits think you are a wimp.

Go around to the South, still holding the wand on high. Visualize it as tracing along the surface of a vertical wall of light that seals off the area as you advance. In the South, face the South, hold the wand aloft, and say, *"By the authority of Hephaistos, Lord of the Flashing Fire, I seal the Southern Quarter against the evil and the profane!"*

Go to the West in the same manner. Say, *"By the authority of Amphitrate, Lady of the Waves and Waters, I seal the Western Quarter against the evil and the profane!"* (Poseidon might seem to be more appropriate for Water, but I am seeking to preserve the "masculine/feminine" balance of the elements.)

Then go to the North in the same way and say, *"By the authority of Demeter, Goddess of the Abundant Earth, I seal the Northern Quarter against the evil and the profane!"* Then come back around to the East to complete your circular wall of protection and finally come back to the center, facing East.

Hold your wand in both hands in front of your chest and say, vibrating the names, *"May this place be under the protection of the gods upon whose names I have called. May it be sealed by the clashing shields of the Kuretes! May the Erinyes pursue those who would violate this sanctuary! Eirene. Eirene. Eirene."* This incantation should be accom-

panied by the appropriate visualizations. The Kuretes were sons of
Rhea who clashed their spears and shields around the infant Zeus to
drown out his cries and hide him from his father, Kronos, who was
intent upon swallowing him. The Erinyes ("ir ANY ease") are the
Furies, who pursue wrongdoers. They are said to be half bird and
half woman. "Eirene" is pronounced (in classical Greek) "Ay-RAY-
nay." It means "peace."

Finally, repeat the centering ritual and throw in another
"Eirene" at the very end.

I confess that this ritual still leans a little too heavily upon modern hermetic practices to be truly ideal, but, in the absence of anything similar in the recorded classical Greek tradition, it was
necessary to use more recent techniques as a sort of paradigm. Any
experienced worker should feel free to change it as he or she feels
appropriate.

Other classical Greek rituals, which are very good, are given in
Dolores Ashcroft-Nowicki's *The Ritual Magic Workbook* (Aquarian
Press, 1986). "The Greek Ritual of Spring" and "The Greek Ritual of
the Summer" are summarized at the end of this chapter. However, I
have to point out that these rituals, too, rely upon the Western Hermetic Tradition. A lemniscate (infinity symbol, ∞) is substituted for
the more usual Western pentagram. Students may also wish to consult Israel Regardie's *Ceremonial Magic* (Aquarian Press, 1980),
wherein he gives instructions for making a dramatic ritual out of *The
Bacchae* of Euripedes. Regardie's invocation of Isis (reproduced in
The Golden Dawn) could easily be adapted to a Greek deity, although, of course, this ritual is squarely in the Western Hermetic/
Rosicrucian Tradition rather than being essentially Greek.

The Greek Ritual of Spring

This ritual appears in *The Ritual Magic Workbook* by Dolores
Ashcroft-Nowicki, copyright 1986, and is reproduced by kind permission of Thorsons Publishing Group (The Aquarian Press), Wellingborough, Northamptonshire, England.

This workbook constitutes an entire program for the aspiring
magician. Theoretically, you are not really ready for this ritual until

you've had a certain amount of practice at lesser rituals, and the ceremony assumes that you have already set up, sealed, and consecrated a temple in a room dedicated to that purpose alone. That, however, constitutes the ideal situation and is simply not practicable for someone living in a small apartment or a small house with wall-to-wall furniture, particularly if children are involved. However, I see no reason why this ritual and the one that follows cannot be performed in whatever temple environment you can contrive, including (especially) an outdoor setting.

Whatever the setting, you will need a central altar and one altar in each quarter. (Small tables will serve if you don't have specially constructed altars.) Pillars are specified, but in a pinch these may be visualized astrally. The prescription for the incense is fairly involved and will require foresight and preparation—it's not something you can throw together at the last minute. However, again, this recipe represents the ideal situation: "sanderac, pine resin, benzoin, with leaves of eucalyptus, pine needles, rosemary, mixed with oil of jasmine. You can add a few bits of rosemary as well." You will also need a bowl of seeds and a wreath. Dress in the Greek style if possible, although your clothing need not be elaborate.

Each of the five altars should be covered with a white cloth and should have a central candle—"a nightlight in a white saucer or bowl is ideal." You should also have four tall candlesticks, which are to be placed between the quarters with alternating green and gold candles. None of the candles are lit at the beginning of the ritual. Other items on the altars in the quarters are:

East—plate holding homemade bread and a teaspoon of honey
South—censer (charcoal lit and ready for incense)
West—jug of red wine and cup
North—bowl of fruit

The fruits in the North should be native to Greece—"apples, grapes, figs, pomegranates, with ready shelled almonds, some raisins and a bowl of mixed flower seeds."

The ritual itself goes like this: Standing behind the Eastern altar, facing East, light a taper and the altar candle. With the taper, trace an infinity sign (lemniscate or "lazy eight"). Visualize the god Hermes between the Pillars, building up the image in detail, and say, "*Son of Zeus and Maia, swift-footed messenger of Olympus, draw near and fill this quarter with the divine pneuma of the Gods."*

When the image is clear, go around the Eastern altar clockwise, go to the Southern altar and go around it to face South. In all these movements, you should pass within (not outside of) the tall candlesticks. "Light the altar light, make the infinity sign, build up the godform of Apollo and invoke."

"Son of Zeus and Leto, god of Delphi and of Delos, driver of the sun's chariot, draw near and fill this place with light."

Proceed to the West in a similar fashion. Note that you don't just go directly from one altar to another. There is always at least a partial clockwise circumambulation involved. What this amounts to is always starting off in the direction opposite to that in which you are going. In each quarter, you light the altar candle, use the taper to make the infinity sign, and build up the god-form. After each evocation, make sure the god-form is as strong and clear as possible before moving on. (The author speaks of "invocation," but, technically, it seems to be evocation that is really involved. There is no attempt to assume the god-forms yourself.)

In the West, the god-form involved is Artemis, and the evocation is this: *"Daughter of Zeus and Leto, night's slender huntress, virgin of the Moon, draw near and fill this place with Tidal power."*

In the north, it's Demeter. Here, you say, *"Daughter of Chronus [Kronos] and Rhea, Earth Mother and giver of bread, draw near and fill this place with strength and growth."*

Go back to the East in the same fashion and light a fresh taper. Now go to the candlestick in the Southeast, circumambulating it as you did the altars. At each of the four tall candlesticks between the quarters, you are going to light the candle with the taper and evoke, formulating the god-images as before. No infinity signs are traced this time around.

Southeast: Iris (Rainbow Goddess). *"Many coloured Iris, servant of Hera, draw near and be ready to take our plea to the halls of Olympus, to the feet of Zeus."*

Southwest: Aphrodite. *"Golden Goddess of Love, Aphrodite of Paphos, draw near and give your aid that we may persuade Hades to return Kore to the Earth."*

Northwest: Hades. *"Dark browed Hades, Lord of the Underworld, give to us your queen, the beauteous Persephone for six short months that the Earth may be fruitful and mankind may grow in strength."*

Northeast: Kore (Persephone). *"Sweet faced Kore, Persephone of the white arms, leave your halls of the Underworld and join us here on Earth bringing new life to the Earth and joy to us all."*

Complete the circle by returning to the Southeast. Bow once there and return to the East. Extinguish the taper. "Take up the piece of bread, dip it in the honey and eat it, offer the plate to the East," saying, *"Great Hermes, take what we offer to great Zeus and ask that Kore may be returned to Earth."*

"Move to the South, lift the incense, smell it, then offer it to the South." Say, *"Golden Apollo halt thy chariot and listen to our plea, take this incense to Olympian Zeus and ask that the Earth Maiden be given back to us."*

Quoting directly from Ms. Ashcroft-Nowicki (with very minor editing of the punctuation):

> (Move to the West, pour the wine into the Chalice and drink, then offer it to the West.)
>
> *Chaste Artemis, Virgin Goddess of the Moon, take this offering to thy immortal father Zeus and plead with him to set free the giver of life.*
>
> (Move to the North, take and eat a piece of fruit, then offer the bowl to the North.)
>
> *Demeter, Corn Goddess, Earth Mother, like you we mourn the loss of Persephone. Ask thy brothers Zeus and Hades to free her that the fields may be blessed.*
>
> (Move to the centre of the temple and lift arms.)
>
> *Hear me, O ye gods, give to mankind the blessing of the Spring.*
>
> (Kneel and place your head in your hands. In your mind build up the sound of running feet; hear them take the twisting labyrinthine path that you have woven in the temple. It is the sacred way of the ancient times, and Kore now treads it on her way to Earth. Feel the Earth beneath you tremble as the whole of nature holds its breath. Let the feeling of imminent Spring and growth build up inside you until the intensity bursts through in a cry of . . .)
>
> *Kore, Kore, Kore, Kore.*
>
> (Stand up and face the quarters in turn giving silent thanks to the gods. Then take the bowl of seeds around to each and hold it up for a blessing. Place your wreath in the centre of the temple and put the bowl inside it. Now go to the East and re-trace the patterns either by pacing, or better still by dancing. Dance until you feel tired, then take up the wreath and the seeds and go to each quarter in turn saying:)
>
> *Go in peace and harmony and with thee go our blessings for the work this night.*

(Put out the lights in the order in which they were lit. Put out bread for the birds, pour the wine onto the Earth, scatter or plant the seeds and share the fruit with family and friends.)

The Greek Ritual of the Summer

This is a ritual for two people, who will take the roles of Hermes and Flora, goddess of flowers. The set-up is essentially the same, but now each of the altars in the Quarters should hold "a small cup of wine and a piece of bread or a honey cake" as well as a central altar light. The predominant colors involved should be rose, green, gold, and blue. Other items on the altars:

East: a small mirror
South: censer with burning charcoal, but no incense
West: a living plant
North: vase of water

Flora has a small basket with some incense, a bottle of water, and some mixed flowers ... Flora waits by the door, while Hermes opens the temple. He faces East and with the Caduceus makes the infinity sign.

Caduceus

The Ritual Magic Workbook contains instructions for making a caduceus for use in this ritual. I will not reproduce those instructions here but will advise the student to use imagination and ingenuity. It will mean more to you if you do it this way rather than following a set of instructions. However, if the caduceus is not going to be used outside one performance of this ritual, you might care to buy the book. I will say only this: Don't use live snakes.

Hermes: *In the name of the All Father, Zeus, lord of Olympus, I open this temple. Grant to me thy son, messenger of the Gods, the power to open the doors of summer and flood the Earth with warmth.*

(He goes to the South and makes the sign.)

In the name of Apollo my brother, I open this temple. Grant to me thy brother the power of the sun that I may ripen the corn.

(Goes to the West and makes the sign.)

In the name of Poseidon, my father's brother, I open this temple. Grant to me thy nephew the power of the oceans that I may feed mankind with its fruit.

(Goes to North and makes the sign.)

In the name of Hades, my father's brother, I open this temple. Grant to me thy nephew the power of the inner earth that I may bestow its riches upon mankind.

(Goes to Flora and takes her by the hand and leads her round the temple in a circle and then to the East.)

Flora: *Hermes of the swift foot, you have summoned me and I am here, what do you wish of my powers?*

Hermes: *Goddess of summer, share with me and with the Earth thy gift of warmth and sweet perfume. Come with me to the Gate of the South and bless it with thy presence.*

(Takes her to the South, here she sprinkles incense on the charcoal.)

Flora: *I bless this gateway with sweet perfume and warmth. Bright Apollo share with me and with thy brother the wine and bread of the Sun.*

(Hermes breaks the bread and shares it with her, also the wine. He then leads her to the West.)

Hermes: *Sweet Flora, pour out thy love upon the life of Earth, bless the Gate of the West with the moisture of thy breath.*

(She pours water on the plant.)

Flora: *I bless this gateway with moisture, great Poseidon share with me and with thy nephew the wine and bread of the west.*

(Hermes shares the bread and wine with her as before. Then he leads her to the North.)

Hermes: *Blessed Flora grant the Earth the colours of thy beauty, deck her with loveliness and brighten the hearts of mankind.*

(She places flowers in vase.)

Flora: *I give my colours to the Earth. Let summer reign as queen. Dark browed Hades open up the richness of the Earth and share it with all men. Share with us also the bread and wine of the North.*

(The bread and wine is shared as before, and Hermes leads Flora to the East.)

Hermes: *Light footed Flora, Golden skinned goddess of summer, let us praise the sky father together and ask his blessing upon the Earth.*

(They join hands and lift arms up.)

Both: *Great Zeus, we praise thee, and that which was before thee, we ask for the blessing of summer upon the face of Earth.*

(Stand silent for a few minutes.)

Hermes: *Daughter of Zeus, sweet sister, have you no gift for the Gate of the East?*

Flora: *To the East I give myself, that I may be one with the Earth and all that lives upon her. Sweet brother take my kiss as a gift for the East.*

(They kiss, and share the bread and wine. Her crown of flowers is placed upon the altar as an offering. Now they circle the temple, Hermes going clockwise and Flora anticlockwise, they cross at the West and continue round and back to the East. Flora goes to stand in the centre and Hermes closes the temple.)

Hermes: *With the power of my father Zeus, I close the temple. To thee, great one, our thanks and blessing.*

(Goes to the South.)

With the power of the sun and my brother Apollo I close the temple. To thee our thanks and blessing.

(Goes to the West.)

With the power of the oceans and my uncle Poseidon, I close the temple. To thee our thanks and blessing.

(Goes to the North.)

With the power of the inner earth and my uncle Hades, I close the temple. To thee our thanks and blessing.

(Back to the East and to the centre, Hermes and Flora kiss, and together put out the lights.)

The only modification I would suggest for this ritual would be to substitute "father's brother" for "uncle" and "brother's son" for "nephew." It sounds better to me, more formal and elegant and magical, probably because the terms "uncle" and "nephew" imply less respect in this country than they do in England.

IV

Classical Greek Philosophy

I'll start this discussion right off with a little disclaimer by saying that I do not intend to give a comprehensive picture of Greek philosophy or to go into it very deeply. That is not my purpose. One of my primary concerns in this book is to show how the central ideas of modern occult philosophy, from Eliphas Levi and H. P. Blavatsky to William Gray and Donald Tyson, were born in Greece and nourished for a thousand years in the Greek language. This is not a crash course in Greek philosophy as a whole. Therefore, I am not going to examine the whole philosophy of any one person, but only the fragments of interest. This will inevitably present a somewhat distorted picture of the totality of the thought of any given philosopher; if you want to know more about any one of them, read a book on Greek philosophy. This isn't one. I would highly recommend *Outlines of the History of Greek Philosophy* by Eduard Zeller. It may be a little outdated here and there—it was originally written in 1883—but, for an informative summary history of Greek philosophy, it can't be beat for the price (at this writing, $6.95 from Dover Publications).

The point in examining Greek philosophy at all is that it is the origin of many ideas and concepts that are more or less taken for granted in modern magic and occultism—or, if they aren't assumed as given precepts, they are sometimes presented as new information channeled from some higher entity as new revelations to humanity.

Pythagoras

It was in the Greek cities on the coast of Asia Minor, in Ionia, especially in Miletus, that Greek philosophy seems to have had its beginnings. The Ionian philosophers started an important trend that had both devastating and constructive effects—the trend of rationalism, materialism, and loss of faith in the reality of the traditional gods. This theme runs in and out of all subsequent Greek philosophy and eventually filtered down to ordinary people who were not philosophers. The subsequent reaction cleared the way for a magical revival, an increased interest in mystery religions, and—alas for Paganism—Christianity.

In any event, it was in Miletus that the idea arose that there was a basic stuff out of which everything is formed. The idea seems to have been that "everything is One"—a familiar statement in most New Age pronouncements as well as occult cosmologies and magical theory. Thales thought this basic substance was Water. He lived c. 624-546 B.C. (All dates given in this chapter are B.C., or, if you prefer, B.C.E.) Anaximander (c. 610-545) said it was something beyond all the elements, out of which the elements arose, something which he called *apeiron*—"the boundless." Students of the cabala will immediately recognize here the concept of *Ain Soph*, a Hebrew term which means the same thing. Anaximenes (c. 585-524) disagreed with the others; he said that the basic substance was Air. A little while later, Heraclitus (c. 544-484) up at Ephesus said it was Fire. Meanwhile, in 494, the Persians took over Miletus.

None of these philosophers except Heraclitus, who lived after Pythagoras, ever either affirmed or denied the existence of a soul. Apparently they'd never heard of such a thing. As far as they were concerned, there was no split between the spiritual and the material. It was all one thing. If someone met a god on the road, it wasn't a spiritual experience. It was just a case of meeting a god on the road.

Pythagoras, the well-known 6th-century B.C. mystic, magus, and shaman from the island of Samos, disagreed with the rest of the Ionians on almost all counts. He said that the basic substance everyone had been theorizing about was Number. Actually, he didn't exactly say that the *basis of the elements* was Number; he said that *the essence of everything* is Number. This idea is reflected not only in modern numerology but also in the cabalistic *Sepher Yetzirah* and in the familiar Tree of Life diagram, which considers numbers as archetypal divine emanations.

Pythagoras was impressed by the musical scale produced by

proportional divisions of the lyre string, and this may have been the basis for his fascination with numbers. He or his followers came up with the Pythagorean theorem about right triangles, and it may well be that he founded the first scientific laboratory, specifically an acoustics lab.

Since the division of a lyre string, or monochord, into proportional parts based on whole numbers up to four produces a harmonious scale, and since four was considered to be the manifestation of three-dimensional space, Pythagoras was enamored of the number four. He represented the numbers one through four with the famous arrangement known as the *tetraktys*, which became a holy symbol for his followers:

```
        *

      *   *

    *   *   *

  *   *   *   *
```

This diagram simultaneously depicts the numbers 1 through 4 and the number 10: $1 + 2 + 3 + 4 = 10$, which is to say the beginning of a new series. Unity, the monad, manifests as the dyad, the triad, and the tetrad, returning to itself in the form of the number 10. The first ten numbers were therefore also considered to be highly important, and attributes and characteristics were assigned to each. The same ideas regarding the progressive unfoldment of unity—into duality (duplication, antithesis), three (multiplication, synthesis), and so on—are still an integral part of almost all occult and magical teachings, as is the idea that there is something unique and deeply meaningful about each number apart from its usefulness in counting.

Something like 800 years after Pythagoras, the Hebrew *Sepher Yetzirah* was written down. The third verse says, "Ten are the numbers (Sephiroth) out of nothing; ten and not nine; ten and not eleven." Did Pythagoras influence the writer of the *Sepher Yetzirah*, or did a prior, unwritten Jewish tradition influence Pythagoras?

Pythagoras also disagreed with the Ionians by affirming the existence of a soul. He taught reincarnation or transmigration (including reincarnation as an animal). His students and acolytes—which were ahead of the times by including women—practiced what is now known as past-life regression.

But if the Ionic philosophers had never heard of a soul, where did Pythagoras get the idea that there was one and that it transmigrated? He is said to have traveled in Egypt. He might have heard about souls there (the *ba* and/or the *ka*), but the Egyptians had no doctrine of reincarnation—at least not one that they were willing to mention to an outsider or a modern archaeologist. Some people have even suggested that he traveled to India, but it's not likely. Scholarly consensus is that he got the idea from the mysteries of Orpheus, which seem to have originated in Thrace. E. R. Dodds advanced the idea that Hinduism, Orphism, and Pythagoreanism had all been influenced by Siberian shamanism by way of Scythia. Indeed, many of the feats attributed to Pythagoras (including, for example, physical bilocation) are precisely those for which the shamans were known. Shamanism, said Dodds, was also probably the source for the ideas that the soul could exist apart from the body and that bilocation was possible in the first place.

Pythagoras was only the second Greek legendary magus or shaman. Orpheus was the first. Despite the fact that Orpheus is a major figure in Greek mythology, there probably was such a person at some time. Unfortunately all we have are some myths about him— how he was the son of the muse Calliope, how he could charm animals with his music and even move trees and rocks around with it, how he was one of Jason's Argonauts, how he traveled to Hades after Eurydice, how he was torn to pieces, how his head became an oracle, and so on. Orphism existed, however, and evidently had a strong influence on Pythagoras. Both Orphics and Pythagoreans were vegetarians, for example. We'll take a look at the Orphic mysteries, along with some others, in the next chapter.

A contemporary of Pythagoras, Xenophanes (570-475), who ended up at Elea in Italy and thus represented what Plato called the Eleatic school of philosophy, didn't have much use for the traditional gods. He foreshadowed the Koran in a way by saying, in effect, "There is no god but God." The deity of Xenophanes was eternal and unchanging—good monotheistic doctrine—but also present in all things, including nature—an idea that would later be labeled by Christian theologians and philosophers as "pantheism." Pantheism somehow became a rather pejorative label for this particular brand of "heresy," but it is now considered acceptable mystical/occult doctrine. If you care to split hairs, saying that God is present in all things is not quite the same as true pantheism, which says that God is *identical* with all things. In any event, the idea now seems to be current that God is somehow both immanent (in all things) and transcendent (above and apart from all things).

The philosophical difficulty with pantheism is that, if God is present in matter, how can it be subject to change? One answer to this problem is to say that the *eternal essence* of a material object does not change, whether this essence is identified with something immaterial or with a modern scientific concept such as atomic particles. Another approach is to say that all change is an illusion.

On the other hand, the difficulty with the pure transcendence idea is that, if God is entirely apart from His/Her creation, then He/She is not infinite and is therefore not God. A good Muslim might say that it amounts to polytheism to say that anything exists other than God, although, particularly if he had no Sufi leanings, he would also regard pantheism as heretical.

Religionists and philosophers, like politicians, can be pretty handy with their labels. Xenophanes said that religious ideas are relative, not absolute—an ox thinks that God is an ox—and that we can really know nothing about God or the gods. "For sure," he said, "nobody knows anything about the gods and other such matters or ever will. Even if somebody said something that was entirely true, he wouldn't know it. It's all guesswork."

Heraclitus, mentioned earlier with regard to Fire, agreed with Xenophanes to the extent that he said that praying to an idol or image is like talking to a man's house instead of the man. He disagreed with Xenophanes, however, by saying that the nature of reality is not constant and unchanging, but rather is in a constant state of flux—like Fire. Nevertheless, he seems to have come up with the idea of compensating balances and "stability through change," another cabalistic and occult doctrine that is still very much current today. He also foreshadowed the cabalistic doctrine of successive emanations, in the same order as that indicated by the divine name YHVH, by saying that Fire produces Water which in turn produces Earth. It is not known why he left out Air, but he did indicate that the sequence Fire-Water-Earth was a "downward path." Since all is change, the upward path of Earth-Water-Fire was also possible. All this sounds rather like the cabalistic/occult doctrine of the descending Lightning Flash of creation and the ascending Serpent of Knowledge. As far as Heraclitus was concerned, however, his ideas were strictly materialistic and had no spiritual connotation.

Heraclitus, by the way, was the first (or among the first) to use the term *Logos* (word) to describe the spiritual principle underlying the world.

Parmenides (c. 540-470) disagreed with Heraclitus about almost everything. He said that that all Being is constant and unvariable and that all change is illusion. More importantly, perhaps, he said that nothing can be created or destroyed and that there is no such thing as empty space; that is, there is no such thing as nothing.

Another half-legendary philosopher/magus in the style of Orpheus and Pythagoras, Empedocles (c. 495-435), was primarily a healer, and miraculous cures were attributed to him—including the ability to raise the dead. He is also supposed to have been able to control the weather to the extent of bringing rain or calming storms.

Empedocles was the one who came up with the notion that there are four elements—Fire, Water, Air, and Earth, which is to say *Pyr, Hydor, Aither* (or *Aer*), and *Gaia*. Aristotle worked this into a system involving four qualities—Hot, Cold, Wet, and Dry. Thus Fire is Hot and Dry, Water is Cold and Wet, Air is Hot and Wet, and Earth is Cold and Dry. There seems to be no particular evidence that the reverence of the Pythagoreans for the number four in any way inspired the number of elements and the number of elemental qualities, but it can't be ruled out. Whatever the case, these doctrines have been with us ever since and play a huge part in modern ceremonial magic as well as in Wicca and other Pagan practices. The Chinese, incidentally, thought along the same lines—except that they came up with five elements, which included Wood and Metal but not Air.

Empedocles also spoke of a world of spirits that exists apart from the material world. He anticipated the Gnostics by saying that matter was essentially inferior and even evil. On this account, like the Cathars of medieval Europe, he was opposed to marriage and sex. To bring a child into this vale of tears is to imprison a free spirit in a tomb of flesh.

In teaching this duality of matter versus spirit, Empedocles was very likely influenced by Orphism. The doctrines of the Orphic mysteries (to be discussed in the next chapter) apparently included a firm idea of spirit versus matter and soul versus body. This dualism was picked up by many Greek philosophers—including not only Empedocles but also Plato and Aristotle, whose influence on Western thought has been so pervasive right down to the present.

The matter/spirit argument still isn't settled. Some say that this idea has led us astray for 2000 years. Others hold fast to it. Some seem to find a way to hold both ideas in mind at once, saying "You are not your body" in one breath and "All is One" or "All is Spirit" in the next. Actually, these two statements may not be as contradictory as they first appear.

Empedocles also anticipated the cabalistic doctrine that we have two souls—the *psyche,* which perishes with the body or shortly thereafter, and the *daimon,* or higher self, which is eternal.

With the apparent exception of Pythagoras, all the philosophers we've considered so far worried a great deal not only about what things were made of but also about what set them in motion. Empedocles said it was love vs. strife. But Anaxagoras (500-428), who was born in Asia Minor and settled in Athens, came up with the idea that the motive power in all things was mind—*nous* (νους).

In the views of Anaxagoras, *nous* was God, or so near to being the same thing as makes no difference. In the beginning, he said, Nous produced the manifested universe out of a disorganized chaos of things—bones, grass blades, pebbles, globules of water, paper clips, coat hangers, and so on and so on. The interesting thing about it is that Nous was supposed to have done this by setting up a rotating spiral motion beginning at a single point. This is *very* reminiscent of the cabalistic doctrine of the "first swirlings" in *Ain Soph,* the beginnings of spiral revolutions, the *Rashith ha-Gilgalim* with its center at *Kether,* the unmanifested Unity.

"Nous" apparently means far more than the individual minds of human beings. It is "mind" considered in an absolute or archetypal sense. Yet, at the same time, it is reflected in or is represented by individual minds. In any event, the notion that *mind* is the universal motive power may not be too far away from the theories of a few modern quantum physicists (John von Neumann, Euegene Wigner, John Wheeler), who say that reality, or at the very least quantum reality, is created or at least structured by consciousness—an idea essential to all magical operations. In any event, hundreds of years later, the Gnostics and Neoplatonists made a great deal out of the concept of *nous,* as we shall see.

And then there was Socrates (470-399). We know that he was an extremely charismatic teacher, that he seems to have been a fully realized human being, that he felt himself to be guided by an inner voice, and that he said he knew nothing. He also wrote nothing. We can only guess as to what philosophical ideas, if any, he taught. He is the protagonist in most of Plato's dialogs (Plato was one of his students), wherein he enacts the "Socratic method" of trying to find the truth by questioning, but we have no way of knowing how much Plato put into his mouth. We do know that he spent his life trying to find some solid definition of "the good" and that he devoted himself to the moral regeneration of his fellow citizens in the wake of rationalistic explanations that had eroded faith in the gods—a situation that sounds fairly familiar to modern ears. He worked by example and tried to get people to think and reflect about what they said and did. He seems to have believed in oracles and prophetic dreams. He must have been doing a lot of good, because he was impeached and condemned to death.

For all their famous enlightened attitude, the Athenians of classical times were intolerant of what they considered blasphemy, perhaps as a reaction against a growing materialism and rationalism. In 412 B.C., it was made illegal to disbelieve in the supernatural or to teach astronomy. Heresy trials were held for the next thirty years. But they at least never resorted to burning people at the stake as did the medieval Christians or beheading them as did the Muslims or stoning them to death as did the ancient Jews. Death was an unusual punishment. The common penalty was banishment or simply being removed from a position of responsibility. Besides Socrates, this 5th-century Inquisition came down on the heads of Anaxagoras, Protagoras, and possibly the playwright Euripedes.

After Socrates, the Cynics and the Hedonists (or Cyrenaics) started up. The Cynics taught that there was only one, invisible God, and they spoke out against temples, prophecy, and initiation. They did not believe in survival of bodily death. Although extremely materialistic in outlook—personifying the anti-spiritual trend that had begun with the Ionic philosophers—and disdaining all knowledge that didn't have an immediate utilitarian application, they embraced poverty. The Hedonists said that good = pleasure and evil = pain, and that one pleasure is as good as another (that is, watching *Gilligan's Island* is as good as going to an Ingmar Bergman film). But one of their number, Hegesias, thought that happiness was unattainable. He was so pessimistic and hated life so much that his teaching brought about many suicides, causing him to be called *Peisithanatos*, counselor of death—a phenomenon that brings to mind the major character of Gore Vidal's novel, *Messiah*. It has been pointed out by dozens of commentators that our own society has Hedonism as its operational philosophy; this would seem to apply both to the ideas of pleasure-seeking and disillusioned pessimism.

Socrates notwithstanding, if there had been no Plato (427-347), there would have been no Neoplatonism and no Platonic Academy. Consequently, it's very likely that Gnosticism, cabalism, Rosicrucianism, modern magic and occultism—even Christianity—would have taken quite different forms. The Neoplatonic ideas embodied in Sufism might have had to be accounted for by some means other than theoretical influence. We might still be using the elements in modern magic, but we'd be more likely to be using the tetraktys than the Tree of Life, and the whole idea of the astral plane along with the associated idea of creative visualization would either not exist or would be much more nebulous than it is.

Plato's idea, you see, was the Idea.

Ideas, or Forms, or Archetypes, he said, have an independent existence prior to manifested phenomena. The whole modern philosophical school of existentialism is founded upon the refutation of this notion, by the way, saying that existence precedes essence. Plato said the Ideas of all things exist eternally and perfectly in some nebulous, supercelestial realm. All the things we see in the "real world" are imperfect copies of the ideal and archetypal Ideas. Somewhere, in the realm of ideas, there is a perfect chair, and all earthly chairs are lame attempts to copy it. This whole philosophy seems to foreshadow cabalistic ideas about the World of Nobility, which is to say the World of Archetypes, the *Olam ha-Atziluth* (called *'Alam ul-Izzah* by the Sufis), although, in this system, the forms of the material world are the result of natural processes.

In any case, the world of Ideas or forms was much more real to Plato than the material world of manifestation. A chair breaks and ceases to be; the idea of a chair remains, eternal. These Ideas also included abstract qualities, "goodness," and so on, as well as objects. The ultimate archetype of "the good," he said, is the one and only true God. He countered the statement of Protagoras by saying that God, not man, is the measure of all things.

From this basic theory, Plato arrived at a sharp dualism between the material world and the world of Ideas, matter vs. spirit, soul vs. body, God vs. world, and so on. In this, he had developed Orphism and Pythagoreanism to their logical conclusion. Everything we see in the "real world" is distinctly inferior. The link between the world

Plato and Aristotle (from a painting by Raphael)

of Ideas and the world of manifestation is provided by the "materia," a sort of formless chaos which nevertheless gave rise through natural causes to the four elements. In order for the Ideas and the materia to interact to form the manifested world, it was necessary for the *Demiourgos*, or Demiurge, to design and create the Cosmos. The Greeks always assumed that the universe had to be created from something pre-existing, from chaos, from something "without form and void"; they could not conceive of its having been created *ex nihilo,* from nothing.

Plato picked up many of the other ideas of the Pythagoreans, including the concept of a soul that survives bodily death. He said that, after death, this soul is judged and either enters eternal bliss, eternal punishment in Tartarus, or some middle state where its sins can be expiated over time. All this sounds very much like Christianity with its heaven, hell, and purgatory. The standard Christian theory is that Plato was wise and blessed enough to be able to predict these spiritual "truths" before they were established by the Church. Pagans might prefer the simpler explanation that the early Christian church borrowed these ideas from Plato. They certainly inspired St. Augustine. In any case, these notions don't seem to have existed in anything like this form in Judaism at the time of Jesus.

Plato adapted the Pythagorean doctrine of transmigration to formulate a theory of reverse evolution that can only strike the modern mind as perverse and bizarre. Evolution for Plato consists not of any upward progress but rather of successive imperfection and degradation as Ideas are subsumed into form. Thus human beings came first, then animals, who are only degraded human beings reincarnated in a lower form. The most pernicious—and typically Athenian—aspect of this doctrine was that men came before women in this scheme, that a woman is just an imperfect man.

At first, Plato considered the soul to be a simple single entity, but he ended up by saying that it has three parts. He correlated these with reason (*Logos,* located in the head and the only immortal soul), will (*Thumos,* in the chest), and desire (*Epithymia,* in the belly). This seems to anticipate a similar and much later cabalistic doctrine; the correspondence to the *Neshamah, Ruach,* and *Nephesh* is not exact, but it is very close. Plato's "error" was in equating the higher soul with the rational intellect.

Plato's theory of knowledge, ethical as well as factual, was of course that the soul simply remembers things from its former existence in the archetypal world. Hence, we all know everything already. It's simply a matter of remembering it. The idea that all knowledge is accessible persists in modern hermetic doctrine, but in a somewhat different form: One has access through the subconscious mind either to other minds or to God or to the akashic record (if there's any difference).

Plato also postulated the existence of a World Soul, created by the Demiurge from the pattern of living creatures, which mediates between the world of Ideas and the material world. (For a more thorough examination of this concept of a World Soul, see Donald Tyson's appendix to *The Three Books of Occult Philosophy* by Cornelius Agrippa [to be published by Llewellyn].)

In his later writings, in the *Laws*, Plato even went so far as say there was also an evil World Soul and thus did his part for the Christian devil hypothesis. However, most modern hermeticists understand that it's impossible to have a devil without limiting God and setting up a Manichaean dualism. The devil is therefore seen as either non-existent or as a misunderstood aspect of God.

Plato set forth these and other doctrines that sound to us today as if they represented a retreat from the arid wastes of materialism into semi-Pythagorean mysticism. He described the dual nature of love—on the one hand, pure and simple lust; on the other hand, a drive toward transcendence in some respects like the Christian *agapē* and in others like the Hindu kundalini. He thought that the stars, and especially the planets, were higher, animate beings. The planets, after all, seemed to move of themselves. The universe as a whole, he said, is the visible form of God.

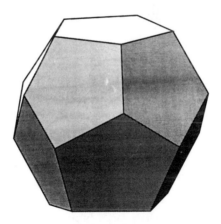

Dodecahedron

Another way in which Plato picked up on Pythagoreanism, incidentally, was in his idea that the five regular polyhedrons—the so-called Platonic solids—correspond to the elements: the cube for Earth, the pyramid or tetrahedron for Fire, the octahedron for Air, the icosahedron for Water, and the dodecahedron for the universe as a whole. (Later, the dodecahedron was assigned to aithēr or spirit.)

Despite all this, however, Plato stood on the side of rationalism. He just tried to extend it to cover metaphysics. Part of the reason may have been that, like Socrates, he was seeking an antidote for the moral degeneration of society that appeared to be an inevitable consequence of the widespread loss of faith in the gods.

Plato's influence on modern occult philosophy is so pervasive that it is tempting to list items of significance one right after another in a vast catalog of ideas—including, for example, Atlantis. For another example, Plato's use of the cave allegory in *The Republic*, which has been examined at length elsewhere (most recently and clearly in *The Inner Guide Meditation* by Edwin C. Steinbrecher, Samuel Weiser, 1988), is meant to illustrate the impossibility of anyone who has seen the true reality of the archetypal world communicating with those who have not, those who continue to take the shadow for the reality.

Also fairly well known is Plato's description of the chariot—Nous as the charioteer drives two horses, one of which, the spirited, the good, pulls upward to the world of ideas, and the other of which, the appetitive, the bad, pulls downward to the world of manifestation. This idea was also expressed in the *Bhagavad Gita* and later seems to have contributed to the design of the Tarot card known as The Chariot.

Despite Plato's undoubted and permeating influence with regard to modern hermetic teachings, many of his ideas seem wrongheaded or even repugnant to the modern mind. The resemblance of his theories of the fate of the soul to Christian dogma is enough to condemn him in the eyes of most Pagans. But there are other difficulties. His political ideas, while perhaps popular with European monarchists and fascists, including those with hermetic leanings, are anathema to anyone who believes in any sort of democracy or equality of opportunity. Most people are upset by his suggestion that children ought to be reared by the state. The word "elitist" seems almost to have been invented especially to describe Plato. There are certain redeeming features, however. For example, he said in the *Timaeus* that women ought to have the same rights, privileges, and obligations as men. At least two of his students were women. Ironically, this is the same document in which he theorized that women are inferior versions of men through a progressively degraded transmigration.

Nevertheless, Plato is the foundation stone of Western philosophy. As his ideas were developed by the Neoplatonists and echoed in Gnosticism, they became the dominant coherent thread of modern occult philosophy as well.

The Pythagorean idea of the holiness of the number ten was combined with Plato's ideas by Speusippus (347-336), Plato's nephew, who took over the Academy after Plato's death. He postulated ten grades of being, again foreshadowing the cabalistic Tree of Life. Students may wish to compare the designations of Speusippus, given below, with their own understanding of the meanings of the Sephiroth:

1. One	6. Beings
2. Many	7. Thought
3. Number	8. Desire
4. Dimension	9. Motion
5. Elements	10. The Good

The major part of the philosophy of Plato's pupil Aristotle (384-322) was concerned with what would now be considered scientific endeavors—logic and empirical investigation—and therefore is beyond the scope of this book. I will just say in passing that he systemized the doctrine of the four elements and the four qualities (hot, cold, moist, dry) and said that the fifth element was aether or aither. He more or less dispensed with Plato's theory of the world of ideas and said that every object contains its own form, which is its essence. Yet all things strive toward God. Things naturally develop or evolve in such a way as to actualize the ideal form of itself, to bring spirit into matter.

Aristotle also described the heavenly spheres, the purity of which, he said, is directly proportional to their distance from the earth. Since all planetary motion had to be accounted for by the influence of these spheres, the higher upon the lower, he calculated that there had to be 56 of them. He believed that the stars and planets were sentient, animate beings. How else could they move? The soul, he said, cannot exist without the body, although he said it has three parts—plant, animal, and human, or nutritive, sensual, and intelligent. However, besides the soul, man has *nous* (thought), and it is immortal.

The fact that I am disposing of Aristotle in so cavalier a fashion should not, however, obscure the fact that his influence on Western philosophy and thought in general was immense. Eighteen hundred years later, church fathers and occultists such as Agrippa were quoting extensively from this great "authority" on subjects ranging from theology to biology. His works on ethics formed the basis of the Christian doctrine of natural law. As far as Christian and Islamic scholars were concerned, Aristotle represented the sum total of human knowledge. It is only in this century that we have begun to see the limitations and errors of Aristotle's logical either/or, black/white thinking.

The following summary lists some of the foregoing Greek philosophers and the chief doctrine(s)-of-interest (to us) that they taught.

Thales—There's one basic substance and it's Water.

Anaximander—There's one basic substance and it's *apeiron,* the boundless *(Ain Soph).*

Anaximenes—There's one basic substance and it's Air.

Heraclitus—There's one basic substance and it's Fire. There is only one God, who manifests stability through change. Descending formation takes place via Fire-Water-Earth (Lightning Flash). The ultimate reality of the Universe is the Logos.

Pythagoras—The essence of everything is Number. We have a reincarnating soul. The numbers 1 through 10 represent manifested existence (the Sephiroth).

Xenophanes—There is only one God, who is immanent and unchanging.

Empedocles—There are four elements: Fire, Water, Air, and Earth. There are two worlds, spiritual and material.

Anaxagoras—The ultimate reality of the Universe is mind, *Nous.* The universe came to be because of the swirling motions generated from a point by Nous *(Rashith ha-Gilgalim).*

Socrates—Know thyself. One may be guided by an inner voice.

Plato—There is a world of Ideas or archetypes of which our world is a second-rate imitation *(Olam ha-Atziluth).* There are three parts to the soul *(Neshamah, Ruach,* and *Nephesh).*

Aristotle—The fifth element is aithēr. The other four are made up of combinations of the qualities Hot/Cold, Wet/Dry. All things strive toward perfection or realization of their true natures.

Now that I have presented this devastating argument "proving" that cabalism and modern esoteric theories were all originated by the Greek philosophers, perhaps I should say that, in the first place, these guys were all influenced by already existing ideas and, in the second place, it's perfectly possible for two people to come up with the same idea quite independently of each other—especially if the idea happens to be true or archetypal and especially if they had common roots (in this case, Central Asia and Mesopotamia). Just because these ideas were born in Greece does not mean that they could not have been born elsewhere as well. The most famous example that can actually be verified of the same idea being arrived at by two people working independently is that Gottfried Leibniz and Isaac Newton both invented calculus. If a Chinese, a Native American, and a Briton all say that rocks (as a rule) are comparatively hard, that does not necessarily mean that any one of them influenced the ideas of the other two.

But it can't be ruled out, either.

Demeter and Kore

V

The Mysteries

I see that I'm not going to get by without talking about the Greek mysteries. That's a shame. Why? Because I don't know the first thing about them. Even though millions of words have been written about them by dozens of people, neither does anyone else. Everything that's been said about them is speculation, pure and simple.

We have a few scattered comments here and there from classical times, but we have no way of knowing if the authors of those comments knew what they were talking about or were just spouting off. The earlier the comment, the less they had to say. The only people who went into detail were early Christian heresy-hunters, and they are probably very far from being the most reliable sources.

We only know that anyone who was initiated into the greater mysteries was absolutely convinced that they had been spiritually reborn into the light through some sort of profound experience and revelation. I'm sorry, but the emotional experiences that people have when they become "born-again Christians" just can't compare. Nine hundred and ninety-nine times out of a thousand, the experience of religious conversion, however deep and meaningful it may seem to the individual at the time, is in essence just a case of overwrought emotionalism. Such does not seem to be the case with the mysteries. Something more took place than just getting worked up by a skillful preacher. Perhaps that is why the authoritarian church of Christian Rome took such pains to extinguish the light of the Greek mysteries. If a competitor is doing what you're doing, but doing it a lot better, it helps to have the Roman legions on your side if you want to stay in business.

Before it became powerful through the conversion of the Emperor Constantine in the 4th century, by the way, Christianity was looked upon by most non-Christians as being "just another mystery religion." But if the early Christian church taught any mysteries beyond the mass, they've been lost somewhere along the way. And the mass ain't what it used to be, although it still has some transformative effect for certain people in certain places at certain times.

A mystery, you see, is not a doctrine. It's not just saying, "Believe this, and you won't die. It says so right here." It's not listening to or believing a narrative concerning someone's life and death and resurrection, be it Osiris or Mithras or Jesus. It is an experience. An experience that utterly blows your mind.

The *mystes,* which is to say the person being initiated into the mystery, was told certain things, saw certain things, perhaps (although we don't know) witnessed a dramatic re-enactment of a divine myth. At the end, the mystes was shown something. The Christian bishop and heresiologist Hippolytus said that, in the Eleusinian mysteries, it was an ear of corn. Big deal. Maybe it was, and it meant a lot more to the ancient Greeks than it would to us. Maybe someone lied to him. Maybe it was something else. Maybe, as a recent book asserts, the big revelation *(epopteia)* of the Mithraic mysteries was the precession of the equinoxes. But I doubt it. At least in the mysteries of Eleusis and Isis, it was a lot more than any astonishing intellectual revelation or the revelation of any secret teaching. It was a lot more than any Masonic or Rosicrucian ceremony in which the hierophant rises from a coffin while impersonating Christian Rosenkreuz (although this in itself is said to occasionally be a fairly profound experience for an aspiring Adeptus Minor).

The central mystery, whatever was shown to the mystes at the climax of the ceremony, was something that took your breath away. It was one huge light bulb lighting up in your head, sort of like, "Oh! Now I get it! Wow!" Only more so. A lightning bolt. It was as if, without there being any chance of anyone's faking anything, the mystes saw the gods walking, witnessed an actual case of death and destruction followed by triumphant resurrection, and/or was spoken to by a numinous entity that could not have been anyone other than the Goddess Herself. Not a priestess playing the role of the Goddess, not even a priestess who had invoked the Goddess, but She Herself, visibly apparent and real, unmistakably divine, an undoubted epiphany, radiant in glory.

A writer named Pausanias said that an intruder once entered the temple during this phase and saw that it was "all full of gods." He lived long enough to tell what he had seen and then fell dead on the spot.

An ear of corn?

I'm not trying to build up this experience into something more than it was, either. I'm just trying to convey the general impression I get from what people who had been through it had to say about it at the time. Initiates (epopts, those who had seen the greater mysteries) were referred to throughout antiquity as "blessed," "thrice blessed," and so on. "Happy is he who has seen it." They no longer feared death, and they felt themselves to have been transformed by the experience.

Of course, all the real superlatives were saved for the mysteries of Eleusis, Isis, and, to a lesser extent, Orpheus. Most of the other mysteries seem to have been just a bit ho-hum by comparison—perhaps as profound as the chief mystery of the Christians, but not much more so, if any.

The oldest Greek mysteries may be those of the Kabeiroi (or Kabiri) at Samothrace, a large island in the northeast corner of the Aegean Sea, off the coast of Thrace. These may also be the mysteries about which we know the least. There seems to be some connection with Hephaestos and elemental Fire—maybe. They seem to have been concerned with some brothers, the Kabeiroi boys (although the term also seems to mean something like "great gods"), who were guilty of some great crime—perhaps two of them killing the third and hiding his head in a cloth. A candidate for the mysteries was asked, "What's the greatest crime against divine justice that you've ever committed in your life?" So maybe it all had something to do with "the forgiveness of sins," perhaps a purging of guilt by fire. Could be. Nobody seems to have gotten as enthused about the Samothracian mysteries as they did about some of the others. To confuse matters further, the mystery was said to have been founded by Demeter and seems to have had something to do with storks or cranes.

The Hermetic Order of the Golden Dawn, a mystical-magical society that flourished in the latter part of the 19th century and that still exists in one form or another, made much use of the "Kabiri" in their initiation ceremony for the grade of Practicus. In this ceremony, the candidate is called Kasmillos. The three Kabiri are called Axieros, Axiokersos, and Axiokersa, and are made to represent different aspects of elemental Fire. Their speeches consist primarily of extracts from the Chaldean Oracles—which were written long after the Samothracian mysteries had ceased to be. All of these characters are represented on the Golden Dawn version of the Tarot trump, Judgment. However, all of this had been written for and adapted to Golden Dawn ceremonial use by MacGregor Mathers and has little or nothing to do with the real mysteries of Samothrace. The only point in bringing it up at all is to once again emphasize that modern magical practices are heavily influenced by what went on in ancient Greece.

The mysteries of Orpheus, which originated in Thrace, were a little different. They were said to have been founded by Orpheus, or in honor of Orpheus, mentioned in the previous chapter in connection with Pythagoras. No doubt some of it had to do with one or another "myth" of Orpheus, but there are several of these, ranging from his adventures with the Argonauts to the use of his head as an oracle, and we don't know which of them were applicable to the mysteries—probably the descent into the underworld, possibly others, but almost certainly the story that he was dismembered by the maenads, followers of Dionysos. In fact, the mysteries of Orpheus did not revolve around Orpheus so much as they did the god Dionysos (not to be confused with the rulers of Syracuse who went by the name Dionysios).

Some people seem to have gotten the impression that any mysteries that involved Dionysos must have consisted mostly of hedonistic drunken orgies and wild dancing, with the key word being "abandonment." This impression seems to be based more on the Roman Bacchus than on the Greek Dionysos—and upon Walt Disney's *Fantasia*. Dionysos may have been the god of wine, but he was far more than just a divine wino. He was a god in every sense of the word. The Orphic mysteries spoke of Dionysos-Phanes, the light bringer, the creator of heaven and earth. The Hymns of Orpheus (a collection of Greek verse assembled in the Christian era) call him Protogonos, the first born. Phanes created Nyx (Night), and the two of them produced Kronos. So Dionysos ends up being the grandfather of Zeus. Zeus devoured Phanes, however, and then begat Dionysos-Zagreus by Persephone, daughter of Demeter. Here we see the beginnings of the doctrine of transmigration: Phanes is reborn as Zagreus, but both are really Dionysos. Another doctrine is hinted at here, too—namely, that we are all "reincarnations" of God; in Hindu thought, avatars necessary for the divine play (*lila*) of Brahman, who is each of us. "Tat tvam asi"—"You are It."

But Dionysos-Zagreus was torn apart and eaten by the Titans while he was still a boy. Zeus got upset over it and destroyed the Titans, creating the third and present human race in the process. Humanity therefore partakes of the evil nature of the Titans—the doctrine of Original Sin.

Athene preserved the heart of Zagreus and brought it to Zeus, who promptly ate it. But this divine cannibalism was for the purpose of preserving Dionysos within himself, for he now begat Dionysos III, Dionysos-Lyseus, by Semele. In the patriarchal Greek myths, Semele was the daughter of King Cadmus; but she was originally an earth goddess in Thrace and Phrygia. It is this Dionysos who is the hero of *The Bacchae* of Euripedes. All the Greek dramas were written in honor of Dionysos, by the way, and were a form of worship at His festival. Believe me, it is impossible to appreciate a Greek tragedy if you're soused; so, again, Dionysos was much more than a god of wine.

It is also this third incarnation of Dionysos who is the soul's redeemer and healer, who has much in common with Jesus in that department. He rose from the dead, too. Twice.

But what went on at the Orphic mysteries? Perhaps, among other things, they involved the ritual washing away of sin (either original or acquired or both). Nobody knows. Those that did know weren't telling.

In any event, Dolores Ashcroft-Nowicki—who is both an adept and a person of uncommon common sense—has included an Orphic group ritual in her book, *First Steps in Ritual*. It can't claim to reproduce any epopteia, but it's certainly worthwhile.

There were also mysteries of Dionysos which did not involve Orpheus. They seem to have been a late development that arose out of the Dionysian religious rites that had already existed for centuries. In its most primitive form, the rites of this religion seem to have

Medieval Illustration of Isis

consisted of a divine frenzy—with or without wine—which led to the dismemberment and devouring of wild beasts and sometimes men. It all fits very neatly into Frazer's theories of a universal vegetation rite, in which the old king is killed and eaten and a new king takes his place. The mysteries are, appropriately enough, rather more mysterious. Divine frenzy seems to have played a part, and the central mystery may have been connected with the divine gift of "speaking in tongues"—raving. Sex and wine are thought to have played a large part; homosexuality has been hinted at as the central mystery; and revelations of an afterlife seem to have been involved. There was no fixed site for these mysteries; they seem to have been conducted by traveling priests. In fact, the more civilized and restrained form of the Dionysian mysteries may have resembled a modern tent meeting in more ways than one.

There were any number of other mystery religions, one of the more important ones being that of Isis and Osiris, or Isis and Serapis, or just Isis, imported from Egypt and thoroughly Hellenized ("Greekified"). Isis and Osiris were Egyptian gods for several thousand years, but the names are Greek. The Egyptians called them Aset or Ast and Ousir or Asar. The mysteries of Isis persisted into Roman times, and there is nothing even remotely Egyptian about the Roman statue of Isis. In *The Golden Ass,* Apuleius (2nd century A.D.) had a few things to say about the mysteries of Isis—but not much. He didn't reveal the epopteia—the revelation of things said, things done, and things seen. He just said that he came near the kingdom of Persephone and returned, saw the sun shining at midnight, and worshiped gods in person. Actually, his comments are fairly cryptic, as are all contemporary comments about the mysteries. Perhaps they just didn't want to give anything away—or perhaps there was really no way they could. Perhaps the experience could not be communicated in words at all.

The best modern account of the mysteries of Isis according to Apuleius is probably that given by Gareth Knight in *The Rose Cross and the Goddess* (Destiny Books, 1985).

But the main mystery religion, the one which most people seem to have experienced (if they experienced any at all), the one spoken of most highly over the longest period of time, was the mysteries of Eleusis—so-called because the center of the mysteries was at Eleusis, near Athens.

The Eleusinian mysteries were very much involved with the

myth of Demeter, Persephone, and Hades. If you've read it before—
and almost everyone with any interest at all in Greek mythology has
read it several times—it gets tedious after about the tenth repetition;
so I'll just give it here in capsule form. Persephone, daughter of the
agricultural goddess Demeter, was kidnapped by Hades, god of the
Underworld. They worked things out so that she would stay on
with Hades six months out of the year and be Queen of the Underworld, but she could come home to Demeter and be a goddess of
spring for the other six months. Demeter was supposed to have been
reunited with Persephone at Eleusis.

There were the Lesser Mysteries and the Greater Mysteries. The
Lesser Mysteries seem to have been a more or less public festival.
The Greater Mysteries took eleven days, but the first eight consisted
of preparatory rituals including purification in the sea, the sacrifice
of pigs, purification by air and fire, floral tributes, processions with
sacred statues, an offering of the first fruits of the harvest, a procession from Athens to Eleusis, fasting, more sacrifices, and so forth.
Then came the mysteries proper, on the final three days, with each
mystes being escorted by a mystagogue, when the gods appeared
and the epopteia was revealed. There seems to have been a re-enactment—by actors, priests and priestesses, or gods—of certain myths
involving Demeter and Persephone. There seems to have been a real
or symbolic descent into the Underworld and a return. There seems
to have been something very mysterious about taking something
out of a basket, using it, and putting it back. Fasting and drinking a
potion seem to have played a part. The mystes may have invoked
the Goddess (that is, identified with Her or been possessed by Her).

Quite a bit is known about the Lesser Mysteries, but they seldom
amounted to much more than organized worship. Some, such as the
mysteries of Mithras or those of Attis and Cybele, involved being
"born again" by standing in a pit under an animal—a bull or a
ram—which was slaughtered so that the candidate was washed in
its blood. It is not unthinkable that this same procedure was used in
early Christianity with a lamb as a symbol of Christ. If so, "washed
in the blood of the lamb" takes on a literal meaning—which it did in
fact have in other mysteries.

Arostides (2nd century A.D.) refers to the "ineffable visions"
seen by Eleusinian initiates. "Happy is he among mortal men who
has seen these things!" says the Homeric hymn—but women and
slaves could be initiated just as well as men. "Blessed," says the poet

Pindar. "Thrice blessed," says the playwright Sophocles. "For them alone there is life."

The Eleusinian mysteries were finally suppressed by the Christian emperor Theodosius and the sanctuary was destroyed by the Goths around 400 A.D.

In the 20th century, Aleister Crowley presented his version of the Eleusinian mysteries in a Paris theater, but this presentation was a combination of guesswork, Golden Dawn dogma, and Crowley's own revealed religion and thus had little or nothing to do with the mysteries from which they took their name.

According to the 17th-century Dutch writer Meursius, whose sources remain doubtful, and according to any number of subsequent authorities, initiates were dismissed at the end of the ceremonies with the words *Konx Om Pax*. That doesn't seem to mean anything in classical Greek. A. E. Waite thought the words had no special significance, but others have equated them with the Coptic *Khabs Am Pekht*, which is said to mean "Light in Extension" and may have been used in the Egyptian mysteries. This formulation was picked up by the Hermetic Order of the Golden Dawn and used in most of its ceremonies—"Khabs Am Pekht! Konx Om Pax! Light in Extension!" The words are explained to the initiate in the Golden Dawn Neophyte ritual: "The Mystical Words—Khabs Am Pekht—are ancient Egyptian, and are the origin of the Greek 'Konx Om Pax' which was uttered at the Eleusinian Mysteries. A literal translation would be 'Light Rushing Out in One Ray' and they signify the same form of Light as that symbolised by the Staff of the Kerux."

According to the Golden Dawn document, "Enterer of the Threshold," probably written by MacGregor Mathers:

> The Mystic Words "Khabs Am Pekht" which accompany the knocks seal the image of the Light. Their significance implies, by various cabalistic methods of analysis, as well as by a certain reading of the Coptic and Egyptian hieroglyphics, "Light in Extension" or "May Light be extended in Abundance upon you." Konx Om Pax is the Greek corrupted pronunciation of this, put here to link it with its right origin.

The matter of Konx Om Pax is, I suppose, of relatively little importance, yet the phrase as it finally came to be understood seems to describe the whole Greek magical and mystical phenomenon—

Light, extending down through something like 2500 years, to illuminate the path of seekers after truth. Light in Extension.

I can tell you what is known of the various mysteries—the purifications, how long it took, what different people said about it—but in the end it's pointless. A hundred other people have described all that at length in a hundred books and articles, so there seems little need for me to add yet another recitation full of half-baked speculation. The only thing really worth knowing is what they saw, what they experienced, and why, and how.

But we can't find out by any amount of research, reading, and mulling it over. Those who experienced the mysteries were sworn not to reveal them, sometimes upon pain of death—death administered not by some hypothetical avenging angel, but by very physical fellow initiates or by the state itself. The Homeric Hymn speaks of "holy mysteries which none may violate, or search into, or noise abroad, for the great curse from the Gods restrains the voice."

Nevertheless, you'd think that someone at some time or another would have spilled the beans. You'd think that someone, seeing that the practice of the mysteries was about to be stamped out, would have written it all down. But no one ever did. For a thousand years or more. No one. Ever.

No doubt there are many among the readers of this book who are quite experienced in pathworking, skrying, traveling in the spirit vision, creative imagination, astral projection, and/or controlled OOBEs—all different names for different degrees of the same thing. Among these there are more than a few who are adept at time travel.

In the British science fiction TV series, Doctor Who travels through time and space in a vehicle called the TARDIS (an acronym for Time And Relative Dimensions In Space). It doesn't always work properly, and, when untrained people try their hands at the controls, they might end up anywhere at any time. Well, we all have our own TARDIS inside us. Once you learn how to get it going, you can easily go to other worlds, to other planes, to other times. But an untrained traveler is liable to end up anywhere at any time regardless of the original goal, and that frequently includes corners of the astral plane that look like the world we know but where things take place that never took place on earth, or ever will.

That's why it takes an adept to travel through time to Eleusis in antiquity and find out what went on at the mysteries. Some people have done it—many in the case of the Egyptian mysteries—but, since no two independent accounts agree, and since no one has come up with a convincing epopteia, we have to conclude that they were all witnessing astral events that weren't accurate representations of what actually went on. Why has no true adept astrally investigated the authentic Eleusinian mysteries and then shared it with the rest of us? The death penalty for revealing the mysteries would be difficult to enact upon an astral visitor from the future, or so one would think.

There are complications. In the first place, as the members of the Golden Dawn proved to the world a hundred years ago, even someone who thinks he is an adept can end up in some strange corner of the astral and take it for an accurate reflection of the world we live in, or can accept the teachings of a "hidden master" who is only some astral drifter having a good joke. That may be what split the order, more than anything else. Abandoned by MacGregor Mathers, they all found their own "secret chiefs," and no two of them agreed about anything. But that's another story, told elsewhere.

The chief difficulty with investigating the mysteries by astral time travel is a sort of Catch 22 proposition. If you aren't already an initiate, a mystes, you won't be admitted. Of course, you would not be present in your physical body, but don't be too sure that the hierophant or mystagogue wouldn't know you were there anyway. And, even if she didn't, you would probably get caught up in the general banishment of all that is profane; everyone who hadn't been initiated into the preliminary stages of a particular mystery was numbered among the profane. You and all the other astral hangers-out would be zapped back to where you came from before you saw anything important—or presented with an ersatz astral version that seemed inspirational in a vague, insipid sort of way.

If, however, you were an initiate, if you had been initiated into this mystery in some past life, then you would be sworn for all time, through all incarnations, not to reveal the secrets!

It really does look as if we'll never know.

VI

Hellenistic Magic

The Hellenistic period runs from 336 B.C., when Alexander the Great succeeded his father, to around 200 B.C., when Rome took over everything in sight. Hellenism, however, meaning Greek thought and customs, lasted well into Roman times and beyond. It was a period that saw, due to Alexander's conquests, the diffusion of Greek ideas from India to Spain—and the modification of Greek thought by the influence of other cultures such as Egypt, Persia, and India. It was a time when the gods were not much revered—they had been neatly disposed of by the rationalism of the philosophers—but it was also a period of renewed interest in magic. This revival may have been in reaction against a failed rationalism and a vitiated religion. It was during this period that some fairly wild mystery religions reached Athens from the East—Cybele and Attis, Bendis, Sabazius, and so on.

The most striking—and unpleasant—feature of the mysteries of Cybele and Attis appears to have been self-castration performed with a flint knife during a period of religious frenzy. It has been theorized that this particular "sacrifice" was performed in order to ensure the fertility of the crops. It is echoed in the somewhat less drastic practices of circumcision and subincision, which have been and are practiced all over the world. Rather than having anything to do with fertility, this practice may have represented an attempt to identify with the Goddess (and/or the female power elite in a matriarchy). Men who had done this were commonly referred to as "she" thereafter. But, since it takes a lot more to make a woman than the absence of male sexual organs, this attempt at identification was foredoomed to failure.

There are plenty of myths about Alexander himself. He is said to have halted his conquests only at the gates of paradise, where he was given an eye or a stone that symbolized himself. He fought fabulous monsters. He searched for the fountain of youth. He was worshiped as a god. He even becomes a major figure in the Koran, as Dhul-Karnain, the Two-Horned One.

Alexander died in 323 B.C., and his generals divided the empire among themselves. They established the Seleucid dynasty in Syria and the Ptolemaic dynasty in Egypt. Yes, Cleopatra was of Greek descent. They didn't manage to hang on to India, though.

The center of magical activity and philosophic learning came to be the Greek city of Alexandria in Egypt—named after guess who—founded in 331 B.C. Perhaps the main thing remembered about Alexandria today was its huge library, which contained all the knowledge of the ancient world, and then some. There is a story that the library was burned by the general Amru when the city was invaded during the period of Islamic expansion under the Caliph Omar. "If the books don't agree with the Koran," he is supposed to have said, "they're heresy. If they do, they're redundant. Burn the library." Aside from the fact that this sounds more like a statement that might have been made by certain Christians (if you substitute "Bible" for "Koran"), there's something fishy about this story. Quite aside from the fact that the Islamic world was responsible for pre-serving what remained of Greek learning throughout the Dark Ages (and not Byzantium, whose emperors banned everything thought to be heretical), it's hard to say just what Amru could have burned. The library had already been burned down by a Christian mob, incited to the atrocity by Saint Cyril the archbishop, in 387 A.D., more than 200 years before the birth of the Prophet Muhammad. There was also an accidental fire in 47 B.C., which burned the original and older collection in one of the royal palaces. So, if Amru burned anything, it probably consisted solely of material acceptable to Christian orthodoxy.

Alexandria was the cultural center of the world in its day, though, and it is entirely symbolically appropriate that it was the site of one of the Seven Wonders of the World—the Pharos of Alexandria, a lighthouse 325 feet high with a light that could be seen from 35 miles away. One of the enlightened facets of Alexandria was that, for the first time in a thousand years, Greek women were considered to be the equals of men.

Alexandria was a bit of a melting pot, and it was here that the influences of all the various cultures within Alexander's empire made themselves felt—most dramatically in the magical rituals of the time. The spells and incantations no longer confined themselves to Greek gods. They began to incorporate the names of foreign gods, on the theory that a name that was powerful in one culture would be powerful anywhere. Most of these incorporated names turned out to be Egyptian or Hebrew, and thus we see Hellenistic magicians calling upon Adonai (lord) and Sabaoth (hosts). The magicians also did not hesitate to use the name "Christ" in their incantations just like any other divine name. They weren't Christians, though.

Here arises an irony: Many people may wish to take up Greek magic in order to get away from the Judaeo-Christian terminology that permeates most rituals and ceremonies in the Western Hermetic Tradition, such as those of the Golden Dawn. But, when you take at look at actual Greek rituals from this period, the first thing you recognize is these same old Hebrew god-names! More than a few of the names became hopelessly corrupted over a period of time, and one suspects that a certain amount of nonsense was thrown in for good measure. One spell for scrying in a basin of water contains the names (or words), *"Naine Basanaptatou Eaptou Menō phaesme Paptou Menōph, Aesimē, Trauapti, Peuchre, Trauara, Ptoumeph, Mourai, Anchouchaphapta, Moursa, Aramei, Iaō, Aththaraui, Menoker, Boroptoumeth, At Taui Meni Charchara, Ptoumau, Lalapsa, Traui Trauepse Mamō Phortoucha, Aēeio Iou, Eai Aēei Oi Iaō Aei Ai Iaō."* From this period, we do have grimoires—or at least magical papyri with single spells on them. We also have protective amulets. It is likewise evident from the papyri that many magicians relied heavily on the use of herbs and potions; the less scrupulous ones did not hesitate to use poison. A drug was a *pharmakon,* in Greek, and a "witch" or sorceress who used drugs (or herbs, for that matter) was called a *pharmakeutria;* a man was called a *pharmakeutes.* The Bible had hard things to say about these people. There were spells for cursing, exorcising, and attracting love.

One common artifact from this period is the *defixiones*—curses or bindings written along with someone's name on metal tablets or pieces of pottery and preferably buried in a graveyard. Hundreds of these things have been found from the 4th century, but few from the earlier 5th century. Apparently, they also used wax images—"voodoo dolls."

Astrology and alchemy were also practiced. Astrology in particular became popular in the 2nd century B.C., and it was from astrology that the doctrine of sympathies arose. Expounded at length by Cornelius Agrippa in the 16th century A.D.—and also by Bolus of Mendes around 200 B.C.—this is simply the idea that earthly creatures, plants, stones, and other objects have an affinity with the planets and signs of the Zodiac. In modern magic, in medieval magic, and presumably in classical magic, you work a spell having to do with something governed by a particular planet by using things that are in sympathy with that planet. Nowadays, these things consist mostly of sigils traced in the air, names vibrated, the appropriate colors, and possibly music. In earlier times, magicians usually thought it necessary to have, for example, the hair of a wolf in order to work a spell having to do with the planet Mars. It certainly wouldn't hurt anything, but it's a little inconvenient in today's world.

Most of the surviving material is from a period well into the Christian era, but it is thought to reflect the earlier Hellenistic period before Christ. Although everything was constantly changing during this time, magical practitioners did have some respect for the power of tradition. It is very doubtful if "Christos" was used as a name of power before the Christian era, and "Iaō" came in with Gnosticism, but we can nevertheless detect Hebrew and Egyptian god names among the "barbarous names" that were probably used much earlier. (Incidentally, to the Greeks, "barbarous" simply meant "foreign.")

The most famous of these rituals today is probably "The Bornless Ritual," of uncertain date, the manuscript of which is in the British Museum. The ritual has been widely reprinted, especially in the version worked out by Aleister Crowley, and it is incorporated into the Golden Dawn format by Israel Regardie in *The Golden Dawn* ("The Bornless Ritual for the Invocation of the Higher Genius"). You might be interested in the original Greek version of the words, which I present here transliterated into the English alphabet for easier readability.

The Bornless Ritual

"Thee I invoke, the Bornless One." *(Se kalo, ton Akephalon.)*

Akephalon (accusative case of *Akephalos*) means, literally, "the headless one." One wonders why they didn't just say *Ageneton*, but it has been proposed that the term refers to Osiris, who was dismembered and decapitated by Set before being reassembled by Isis. There were also various headless gods in Egypt who were associated with disease and healing.

"Thee, that didst create the earth and the heavens:" *(Ton ktisanta gen kai ouranon:)*

"Thee, that didst create the night and the day." *(Ton ktisanta nykta kai hemeran.)*

"Thee, that didst create the darkness and the light." *(Se ton ktisanta phos kai skotos.)*

"Thou art Osorronophris: Whom no man hath seen at any time." *(Su ei Osoronnophris, on oudeis eide popote.)* This seems to indicate that the god meant is Osiris.

"Thou art Iabas/Thou art Iapos:" *(Su ei Iabas, su ei Iapos:)*

"Thou hast distinguished between the just and the unjust." *(Su diekreinas to dikaion kai to adikon.)*

"Thou didst make the female and the male." *(Su epoiesas thelu kai arren.)*

"Thou didst produce the seed and the fruit." *(Su edeixas storan kai karpous.)*

"Thou didst form Men to love another, and to hate one another." *(Su epoiesas tous anthropous allelophilein kai allelomisein.)*

"I am Moses Thy Prophet, unto Whom Thou didst commit Thy Mysteries, the Ceremonies of Israel:" *(Ego eimi Mouses o prophetes sou, ho paredokas ta mysteria sou ta synteloumena Istrael.)* The author of the ritual decides to throw in a little Hebrew mythology along with the Egyptian.

"Thou didst produce the moist and the dry, and that which nourisheth all created life." *(Su edeixas hygron kai xeron kai pasan trophen.)*

"Hear Thou me, for I am the angel of Paphro Osorronophris:" *(Epakouson mou ego eimi angelos tou Phapro Osoronnophris:)*

"This is Thy True Name, handed down to the prophets of Israel." *(Touto estin sou to onoma to alethinon, to paradidomenon tois prophetais Istrael.)*

"Hear Me:—Ar: Thiao: Rheibet: Atheleberseth: A: Blatha: Abeu: Ebeu: Phi: Thitasoe: Ib: Thiao." *(Epakouson mou, ar, thiao, rheibet, atheleberseth, a, blatha, abeu, eben, phi, chitasoe, ib, thiao.")*

The variations in some of the barbarous names may be due to misprints or mistakes in the Greek transcription. The first published version, in 1852, has ellipses (dots) after *"Ar," "A,"* and *"Ib,"* indicating that some material may have been missing or indecipherable.

Then comes the primary invocation, which, in the modern version, is repeated throughout as a refrain—but, in the original document, this invocation occurs only once, at the very end, and lacks the initial "Hear Me" (which would evidently be *Epikouson mou).*

"Hear Me, and make all Spirits subject unto Me: so that every Spirit of the firmament and of the Ether: upon the Earth and under the Earth: on dry Land or in the Water: of Whirling Air, and of rushing Fire: and every Spell and Scourge of God may be obedient unto Me." *(Hypotaxon moi panta ta daimonia, hina moi he hypekoos pas daimon ouranios kai aitherios kai epigeios kai hypogeios kai enudros kai pasa epipompe kai mastix theou.)*

At this point, the original document contains the sentence *Eisakouson mou kai apostrepson to daimonion touto*—"Hear me and drive away this spirit." This doesn't make any particular sense in the context unless the ceremony was at least partly intended as a rite of exorcism—or unless the speaker is referring to his own spirit, which is to be replaced by that of the god. But to continue:

"I invoke Thee, the Terrible and Invisible God: Who dwellest in the Void Place of the Spirit:—Arogogorobrao: Sothou: Modorio: Phalarthao: Doo: Ape, The Bornless One:" *(Epikaloumai se ton en to keno pneumati deinon kai aopaton theon, arogogorobrao, sochou, modorio, phalarchao, ooo, ape, akephale.)*

In the modern version, the refrain ("Hear me, and make all Spirits" etc.) is repeated at this point. In the original, we have another phrase of exorcism: "Deliver such an one from the spirit that possesses him." *(Apallaxon ton deina apo tou synechontos auton daimonos.)*

The ritual continues: "Hear me:—Roubriao: Mariodam: Balbnabaoth: Assalonai: Aphniao: I: Thoteth: Abrasax: Aeoou: Ischure,

Mighty and Bornless One!" *(Roubriaō, mariōdam, balbnabaōth, as-salōnai, aphniaō, i, thōleth, abrasax, aeōou, ischyre, akephale.)*

Then we again have, in the original, *"Apallaxon ton deina..."* and so on; that is, "Deliver such an one from the spirit that possesses him." In the modern version, however, the refrain about "all Spirits subject unto me" is repeated.

"I invoke Thee:—Ma: Barraio: Ioel: Kotha: Athorebalo: Abraoth:" *(Ma, barraiō, iōel, kotha, athorēbalō, abraōth.)* In the original, we have *"apallaxon ton deina"*—"deliver such an one." In the modern version, the refrain is repeated.

"Hear me: Aoth: Abaoth: Basum: Isak: Sabaoth: Iao;" *(Aōth, abaōth, basum, isak, sabaōth, iaō.)*

"This is the Lord of the Gods: This is the Lord of the Universe: This is He Whom the Winds fear." *(Outos estin ho kyrios tōn theōn, outos estin ho kyrios tēs oikoumenēs, outos estin on hoi anemoi phobountai.)*

"This is He, Who having made Voice by his Commandment, is Lord of All Things; king, ruler, and helper." *(Outos estin ho poiēsas phōnēn prostagmati eautou, pantōn kyrie, basileu, dynasta, boēthe.)* The original goes on, "Save this soul" *(sōson psychen).* The modern version repeats the refrain.

"Hear Me:—Ieou: Pur: Iou: Pur: Iaot: Iaeo: Ioou: Abrasax: Sabriam: Do: Uu: Adonaie: Ede: Edu: Angelos ton Theon: Anlala Lai: Gaia: Ape: Diathanna Thorun." *(Ieou, pyr [fire], iou, pyr, iaot, iaēo, ioou, abrasax, sabriam, oo, uu, eu, oo, uu, adonaie, ede, edu, angelos tou theou, anlala, lai, gaia, apa, diachanna chorun.)* Here we see some interesting variations between the original and the modern version. To complicate matters, some printings consistently err in rendering the good old reliable Gnostic name, Abrasax, as "Abrasar." Crowley knew better.

The climax of the ritual: "I am He! the Bornless Spirit! having sight in the feet: Strong, and the Immortal Fire!" *(Egō eimi ho akephalos daimon en tois posin echōn tēn opasin, ischyros, to pyr to athanaton.)*

"I am He! the Truth!" *(Ego eimi hē alētheia.)*

"I am He! Who hate that evil should be wrought in the World!" *(O meisōn adikēmata geinesthai hen tō kosmō.)*

"I am He, that lighteneth and thundereth." *(Egō eimi ho astraptōn kai brontōn.)*

"I am He, from whom is the Shower of the Life of Earth:" *(Egō eimi ou estin ho idrōs ombros epipeipton epi ten gen hina ocheue.)*

"I am He, whose mouth ever flameth:" *(Ego eimi ou to stoma kaietai di olou.)*

"I am He, the Begetter and Manifester unto the Light:" *(Ego eimi ho gennon kai apogennon.—*"I am the begetter and the bringer forth." There's nothing in the original about "Light.")

"I am he; the Grace of the World:" *(Ego eimi he charis tou aionos.)*

"'The Heart Girt with a Serpent' is My Name!" *(Onoma moi kardia perizosmene ophin.)*

"Come Thou forth, and follow Me:" *(Exelthe kai akoloutheson.)*

The modern ritual continues with, "...and make all Spirits subject unto Me," and so on, concluding "Iao: Sabao: Such are the Words!" But, after "Come forth and follow," the original continues (in the 1852 translation of Charles Wycliffe Goodwin), "The celebration of the preceding ceremony.—Write the names *[onomata]* upon a piece of new paper *[chartarion]*, and having extended it over your forehead from one temple to the other, address yourself turning towards the north to the six names, saying: Make all the spirits subject to me..." and so forth, as in the refrain, ending, "And all the spirits shall be obedient unto you."

To make matters even more puzzling, the entire ritual is headed "An address to the god drawn upon the letter" *(Stele tou Theou tou zogr, eis ten epistolen).* It appears to have originally been a ritual for the invocation of a headless god *(Akephalos)* for the purpose of casting out spirits and/or healing, although there is some ambiguity here. *Akephalos* also means "without beginning." In any event, the modern version is a ritual for, as Regardie says, "the invocation of the higher genius," which is to say the Holy Guardian Angel or *augoeides.*

As Regardie said, you can't expect to read through this ritual and suddenly become enlightened. It takes lots and lots of practice and many repetitions. It would also help if you'd had a year or two experience in basic ritual before you even attempted it. I don't know of anyone who's ever suffered any ill effects from it, but trying to run a ritual of this nature without having built up some reserve of magical power (baraka, mana, Light, or whatever) has approximately the same results as trying to drive your car with no gasoline. You just don't get anywhere.

On the other hand, I'm not sure I endorse the way Regardie recommended going about it. The whole ritual is based on the idea that you should "enflame yourself with prayer," and stopping to trace pentagrams, vibrate divine names (other than those in the ritual itself), give grade signs, and circumambulate a few extra times tends to break the momentum of the emotional/magical buildup. I would recommend simply using a standard opening and closing procedure (preferably the Golden Dawn's Opening by Watchtower, if you're up to it—it's not for beginners) and just facing the appropriate quarter for each part of the ritual. Make the applicable invoking pentagrams if you wish and if you can do so without interfering with your concentration, but leave out the extra divine names, the grade signs, and so on.

If you have no earthly idea what I'm talking about, consult the ritual in *The Golden Dawn* (pp. 442-446) and you'll see what I mean.

VII

Hellenistic Philosophy

During the Hellenistic period and on into the Roman period, Greek philosophy gradually became more syncretic and eclectic, drawing, like the magic of the period, from the traditions of conquered peoples and seeking to reconcile differences in all-inclusive systems. To begin with, scientific theories and investigations now tended to separate from the philosophy of which they had formerly been an integral part. Philosophy and religion, on the other hand, tended to get closer together. Like certain modern Christians, philosophers took to the streets to proselytize their ideas, and, for many, philosophy became a substitute for a moribund religion.

In many ways, this era resembled our own times. The materialism and cold reason of philosophy, which began with the Ionian seekers for the ultimate substance, had in the end totally devalued religion only to find *itself* equally bankrupt. The spiritual and moral needs of the people were simply not being met, and classical philosophy proved altogether inadequate to deal with the exigencies of day-to-day living. Consequently, as we shall see, the road was left wide open for a resurgence of spiritual values in the form of myriads of new or imported cults (such as some of the more eccentric forms of Gnosticism), mysteries (such as those of Attis and Cybele), religions (such as Christianity), and mystical philosophies (such as Neoplatonism).

Probably the most important school of traditional philosophy during this period was Stoicism, originating with Zeno of Citium (c. 333-261 B.C.). The Stoics were strict materialists and, for the most part, probably had more in common with modern scientism and existential philosophy than any other classical system. They scoffed at Plato's world of Ideas and said perceived reality is the only reality; they emphasized scientific research.

The Stoics, however, said that things and qualities came from a permeating Logos or rational force, a World Soul, a universal Nous. The soul was seen as being breath *(pneuma)* or fire—a sort of artificial fire, a technological fire *(pyr technikon)*. God was considered to be composed of a fiery vapor, and was identified with Zeus. In any case, there was no dichotomy between God and the material world; it was all one thing. God and the soul were strictly material and in no way supernatural or supermundane. In this, they returned to the view of the old Ionic philosophers, but their reasons were skeptical rather than innocent or naive.

Zeus could be worshiped, they said, under that name, with the understanding that He was the creator and sustainer of the universe. But Zeus could also be worshiped indirectly by reverencing the other gods of mythology, which were said to represent divine forces.

In cabalism today, at least within the Western Hermetic Tradition, all the gods and god names of the Tree of Life are seen as aspects of the One. Thus in calling upon Hermes, you are really calling upon Elohim Tzabaoth, the Lord of Hosts—or vice-versa—since both names are associated with the Sephirah Hod. And, of course, Elohim Tzabaoth is just one aspect or face of the One True God—the eighth emanation, to be exact. These gods or divine aspects could be seen, said the Stoics, in natural phenomena such as the stars, the elements, a bountiful nature, and exceptionally good men.

Meanwhile, the Stoics refused to take any of the myths seriously and strove to give them an allegorical interpretation to reveal their philosophic truth. They were not the first philosophers to do this, but they carried the technique to its furthest extent.

The creation of the world by Zeus was accomplished by a progressive transmogrification of the elements. He began by transforming a part of Himself into air and the air into water, in both of which He was still present as Logos. From the water, He formed earth and air, though a part stayed water. Part of the air was made into fire. The only way in which the material world can be distinguished from God is that He is its soul; that is, God is to the world as the soul is to a human being—but all are strictly material and in no way spiritual. Yet the fundamental basis of the universe was thought to be its own Nous (reason) and Logos. In all this, we seem to see an anticipation of the cabalistic doctrine of emanations.

After the world has run its course, Zeus will dissolve everything back into Himself in a universal conflagration. At some predetermined time, He will start the whole thing all over again. This idea also exists in Hinduism, with its Day and Night of Brahman, and indeed may have been adapted from it. The idea also exists in modern physics as the oscillating universe theory, but God is left out of it.

But the Stoics said that, since the same causes always have the same effects, the regenerated universe would be identical with the old one, even to the point that we would all live our lives over again identically in an endless succession of universes. The idea of "eternal recurrence" was therefore not original with the German philosopher Friedrich Nietzsche. The individual soul, however, would exist independently except for the periods when it was reabsorbed by God along with everything else. Some said this happened to everybody, others that it was the privilege of the wise only.

Like Socrates, the Stoics thought that happiness arises naturally from virtue. Perhaps because of the influence of Aristotle, they tended to see virtue as an either/or proposition. Either you were wise or you were a fool. Anyone "on the path" toward wisdom was still in the fool category. They thought that hardly anyone was wise and that the population of the wise was in rapid decline.

They anticipated the Christians not only with their pronouncement that you should forgive your enemies and do good to them, but also by describing the extremes and pits of human imperfection and depravity, often approaching the tone of Jonathan Edwards' sermon about "Sinners in the Hands of an Angry God." In this famous sermon, which generations of high school English students were forced to read, man is depicted as a loathsome insect being held in the hand of God above the coals of a fireplace.

Aside from that, the Stoics were rather fatalistic. They said you should follow the line of least resistance and obey the laws of the universe and submit to your destiny—a sort of dark version of Taoism, which emphasizes harmony, or Islam, which teaches submission to God. Their pessimism extended to life itself, which, along with everything else, they considered to be a matter of indifference. They said that suicide is advisable if it seems to be a good idea at the time, and several of them, including Zeno and Eratosthenes, took their own advice.

In any event, the Stoics assumed that humanity is a product of nature and cannot act contrary to nature. Hence they were firm believers in fate and determinism.

Despite their hard-nosed materialism, however, the Stoics probably did more than anyone else to provide the logical underpinnings of magic and astrology. This they did with the doctrine of cosmic sympathies. Everything in the universe is connected with everything else in an ordered and systematic way. It's only one step from this idea to sympathetic magic and the cosmic interconnectedness of astrology.

Aside from the Stoics, Hellenistic philosophy did not amount to much. Despite the appearance of several new schools with new names, it was essentially a watered-down rehash of things that had gone before when it was not downright degenerate. Any sort of survey would be rather dull, would quickly become little more than a sort of list or citation of names and doctrines, and would be largely irrelevant to the theme of this book. For example, Epicurus (341-270 A.D.) and the Epicureans advised independence from worldly concerns such as honor, glory, and wealth. And like the later Christians, they said that it is better to perform a kindness than to be the beneficiary of one. The Skeptics, led by Pyrrho of Elis (d. 275 A.D.), revived the idea that perception is deceptive and that the true nature of things cannot be known. They said that we should never make a dogmatic statement such as "Fire is hot." Instead, we should say something like "Fire seems hot to me." This sentiment is echoed in contemporary thinking by Robert Anton Wilson (see, for example, *The New Inquisition*). It was also sympathetically satirized by Douglas Adams in his *Hitchhiker* trilogy.

When Greece officially became a part of the Roman Empire in something like 168 B.C., the tendency toward eclecticism picked up momentum. This was an attempt to reconcile the various schools of philosophy by emphasizing their similarities and overlooking or explaining away their differences. They were pragmatic, in that they were more interested in practical application than the validity of philosophic argument or scientific proof. Despite these efforts, however, they provided most people with very little to cling to in terms of "philosophic consolation" in the face of the ever-present terrors of life and death.

One idea important in later mystical thought was expressed by Posidonius of Apamea (133 B.C.-51 A.D.), a major representative of the Eclectic school, who said that the sun was the source of an essential life force that was infused throughout the entire world. He also came up with an interesting version of dualism, in that he said the mundane world existed beneath the moon and the heavenly world above it. To this day, the moon represents the transition point between ordinary existence and the higher realms, inasmuch as it is associated with the astral plane. In cabalism, the sphere of the moon is in Yesod, which mediates between Malkuth and the rest of the Tree. According to Posidonius, however, the moon was merely the borderland; the bridge between the worlds was man himself.

The soul, he said, is composed of light and fire and is of the nature of a daimon. After death, it may evolve into a being of air, a hero. A god, on the other hand, is composed of fiery breath.

One of the more important phenomena of the Hellenistic world was the mutual influence between Greek thought and Judaism. The philosophic Greeks were attracted to Judaism because the Jews worshiped an immaterial deity who had no image, unlike their native Zeus, whom it was necessary to divest of human qualities and forms in order to think of Him seriously as God.

The influence was mutual, however. Jewish books began to appear which were attributed to Solomon and which incorporated Pythagorean and Platonic ideas. The Jews of Alexandria became so Hellenized that they had to have a Greek translation of the scriptures, technically referred to as the Septuagint. A man named Philobulus tried to trace the ideas of Pythagoras, Socrates, and Plato to Mosaic writings, but he had to resort to strained allegory and deliberate faking to bring it off.

We've all heard of the Essenes, I presume. An examination of their doctrines makes it quite clear that they borrowed heavily from Orphism, Pythagoreanism, and Platonism: They were vegetarians and teetotalers, and they preached the pre-existence and survival of the soul. They taught a sharp dualism between matter and spirit. They not only emphasized the traditional Hebrew belief in angels, but also and saw the sun and the elements as manifestations of God. The Essenes had a great deal to do with writing and/or preserving the Dead Sea Scrolls, which have finally been made available in translation more than 45 years after their discovery. Their availability will undoubtedly cast a great deal more light on the nature and beliefs of the Essenes.

There has been some speculation that John the Baptist, if not Jesus, was an Essene. Stephan Hoeller (*Jung and the Lost Gospels*) doesn't say much about Greek influences on the Essenes, but he feels that this group formed the seedbed of Gnosticism. In any event, in the next chapter, I propose to show that Christianity is not a Jewish sect, but a Greek one, which has more in common with the Greek mystery religions than with the synagogue.

Along with the Essenes, the Jewish Therapeutes in Egypt were much influenced by Greek philosophical ideas. The Therapeutes went in for asceticism, piety, allegorical interpretations, and theological speculation. According to Hoeller, they and the Essenes were one and the same, the Egyptians being a group that emigrated after the disastrous Roman-Jewish war.

Philo of Alexandria (20/30 B.C.-40 A.D.), perhaps the most famous of the Hellenistic/Jewish philosophers (next to Paul of Tarsus), said that the same truth was to be found in both the sacred writings of the Jews and in Greek philosophy. He laid particular emphasis on Pythagoras, Plato, Parmenides, Empedocles, Zeno, and Cleanthes. To prove his thesis, he resorted to interpreting everything as an allegory to such an extent that most modern critics find his proofs useless if not laughable.

He did observe, however, that God is beyond all definition and description. His existence can be affirmed, but nothing beyond that (including the use of masculine pronouns to refer to Him/Her/It). In this, he anticipated Plotinus and Neoplatonism.

Since God is beyond all human comprehension, intermediate beings are required in order for God to communicate with the material world. These are the *dynameis* (Powers), qualities, ideas, or thoughts of God, which are also angels, daimons, and souls. All of these entities are comprehended in a World Soul, which is the wisdom and reason of God, which is the Logos. Philo's Logos is described by Zeller as "the idea which comprises all ideas, the power that comprises all powers, the representative and ambassador of God, the instrument of creation and government of the world, the highest of the angels, the first-born son of God, the second God (*deuteros theos*), original pattern of world and force that creates everything in it, the soul which is clothed with the body of the world as with a garment."

Philo was not a hundred percent original, of course, and this cannot be legitimately expected of any philosopher. He borrowed a great deal from older philosophies, building on what had come before. Like Aristotle, he said that the stars are visible gods. Like Pythagoras, he affirmed that everything is arranged according to numbers. Like the Orphics, he considered the body to be the tomb of the soul. Sin arises because of the combination of the two, and humanity is hopelessly corrupt. He said that God is the only source of virtue or goodness. He followed the Stoics in advising the rejection of all sensual pleasure and passions. Like the Cynics, he advocated an extreme simplicity of life.

Philo said that you have to bypass all the *dynameis*, even the Logos, in order to become illuminated and see the pure unity of God, and that this is accomplished by the infusion of God's pneuma. You can't do this by studying anything that can actually be learned; it is the Ethereal Wisdom (*aitherios sophia*) given by God. Philo carefully avoided using the term "gnosis," but this is a pretty good description of the concept.

In other words, Philo departed from the rationalism of traditional classical philosophy and transformed it into mysticism, where revelation was more important than reason, God's grace more important than mental effort, and the prophet greater than the wise man. He rejected the immanence of God (pantheism) that the older Greek philosophers had advocated and insisted on a dualistic transcendence, God vs. the world. In affirming all these things, Philo had turned traditional Greek philosophy upside down. Most people think that was "bad," but maybe not. He at least set currents in motion that would pave the way for Neoplatonism.

The so-called Neo-Pythagoreans, like Philo, taught the dualism of mind vs. matter and God vs. the world. Revelation from angels and daimons was the only way to know anything, since, as the Skeptics affirmed, we can't figure anything out for ourselves because we don't have anything reliable to go by.

Some said that God was the monad, others that God was partly the first cause, combining matter and form as per Plato, and partly beyond number (like Ain Soph), giving rise to both the monad and then the dyad. By combining the monism of the Stoics with the dualism of Plato and Aristotle, they further paved the way for Neoplatonism.

The Neo-Pythagoreans said that the Ideas of Plato were numbers and were the thoughts of God and that they were the pattern for our inferior material imitations rather than being the inner essence of things. Like Plato, they said that a World Soul necessarily intervenes between Ideas and matter. Like Xenocrates, they conceived of the soul as a self-moving number. Also like Plato, they said that the soul was pre-existent and eternal and, as Plato said, had three parts. They laid much less stress on transmigration than had the original Pythagoreans, and they followed Philo in affirming the necessary intermediary function of daimons, which they equated with Hebrew angels.

The most famous Neo-Pythagorean—if, indeed, that's what he truly was—was Apollonius of Tyana, who lived in the second half of the 1st century A.D. (Tyana was in Cappadocia, in Asia Minor.) Just about everything we know about Apollonius was set forth more than a hundred years after his death by Philostratus, and his biography is thought to be less than reliable. According to Philostratus, Apollonius was a wandering teacher who traveled all over the Roman Empire and spent time in India with the Brahmins. He was a vegetarian and advocate of animal rights in that he wouldn't wear any clothing that came from animals and condemned animal sacrifice. If he were alive today, he'd be right out there demonstrating against the use of laboratory animals. But he was also an ascetic, renouncing wine and women along with the flesh of animals.

Apollonius was supposedly put on trial sometime around 90 A.D. by the emperor Domitian. When he saw things were going against him, he simply teleported out—vanished. Among other feats, he rescued a young man from a lamia (a man-eating monster disguised as a woman) and ended a plague at Ephesus by getting the citizens to stone an old beggar who was in reality the plague demon. When they removed the rocks, they found no beggar but only a dog-monster.

He is supposed to have remained silent for six years, during which time he nevertheless quelled several riots merely by the force of his personality. He understood all languages, including that of birds, without having to learn them. He performed miracles of healing and raised the dead. Long after his death, he appeared as an

Apollonius of Tyana

oracle to Marcus Aurelius. After relating about half a page of these marvels, Francis Barrett (*The Magus*, 1801) says he won't bother to repeat anything Philostratus said because it's too fantastic.

In the early 4th century, there was an attempt by the Pagan opponents of Christianity to set up Apollonius as a rival to Jesus in an effort to limit the growth of the relatively new religion, but this scheme failed to have the desired effect. Needless to say, Apollonius of Tyana was not the same man as Saint Apollonius the Apologist, a Christian martyr who was killed around 185 A.D.

In the 1st century, there developed a school now referred to as Middle Platonism. Plutarch of Chaeronia (45-125 A.D.) said that, since evil cannot come from God, the intermediary between God and the world must be an evil World Soul. The most famous representative of the Middle Platonic school, Plutarch seems to have been a prototype of modern theologians in that he tried to reconcile religion with rationalism while remaining traditional. He really didn't have much to say that was original, but tried to pick and choose the best from each system. He taught, for example, that God is so far above the world that interaction is only possible through intermediate beings or daimons (both good and evil), that the stars and planets are gods, that the soul has several parts (psyche being superior to the body, but nous being superior to psyche), that the soul survives the death of the body and meets relatives in the hereafter, that suicide is permissible, that there are five elements with the fifth being aither, and so on. In his effort to reconcile all philosophies, he said we should strive for a golden mean between excess and strict asceticism. Plutarch's greatest historical importance lies not in his rather colorless melting-pot of eclectic philosophy but in the fact that he wrote biographies of all the important people of his time in his *Lives*.

Less famous than Plutarch but possibly more important was Gaius, who lived in the first half of the 2nd century. He anticipated Plotinus and Neoplatonism by enunciating the three principles of *protos theos* (the first god), ideas (his thoughts), and *hylē* (matter).

The Chaldean Oracles of Zoroaster and the writings attributed to Hermes Trismegistus are, strictly speaking, developments of Neo-Pythagoreanism and Middle Platonism, but I am already getting way ahead of the story. So let's back up to Christianity. Without Hellenistic philosophy, Christianity might still be an obscure and heretical Jewish sect. This debt is even greater in the case of "orthodox" Christianity than it is for Gnosticism—the version of Christianity that lost out.

VIII

Gnosticism

It may seem strange to discuss Gnosticism—that great Christian "heresy"—before considering mainstream Christianity itself, but I'm taking that approach here for the simple reason that, although Gnosticism, in the form that we know it, came after Jesus Christ, it also originated and had become an ongoing concern before any part of the New Testament was committed to writing. Therefore, the Christian scriptures, written in Greek, not only refer to Gnosticism, but also make use of it and incorporate many features of it. One of the first Gnostics, Simon Magus, is a minor character in the book of Acts.

Why consider Gnosticism at all in a book on Greek magic? After all, its most important centers were in Egypt (Alexandria) and Asia Minor (Ephesus). The language of its scriptures was not only Greek, but also Coptic (a late form of vernacular Egyptian that incorporated many Greek words), Aramaic, Persian, and other languages—even Chinese! It arose in the period of Roman domination hundreds of years after Alexander's empire had broken up. Greek religion contributed next to nothing to it, and Greek philosophy was only one of many influences. In fact, the primary constituents of Gnosticism were Eastern and were contributed to by the religions and philosophies of the conquered peoples—viewpoints finally reasserting themselves after a long period of dormant silence.

But it took place within the Hellenistic world, the world that had been Greek and that still expressed itself in the Greek language in most of its literature. Most of the terms and names of Gnosticism are Greek, although Hebrew and other languages play a large part. The Nag Hammadi scrolls are Coptic translations from Greek documents. Although Gnosticism was far more than Hellenized Christianity, as was once thought, the Greek tradition is nevertheless the largest tributary of the river of Gnosticism.

Some people lament the fact that Christianity today is fragmented into numberless denominations and sects; they long for the early days of the religion, when it was a single, unified church. Alas, such a golden age never existed. In the first few centuries after Jesus, there were just as many sects as there are today, and the differences among them were much greater. At that time of discontent, confusion, and turmoil, there were hundreds of religions and hundreds of variations within each religion. Then as now, only much more so, one person's truth was another's heresy. It was not a case of a monolithic, established Christian church fighting against a strange heresy in the form of Gnosticism.

But Gnosticism was not a monolithic religion, either. There were plenty of sects—the Simonians, the Basilideans, the Valentinans, the Ophites, and so on—some of them with opposite versions of the same doctrines. Thus one group venerated the serpent and assigned the god "Sabaoth" to a lesser position. Another group, more oriented toward Judaism, did just the reverse. Other groups didn't see fit to make much mention of either of them.

Furthermore, the Gnostics did not call themselves "Gnostics." Some of them called themselves "Pneumatics." Some were content to call themselves "Christians." Others left Christ out of things altogether. Gnosticism was not necessarily Christian. It was a religion in its own right, with some of its sects incorporating the persons and some of the doctrines of the Christian myth.

The Gnostics believed that revelation was an ongoing process rather than a set of doctrines established for all time. Any individual could preach and prophesy. In fact, the ability to "channel" Jesus or the Apostles with new revelations was considered to be a sign of spiritual maturity that non-Gnostic Christians lacked. For the Gnostics, revelation was a continuing process, not a crystallized and eventually lifeless dogma that had to be believed or else.

The most important idea that all Gnostic sects had in common, though, was that God is unknowable by any normal means of seeking or knowledge. God was beyond reason—and beyond faith, as well. Besides intellectual knowledge of the true state of the universe, beyond the passwords and words of power to be used in passing through the heavenly spheres after death, you had to know God by direct revelation, by a transcendental experience. This was called Gnosis—knowledge. (In most cases, "Gnosis" meant experiential knowledge as opposed to book learning or intellectual knowledge, although in some cases it seems to have meant no more than having been informed of the true state of things.)

Other ideas that all, or almost all, of the Gnostic sects held in common included the doctrine that the world is imperfect because it was not created by the real God. It had been made by an imperfect Demiurge *(Demiourgos),* who, depending on which sect you belonged to, was either evil or just plain stupid and inept. Note that the term itself—Demiurge, meaning a creator god—was borrowed from Plato.

The real God was so far removed from the manifested world that God had nothing to do with it. God did not create it nor sustain it, and there was no such thing as heavenly Providence. God and the world were two entirely different things; God was completely Other, alien, unknowable except by direct experience. The world had been created not by God, but by misguided actions on the part of entities that naturally evolved or emanated from God in successive steps. Nevertheless, in most systems, it was believed that God intervenes to the extent of providing a means of Gnosis, usually a redeemer figure.

The Gnostics were in rebellion against the Demiurge and were loyal to the transcendental God. In this, they were somewhat like Huckleberry Finn. When faced with a decision involving the accepted church morality of his time and place, versus what he intuitively knew to be right—helping a slave to escape—he said, "All right, then, I'll go to hell!"

This devotion to the true God over and above the false and limited conceptions promulgated by any organized religion ("The Tao which can be described is not the Eternal Tao"), along with the egalitarian practices of the Gnostics, led to a lack of respect for ecclesiastical authority. The organized church, with its more-or-less permanently installed bishops, priests, and deacons based on the apostolic succession, was accused of playing power games. Most bishops, being all too human, lusted after power and authority. The Gnostic system, wherein there was no authority that superseded personal revelation, undermined that desire. Some bishops, as it turned out, were Gnostics; most, however, opposed it to the limits of their ability to do so.

In Gnosticism, a human being was a spark of the divine light, a tiny piece of God, a *pneuma* (spirit) imprisoned in a body of flesh and burdened with an appetitive soul (the *psyche*, Plato's term for the soul).

Body and soul had been created by lesser beings to imprison the divine spark. The whole material world and its gods—usually personified as rulers or Archons of the heavenly spheres—was geared toward the tyrannical perpetuation of this grim imprisonment in matter. The goal of Gnosis was first to realize this situation and then somehow to escape it.

Incidentally, the pneuma was considered by most Gnostics to be female, and the idea of all souls being female has persisted in various traditions. This is in contradistinction to the attitude which regards spiritual matters as masculine and the body and/or matter as feminine, a doctrine reflected in some of the writings attributed to Paul wherein man stands between woman and God. This in turn may be a natural outgrowth of the classical tendency to regard earth deities as female and sky/sun deities as male. On the other hand, the idea that woman-man-God forms an ascending hierarchy is right out of Plato.

God wanted to recover the lost parts of Itself—the divine sparks that were the spirits of human beings; otherwise God was completely indifferent to the world. (In some systems, however, the divine Sophia, behind the back of the Demiurge, infused all of creation with traces of Light.) Accordingly, God and the more exalted emanations sent down a redeemer to reveal the truth and guide humanity back to the Light. In some forms of Gnosticism, this redeemer was Christ—incarnated, according to some sects, as the man Jesus. In other sects, he was called something else, such as Manda d'Hayye or Hibil-Uthra or simply Logos.

The Zoroastrian symbolism of light vs. darkness was widely used, God dwelling in the realm of Light and the world being the realm of Darkness. It was also said—1900 years before George Gurdjieff gained a reputation for profound wisdom and insight by saying the same thing—that humanity is asleep and needs to be awakened.

In the ascent of the spirit after death—assuming she was in possession of Gnosis—various attributes or accretions were shed like garments, lesser souls or shells abandoned in the planetary realms of the same nature. This feature was held in common with many of the mystery religions, where initiates shed successive layers of clothing. The ascent through the seven heavens, sometimes by means of a symbolic ladder or staircase, was also a feature of many mysteries.

The great scholar Charles William King, writing in the last century, made a good case for a strong Buddhist influence on Gnosticism. Others have since done the same. However, it now seems that, if such were the case, it was Buddhist influence that had first been ground in the mills of Persian theology and Greek philosophy. Whether that is the case or not, just about all the religions in the Hellenistic world of the time had at least some influence on Gnosticism. Various scholars have found its origins not only in Buddhism, but also in Judaism, Zoroastrianism, Hellenistic philosophy, the Essenes, and anything else that occurred to them. The truth is that all these cultures contributed; the religion of the period, like its philosophy, was extremely eclectic and syncretistic—and that applies to Christianity as well as everything else.

It's certainly worthy of note that the partriarchal nature of both Athenian mythology and orthodox Judaism was abandoned by at least some Gnostics in favor of the idea of a great Goddess, Sophia or Barbelo, although She was usually thought to have been emanated or produced by a transcendent being identified as either male, androgynous, or transcending sexual distinction. Many were agreed that the salvation of the world depended entirely on a Goddess, the lesser Sophia or Achamoth, who would be redeemed by her brother and/or mate, Christos. (The name Sophia means "wisdom.") When combined with the relative liberation of women in Alexandria, one of the major centers of Gnosticism, we see a reversal of the old Athenian and Yahwist patriarchies—a reversal that was eventually stamped out by "official" Christianity.

The version of Christianity that we know did not win out over other versions because it was somehow "better," because it was "true" and the other doctrines "false," because it was the "real thing" and the others were imitations or "heresies," but because it maintained a strict authoritarian hierarchy, and because it was the version that eventually received Roman imperial sanction with the conversion of the emperor Constantine. At the Council of Nicea in 325 A.D., called by Constantine, Christianity became a monolithic, imperial, doctrinaire religion. Any organized, hierarchical, authoritarian organization has a definite advantage in any conflict with a group that is disorganized, free, and without unquestioned authority figures. Even libertarian democracies have rigidly authoritarian armies. Nevertheless, the suppression of Gnosticism and, even more so, Paganism was a gradual process that required centuries to get into full swing.

And that was another distinguishing feature of Gnosticism. Even though it had its important spokesmen, such as Basilides and Valentinus, it recognized no authority as final except the authority of an individually bestowed Gnosis. Aside from a few verbal attacks, it lacked either the machinery or the inclination to persecute those who disagreed with it. Furthermore, it tended to be elitist, distinguishing those in the know from the great unwashed. Of course, another way of looking at this distinction is to point out that it represented a "search for excellence." You couldn't just be dunked in a river or eat a wafer and expect to be automatically saved or enlightened. You had to show some evidence of spiritual attainment to be considered "mature."

Gnosticism was also weak in the area of evangelistic proselytization. In this way, and because it demanded proven quality rather than quantity for its membership, it cut itself off from the mass of humanity and prevented itself from becoming a widespread popular religion. Imperial Roman Christianity had none of these drawbacks.

But, if organized Christianity had not survived, Mithraism would probably have taken its place rather than any of the Gnostic sects. There were no women in the Mithraic system, either—outside of Medusa as a slain monster—and Mithraism had its main strength within the ranks of the military. The initiation ceremonies, reminiscent of both shamanism and modern fraternity initiations, were very macho. And if certain Gnostics had taken the day, things might have been much worse. Some of them thought propagating the human species was sinful. That might be a useful doctrine in today's overcrowded world, but it wasn't too good an idea at the time. In any event, they were never organized enough to become a major world religion in the material world. If mainstream Christianity had gone down the tubes, we might all be praying toward Mecca five times a day—although Islam would probably have taken a somewhat different form, too.

For a long time, all we knew about the Gnostics was what their enemies had said about them. The early Christian church did an excellent job of destroying Gnostic manuscripts. A lot of them were probably lost when they burned down the library at Alexandria. The only authorities on Gnosticism were the Christian heresiologists (heresy hunters), mainly Irenaeus (c. 125-203 A.D.), born in Asia Minor but winding up as bishop of Lyons in Gaul (France), and Hippolytus (died in 235 A.D.), who was a priest at Rome. Others included Origen, Justin Martyr, Tertullian, and Epiphanius. Then a late Gnostic manuscript written in Coptic (a form of late Egyptian written with characters modeled on Greek) was found in the 18th century—the *Pistis Sophia* ("Faith-Wisdom"). Other, minor documents, such as the *Apocryphon of John,* turned up from time to time.

Still, nobody really knew a whole lot. After all, people with axes to grind are not always the most objective authorities—although, to give them credit, they did quote the original Gnostic scriptures, and at length. The Gnostic documents we had were few and mostly fragmentary.

Fortunately, all this changed in 1945 with the discovery of a huge cache of Gnostic writings—again, in Coptic—at Nag Hammadi in Egypt. Even then, it took a ridiculously long time for the manuscripts to be fully translated and published. We didn't get a complete English-language version until 1977, although bits and pieces showed up before then. Even so, these documents were the library of one sect in one part of Egypt; they don't tell us much about the beliefs of the Gnostics at Ephesus and elsewhere.

Simon Magus, who apparently lived sometime in the 1st century A.D., was the first teacher we know about who taught what came to be known as Gnostic doctrines. That doesn't mean he invented them or that there weren't others before him, but he's the first one who became well enough known to be recorded by history. He must have been good at what he did, because he even made it into the Bible.

When he did his write-up on Simon Magus, Hippolytus mentioned a strange character called Apsethus the Lybian. Apsethus tried and failed to become God, so he gave up and just *told* everybody he was God. He hit upon a strange scheme to convince people of it. He kept a room full of parrots and trained them all to say,

"Apsethus is a god." When the parrots were well trained, he let them loose to fly all over the countryside. People heard parrots all over the district saying, "Apsethus is a god." It had quite an effect. Unfortunately for Apsethus, some anonymous Greek caught on to the trick and caught a bunch of the parrots. He "deprogrammed" them and taught them to say, "Apsethus shut us up, and forced us to say Apsethus is a god." He then let loose these retrained parrots and exploded the Apsethus balloon. The result was that the Libyans burned Apsethus at the stake.

That little tale doesn't have much if anything to do with Gnosticism, but, besides being an interesting story, it serves to show just how reliable Hippolytus really was. "Apsethus is a god"—well, maybe. But that long speech which the Greek taught the parrots is altogether unbelievable. You might train a parrot to say, "Polly want a cracker," but you're going to have difficulty getting it to recite the Gettysburg address. Maybe the Greek just taught them to say, "Apsethus is a liar." It's much more likely, however, that the whole story was just made up out of someone's vivid imagination.

According to the Bible (Acts 8:9-24), Simon—who hailed from Samaria in central Palestine—was baptized and became a nominal Christian. When he saw the Apostles ordaining priests by the laying on of hands, he tried to buy the right to do the same thing. Simon Peter set him straight, saying the power to bestow the Holy Ghost came only from God, and Simon Magus sort of repented. But, after all, buying a religious office was far from unknown in the region at the time.

Anyway, the account given by Hippolytus is a lot more colorful and detailed. All along, he says, Simon had been gaining followers partly by legerdemain (magic tricks) and partly by performing miracles with the aid of demons. After he backslid from "orthodox" Christianity (which, remember, was the doomed Jewish Christianity of Peter rather than the gentile Christianity of Paul), he went to Tyre and bought a prostitute named Helena. He said that she was the reincarnation of Helen of Troy, and, much more than that, Epinoia or Ennoia, the Intelligence of God. He himself was none other than Nous, the Thought of God.

Everybody accepts Hippolytus's assertion that Helena had been a prostitute and that Simon preached promiscuity. He's supposed to have gotten the story from Justin Martyr (100-165), whose writings have not survived. On the basis of the parrot story—and on the basis of the fact that Hippolytus was doing his best to make Simon look bad—permit me to consider the possibility that Helena might not have been a Tyrian prostitute after all—or that she went and sinned no more after meeting Simon. It has even been suggested that there was no such person; that Helena was a personification of Simon's ideas about Epinoia. On the other hand, it has been said that Helena was a necessary adjunct to Simon's teaching, and that she had to be a prostitute—*Sophia-Prunikos*—in order to demonstrate how far Sophia had fallen into the prison of matter.

Orthodox Christians doubtless consider it an invidious comparison to draw parallels between Simon and Helena on the one hand and Jesus and Mary Magdalene on the other, but some of the Gnostic scriptures might lead one to suppose the difference between the two pairs wasn't all that great. After all, here were two redeemers, two religious leaders with a message, both accompanied by women who had been prostitutes. And there were other such pairs abroad in those days! This pattern was aped in modern times by Aleister Crowley and his "Scarlet Woman." It may not be an insignificant detail that—at least according to Mark (the earliest canonical gospel) and John—Mary Magdalene was the first to see Jesus after his resurrection. It's not for me to say whether this parallel is demeaning to Jesus, favorable to Simon, or simply reduces the size of the perceived yawning gulf between the two.

It might also be well to remember that we only have the word of Hippolytus that Simon claimed to be Nous while claiming that Helena was Epinoia. But just who or what are Nous and Epinoia?

In the Simonian system, Silence—which is One and unmanifest, neither male nor female—produces Mind and Thought; that is, Nous and Epinoia, Father and Mother, male and female. Silence accomplished this feat by the simple act of reflection. Already containing the seed of the Father, Epinoia produces archangels, angels, powers, and so on, who in turn produce the world in a series of progressive degenerations.

In Persian Gnosticism, of course, no such Fall was required—the duality of the world, good versus evil and light versus darkness, had been there from the very beginning.

According to Irenaeus and Hippolytus, Simon taught that anyone who believed in him and Helena as Nous and Epinoia was already redeemed and could therefore do as they liked. The heresiologists evidently thought this was a pretty damning indictment,

The Christian Version of the Death of Simon Magus

but it's really not so far from some forms of primitive, folk "Christian" belief as folowed by some errant souls to this very day. Since, said Martin Luther, we are saved by faith and not by deeds, believe and sin heartily. This doctrine has been taken to extremes by some individuals, who firmly believe (and say so in so many words) that they have already been saved and that they are therefore blameless when they get drunk, beat their wives, or cheat their employers. The sins have already been paid for. All they have to do is repent once in a while, which means occasionally feeling a little guilty about it. (To be fair, I also have to say that I have never known any brand of minister to condone carrying things quite that far, and no organized religion holds the doctrine in quite this form.)

Simon is said to have come to a bad end, either by trying and failing to fly or ascend to heaven or by allowing himself to be buried with the prospect of rising again in three days like Jesus. Again, permit me to doubt it. Still, there is no evidence whatever that he lived to a ripe old age. In any event, Simon Magus is supposed to have been the prototype for the Faust legend.

Simon bashing turned out to be a sort of historical cottage industry. Not only did the Bible, Justin, Irenaeus, and Hippolytus get in on the act, but Warner Brothers joined their ranks in 1955 with *The Silver Chalice*. In this "epic that wasn't," Simon Magus is played by Jack Palance and meets his end in the flying stunt when his apparatus fails. Virginia Mayo plays Helena as a "right whore" who tries to seduce Victor Mature—a lost cause from the beginning. The film does not examine Gnostic doctrine.

Simon's doctrines were more fully developed by Basilides and his followers. According to Basilides (according to Hippolytus), in the beginning there was a great big nothing which was nevertheless not nothing. Out of it came the Seed of the World which contained absolutely everything in potential. These are analogous to the *Ain* and *Kether* of later cabalism. It's also pretty accurate in describing current cosmological theories about the origin of the universe, except that, in the scientific view, this Nothing and this Primordial Point or singularity were altogether mindless. Anyway, the Seed produced three sons, one subtle, one gross, and one impure. The Holy Ghost, or Boundary Spirit, separated the upper and lower worlds.

The Seed also produced the Great Archon, ruler of the Ogdoad (the eighth heaven), who supposed himself to be the highest God—

the Demiurge again—and he created everything in the ethereal world. He also produced a son, who turned out to be one and the same as the third son of the Seed. Nevertheless, the son was far more nearly perfect than the father.

Then a Second Archon arose, ruler of the Hebdomad (the seventh sphere on down), and He created the material world. The whole scheme of redemption lies in restoring everybody's pristine ignorance so that they will know their place and be content in it—which they might as well be, since they cannot go higher. This doctrine is at variance with all the rest of Gnostic thought, which said that a part of us is divine and can be redeemed to the Light despite the machinations of the Demiurge.

Basilides deduced that, since God is so distant from the world, a simple Simonian scheme of Nous-Epinoia-angels-world was too intimate. He said there were 365 heavenly spheres or Aeons (Eons, Aions) and that the lowest one was ruled by the Jewish god.

The one sect about which we seem to know the most—from Hippolytus, anyway—is the Ophites. Here we have an elaborate theology (or Gnosis) in which Bythos (the Deep) and Ennoia (or Sigē) produce Pneuma (or the higher Sophia), the mother of all living (Eve, who redeems Adam) and the intermediary between the intellectual and natural worlds (above and below the Moon, respectively). They also produce Ecclēsia, the Idea of the church. Sophia produces Christos, who is perfect, and the lower Sophia, Sophia-Achamoth, who is imperfect. In a desire to do a little creating of her own, Achamoth produces Ialdabaoth, and that's where the trouble begins.

Ialdabaoth (or Ildabaoth) produces the planetary rulers Iao, Sabaoth, Adonai, Ecoi, Ouraios, and Astaphaios. He is evil. He is not too bright. He thinks he is the highest God. He creates the world. He is the god of the Old Testament; that is, of the Jewish scriptures. You'll note that some of the names of his Archons are Jewish names for God. Like Judaism before it and Christianity afterwards, Gnosticism sometimes identified the gods of other religions as devils, or at least as distinctly inferior and selfish.

When Ialdabaoth creates humanity, he is dismayed that they, because of an infusion of Light from the higher realms, are in fact superior to himself. He therefore imprisons them in bodies of flesh. His hatred and rancor reflected in the Abyss produce the serpent Ophionophos, who is more or less "the devil," but whom the

Ophites say is also Michael or Samiel. The higher gods have mercy and create Ophis, the serpent of the Garden of Eden, who lets the cat out of the bag by getting Eve to eat the forbidden fruit and thereby find out the truth about Ialdabaoth and the higher deities. But then, at least according to one branch of the Ophites, Ophis himself goes bad and tries to keep humanity imprisoned in the flesh through ignorance.

Meanwhile, Sophia-Achamoth is imprisoned in the world of matter, like Simon's Epinoia, and it's up to Christos to get her out. Jesus is a man who becomes infused with the spirit of Christos for just that purpose. Other versions say that Achamoth was left behind by Sophia to redeem humanity.

The most influential, some say the greatest, teacher of Gnostic ideas was Valentinus, who lived in the 2nd century. He was born in Egypt and educated at Alexandria, but he taught at Rome. He may have been a Christian bishop, and he came within an inch of being elected pope. In any case, he considered himself to be a true Christian and his opponents to have gone astray. At that point in church history, there was no objective reason to say that one or the other side of this conflict represented the "true church" and the other heresy. Those who lost out were heretics; that's all. Slave-holders, many of them fighting for the right to keep slaves, were heroes in the Texas War of Independence against Mexico in 1836 but villains in the Civil War of 1861-65. Heresy and villainy are too often defined by who wins and who loses.

According to the heresiologists, Valentinus postulated a hierarchy of thirty "Aeons" (gods, emanations, or ideas personifying the abysses of space and time that separate humanity from God) in fifteen male-female pairs, divided into an Ogdoad plus a Decad plus a Dodecad (8 + 10 + 12).

The Ogdoad

Depth (Bythos)	Silence (Sigē)
Mind (Nous)	Truth (Aletheia)
Reason (Logos)	Life (Zōe)
Man (Anthrōpos)	Church (Ecclesia)

Scholars writing in German or English are apparently unanimous in not bothering to give the Greek names (used by the heresiologists) for the Aeons of the Decad and Dodecad, although, even with a layman's lack of access to the original Greek documents (or even English translations), we can make educated guesses at some of them. In the following list, some of the variant English translations are given. There are others.

The Decad
(produced by Nous and Aletheia)

(1) Profundity, Depthlike, or Deep and (2) Mixture, Commingling, or Mingling

(3) Unfading, Unaging, or Undecaying and (4) Union

(5) Self-born, Self-productive, or Self-existent and (6) Temperance or Bliss

(7) Immovable and (8) Unity, Blending, or Composition

(9) Only-begotten or Alone Begotten *(Monogenes?)* and

(10) Pleasure or Happiness

The Dodecad
(produced by Logos and Zoe)

(1) Comforter and (2) Faith *(Pistis)*

(3) Fatherly, Father-like, or Paternal *(Patroos?)* and (4) Hope *(Elpis)*

(5) Motherly, Mother-like, or Maternal *(Metroos?)* and (6) Charity or Love *(Agape)*

(7) Eternal, Everlasting, or Ever-thinking and (8) Intelligence or Understanding

(9) Eucharistic, Church-like, or Ecclesiastical and (10) Beatitude or Happiness

(11) Longed-for or Light and (12) Wisdom *(Sophia)*

Epiphanius (315-403 A.D.) gets the order switched around on some of these, and it is he (apparently) who says "Light" when the others say "Longed-for." But perhaps this is the fault of the translator.

Epiphanius cites "barbarous names" for the Aeons, as follows: The Ogdoad: Ampsiu, Ouraan, Bucua, Thartun, Ubucua, Thardedia, Metaxas, and Artababa; the Decad: Allora, Dammo, Oren, Lamaspechs, Amphiphuls, Emphsboshbaud, Dexariche, Belin, Assiouache, and Massemo; and the Dodecad: Udu or Udua, Casten or

Vacastene, Amphian, Essumen, Vannanin, Lamer, Tarde, Athames, Susua, Allora (again, both "Profundity" and "Beatitude"), Bucidia, and Damadarah. The best guess as to the origin of these names is Persian angelology, with the names having been sifted through several languages until they are no longer recognizable, although they may instead have been artificially constructed abstract terms.

Other than Sophia and the entities of the Ogdoad, the theological or magical importance of these names has not, to my knowledge, been determined. Some experimentation in invocation—preferably by people who know what they're doing—appears to be in order. Be that as it may, remember that this is a hostile second-hand report on only one system out of dozens. The names of the Valentinian Aeons are really very much secondary to the myths, legends, and religious philosophy of the Gnostics. Other sects had Aeons, too—sometimes seven, sometimes twelve, sometimes some other number, most of them with different names—and Archons as well. In some systems, such as that presented in the *Hypostasis of the Archons*, one of the Nag Hammadi manuscripts, Zōē is the daughter of Sophia and is identical with Eve, a goddess who enlightens Adam.

The myth of Eve having been created from Adam's rib is not necessarily another instance of patriarchs denying the creative power of women. It was not understood as such by the Sethian Gnostics (so-called because they saw Seth as a redeemer figure). In the first place, looking at it from a somewhat more modern standpoint, Eve represents second-generation technology. Adam was created from dust, but Eve from organic material; thus Eve is the superior creation. But, from the Gnostic viewpoint, Eve is a figure of redemption sent by the Aeons. Hiding from the Archons, she enters Adam and then comes forth from his side. She induces him to realize his true nature by eating from the Tree of Knowledge, forbidden to him by the Demiurge. The work of redemptive Gnosis is carried on by their children, Seth and Norea (or Horaia), the latter being the Gnostic version of the Biblical Naamah.

In her longing for the ultimate, for Bythos, Sophia experienced various emotions which took on an existence of their own. There are many different versions of just what these emotions were, but they are usually listed as Ignorance, Fear, Grief, and Bewilderment. These feelings were the origin of the four elements (Fire, Water, Air, and Earth, respectively).

Sophia was prevented, of course, from reuniting with Bythos because of Her lower nature (compared with the ultimate Unmanifest) and because She was prevented from doing so by a personified limit (Horos), who not only separates Bythos (or Bythos and Ennoia) from the rest of the Aeons but also separates the Pleroma from the cosmos.

Since the emotions of Sophia and the necessary manifestation of Horos had upset the harmony of the Pleroma, two more Aeons— Christ and the Holy Spirit—were produced by the rest of the Aeons to set things right again. Christ (or Christos) reconciled the Aeons to their place in the scheme of things and got Sophia straightened out.

But the desire or intention of Sophia had already become personified as a separate entity, the lower Sophia or Achamoth (from the Hebrew *chokmah*, wisdom). The lower Sophia longs to re-ascend to the Pleroma, but is prevented by Her own nature and by Horos. She has to remain alone in the cosmos, where She suffers everything there is to suffer—not as a punishment, but just because that's how things are by their natures. But the Aeons take pity and send Jesus (who, in this system, was considered to be an altogether different entity from Christ) to redeem Her. She is in fact redeemed by being purged of Her disturbing passions, but these passions still have an existence of their own. They remain behind in the form of the manifested world, matter. Out of this lower psychic substance, Sophia creates the Demiurge, who in turn creates the seven heavens and their Archons. The relationship between Sophia and the Demiurge is the same as that between pneuma and psyche.

One variant of Valentinism is represented by the *Apocryphon of John,* which starts out with a long description of the transcendent first principle. What it amounts to is very similar to the Chinese Tao. The thought of this divinity becomes personified as the goddess Barbelo, corresponding to Ennoia in other systems. Barbelo creates other Aeons (but not in male/female pairs as in mainstream Valentinism), including Sophia. Sophia also wishes to create, but makes a mess of it—because she tries to do it alone without a pair-mate, according to one theory. The best She can do is Ialdabaoth, the first Archon, who becomes the Demiurge. Sophia is so disgusted with Her creation that she pushes it away from Herself and tries to hide it.

Ialdabaoth, also known as Saklas or Samael, adheres to the usual pattern by being ignorant of his own nature and supposing himself the supreme god. He creates twelve Archons, five of whom rule over the nether world and seven of whom rule over the heavens.

These seven are given Hebrew names of God (showing just what this particular school of Gnostics thought about orthodox Judaism):

Athoth, the sheep-faced
Eloaiou, the donkey-faced
Astaphaios, the hyena-faced
Iao, the serpent-faced (with seven heads)
Sabaoth, the dragon-faced
Adonin, the monkey-faced
Sabbade, the fire-faced

"This is the sevenness of the week," says the Apocryphon. Evidently, these powers correspond to the seven planets or heavenly spheres, but no exact correlation is given. However, various clues would seem to indicate that Athoth corresponds to Saturn, Eloaiou to Jupiter, and so on in the traditional order through Sabbade and the Moon.

Finally, Iadlabaoth creates "man" *(anthrōpos)* in the image of God, some dim reflection of which he has seen in a vision. "Come," he says, "let us make man in God's image."

As for Gnostic morality according to the traditional authorities (including most modern pre-Nag-Hammadi scholars), it was either extremely ascetic or else libertine. Once you find out that the Archons and the Demiurge are evil, their laws don't count for very much. Something like the Mosaic code, they believed, was designed to make us miserable and keep us imprisoned. Since matter was the evil creation of evil beings, it is said, most Gnostics supposedly renounced the world and had as little to do with material concerns as possible—including, of course, sex and procreation. Some, however, decided to fight the Archons by breaking all the laws.

But, like every other statement that can be made about the Gnostics, these ultimately Christian observations of Gnostic morality may have been exaggerated or may have been true only in the case of a few sects. There are, after all—as we know now—Gnostic scriptures which do not assert that matter is evil in itself and that it, too, can be redeemed through Gnosis.

Surprisingly, there is one Gnostic sect that has survived to the present day—the Mandaeans in Syria. They evidently hold it as a central tenet of their faith that John the Baptist was the real Savior and that Jesus was an evil impostor who sought to distort his message.

Before leaving the subject of Gnosticism, let's look at a few other "heresies" and traditions that incorporated Gnostic ideas or that were heavily influenced by Gnosticism.

Marcion (2nd century), a Christian "heretic"—that is, someone whose views varied from what eventually became accepted doctrines—rates a mention in spite of the fact that he was not really a Gnostic. Marcion considered himself a follower of Paul, although Paul would probably have disowned him. Nevertheless, he used some of the same ideas as the "real" Gnostics.

According to Marcion, there were two gods, the god of justice and the god of mercy, who existed independently rather than one having emanated from the other. Certainly, according to him, they could not both be manifestations of one god. In cabalistic terms, although these concepts did not arise until much later, he denied the existence of the Middle Pillar of the Tree of Life. The just god was the god of the Old Testament, the creator of heaven and earth. But Christ had been sent by the god of mercy, the good god, to rescue humanity from the clutches of the vengeful and unmerciful just god. Since humanity had been created by the just god and did not even contain a spark of the merciful god, the rescue attempt was an act of grace, pure goodness and mercy. Also, since ownership of humanity resided in the just god, a price had to be paid—the blood of Christ on the cross. Note that the question of sin does not even arise; the blood is simply the purchase price.

What all this has to do with Gnosticism is the idea of a redeemer who rescues humanity from the inferior world of manifestation. The idea of salvation by grace alone is definitely un-Gnostic. However, like some of the Gnostics, Marcion advocated fighting back against the creator god by having as little as possible to do with his creation—that is, the practice of completely asexual asceticism.

Marcion started a trend, however, in deciding which scriptures were canonical ("true") and which were not. In the end, he accepted only some of Paul's epistles and an expurgated version of the Gospel of Luke. The Old Testament, being a product of the old regime (that of the just god), had to go. Nevertheless, he thought people ought to adhere to the Mosaic code as long as they were subject to the just god.

Another movement that incorporated Gnostic elements without being exactly Gnostic itself was Hermeticism, a philosophical religion based on the alleged writings of Hermes Trismegistus (Thrice-Greatest Hermes), a legendary figure associated with the Egyptian god Thoth. It has been said that the Hermetic writings represent the wisdom of ancient Egypt. If so, it is strange how they so nearly reflect the religious climate and thinking of the times in which they first appeared.

Whereas it might be said that the ideas of Marcion are a radically Christianized version of Gnosticism, the Hermetic writings contain almost nothing Christian. They are entirely a product of Hellenistic Paganism.

The Emerald Tablet of Hermes Trismegistus might be called a basic document in the history of Western Hermetic philosophy, but it did not appear publicly until the alchemist Geber published it in Arabic in the 8th century. No earlier version is known.

The most important Hermetic work of the earlier centuries being considered here was the Poemandres, which in the Middle Ages took on the slightly corrupted title of "The Divine Pymander." The title comes from the name of the divine being who reveals the secrets of the cosmos to the author. It means Shepherd of Men. Poemandres identifies himself as the Nous of the absolute power.

In the beginning was Light. Somehow—it isn't explained very well—a swirling, serpent-like darkness comes to be. The Nous produces the Logos, the "Son of God," who effects a partial separation of the elements in the darkness so that Fire and Air ascend above the Earth and Water. The elements evidently originated in the first place from the will *(Boule)* of the Nous.

The Nous then produces a Demiurge to govern the elements, and he in turn produces seven governors. The Logos unites with the Demiurge, who produces animal life while the Nous produces Man, an entirely spiritual being who is androgynous. Man sees his reflection in the world of nature, falls in love with it, and becomes drawn into it and trapped there. Thus love is seen as the cause of the Fall of Man. To ascend again to the Nous, Man must abandon his love of the body.

Another movement that seems to have incorporated Gnostic ideas was 3rd-century Manichaeism, the Persian religion of Mani. All of the least attractive features generally attributed to Gnosticism as a whole by its critics seem to have crystallized for real in Manichaeism—extreme dualism (the universe as good vs. evil, light vs. darkness), extreme asceticism and anti-sexuality, the idea that matter was evil by nature, and so on. Unlike the Gnostics, however, Mani did not try to explain the existence of evil by a series of progressively less perfect emanations from an unknowable God. Instead, in line with the traditional Zoroastrianism which formed the basis of Manichaeism, the eternal pre-existence of good (light) and evil (darkness) is assumed. Darkness tries to take over the realms of Light, and that's where the trouble starts and the world begins.

What seems to distinguish Manichaeism from the older Zoroastrianism is that, first of all, it tried to incorporate all the major religions existing at that time—Judaism, Christianity, Buddhism, Zoroastrianism, Gnosticism, and so on. Secondly, it made use of the idea of Aeons or divine emanations, which, in Manichaeism, generally come in sets of five. Thus the good God is accompanied by Deliberation, Intelligence, Knowledge, Resolution, and Thought. The whole thing gets at least as complicated as the system of Valentinus, but this isn't really the place to go into it; the phenomenon was Persian with only very diluted Greek elements. Nevertheless, Manichaeism owed a lot to Gnosticism and was extremely influential in its day. It spread all over the Greek-speaking world as well as in the East, and St. Augustine himself started out as a Manichaean. Although he "saw the light" and switched over to Christianity, surely Manichaean ideas helped shape Augustine's extremely influential pronouncements on the Christian religion. The practice of shaking hands is supposed to have originated with the Manichaeans.

Some people in our own time find Gnosticism at least interesting because they are fed up with the current state of the traditional monotheistic religions, because they see some truth in Gnosticism that orthodox religions lack, or because they are attracted by some outstanding feature of Gnosticism such as its anti-authoritarian attitude. But, if you believe the accounts of the heresiologists—backed up by the opinions of modern scholars such as King and Hans Jonas, who wrote before the availability of most of the Nag Hammadi material and had to use the heresiologists as their primary sources— Gnosticism in its original form is not very well suited for modern times. Consider some of the more prevalent (if not absolutely universal) doctrines of Gnosticism as they were understood to have been not so very long ago:

1. Matter is evil. The body is evil.

2. Renunciation of the world; extreme asceticism.
3. Pronounced duality between God and the world, light and darkness, spirit and flesh.
4. Elitism ("We're in the know; you're just a peasant.")

The business about duality, for instance—carried to its logical consequence in the religion of Manichaeism—runs exactly opposite to more modern and hopefully more enlightened ideas that all is One, that matter is just a limited way of seeing spirit, and that God is immanent in all things or perhaps identical with all things.

It must be said, however, that there is not one of these points that has not been more or less refuted by more recent authors such as Stephan Hoeller who have now had the opportunity to study the Nag Hammadi corpus in translation. Various statements in the Gnostic Gospel of Philip, for example, flatly contradict most of the assumptions listed above.

Part of the confusion may arise from the fact that, among the Gnostics, individual interpretation was not only allowed, it was encouraged and was considered a sign of enlightenment.

It is probably impossible to say anything at all about the Gnostics that cannot be disproven by one or more counter-examples from historical record or Gnostic scripture. Gnosticism itself begins to resemble the God of the *Aprocryphon of John*—unknowable and inexpressible except to say that it is not this, not that.

But that doesn't mean that certain Gnostic ideas cannot be adapted for our own times. As with all myth, mysticism, and religion, the danger comes in insisting upon the literal truth of every detail. Analogously, though on a somewhat lower level, it isn't necessary to believe in talking swine in order to draw the moral of practicality from "The Three Little Pigs." At the other extreme are teaching stories and myths. The prime example of this, which says all you really need to know about Gnosticism or about the meaning of life in general, is "The Song of the Pearl."

Cast in the form of a fairy tale or classical hero myth, "The Song of the Pearl" concerns a prince who journeys to Egypt in quest of a pearl guarded by a dragon. It has been presented in the Nag Hammadi Library (as part of the Acts of Thomas) and has been retold and explained by Hans Jonas and by Stephan Hoeller (see bibliography). But the immediate impact of the story needs no explanation. Neither your intuitive mind nor your subconscious mind require one. If you never read anything else having to do with Gnosticism, read "The Song of the Pearl."

In the present day, Gnosticism is perhaps best understood and appreciated if everything is interpreted in psychological terms (for example, Ialdabaoth = the ego). We'll examine that approach a little more closely in Chapter XII.

A Gnostic Ritual of Spiritual Development

There is no surviving step-by-step description of any Gnostic ceremony or ritual, and we cannot always trust even the general descriptions given by the opponents of Gnosticism. It is probably safe to assume that most Gnostic rituals were group religious ceremonies not totally unlike those performed today in various Christian churches, bearing in mind that any Pneumatic was qualified to administer the ceremonies and deliver the "sermon."

Rather than attempting a conjectural reconstruction of such a religious ceremony, I have here tried to use Gnostic ideas in the construction of a ritual aimed at spiritual development. The myth-structure is that of the *Apocryphon of John*. The idea is to confront each of the seven planetary Archons in turn and bypass all of them to reach the Pleroma. These Archons represent negative aspects of your own personality that bar you from spiritual realization. Their images have been formulated by a combination of logic, intuition, and a little exploratory astral investigation. Feel free, however, to visualize any image that you feel to be more appropriate. It is to be hoped that this ritual will at least make you aware of some of your own shortcomings—and we all have each and every one of those enumerated here to some extent—and perhaps result in their noticeable abatement. At the same time, the ritual, if performed properly, should give you a feeling of freedom and well-being at its conclusion.

If you find the ritual uncongenial because of the inherent negativity of banishing everything in sight—although that is the goal of true meditation—or if you find the use of the names of the Archons offensive because they are holy names in other traditions, you are under no sort of obligation to perform this ritual. You may, on the other hand, see fit to modify it to accord with your personal preferences.

The altar should be covered with a white cloth. On the altar should be a small piece of bread on a plate and a cup of wine. Seven images or objects should be placed about the room to represent the planets. These can be candles of the appropriate colors or simple objects of a planetary character (for example, gemstones, the planetary emblems painted on poster board, and/or specific objects such aspen and paper for Mercury, a mirror for Venus, and so on. Correspondences may be found in Denning and Phillips' *Planetary Magick* or in Crowley's 777.) If you know how to cast a horoscope for the time of working, do so and place the objects in the directions of the planets in the heavens. Otherwise, simply space the objects evenly about the room with the sun in the East.

Some sort of opening protection ritual ought to be performed—the Lesser Banishing Ritual of the Pentagram, if nothing else. I have mentioned this basic ritual before, so I might as well say now that it was apparently invented—or channeled—by MacGregor Mathers for the Golden Dawn. Since then, its use has become widespread—almost universal—among all practitioners of magic, including some Wiccans and Neo-Pagans. It is described in *The Golden Dawn* by Israel Regardie, but far more meaningful directions for actually performing it are given by Donald Michael Kraig in *Modern Magick*, who, for the sake of convenience, refers to it as "the LBRP."

However, if you do use the LBRP for a Gnostic ritual, do not use the usual Hebrew God-names and archangels. From a Gnostic standpoint, these names represent the Demiurge and his Archons. However, the ritual as it stands is adequate if certain names are substituted. You may prefer to use the Greek form of the cabalistic cross (*"Eis, hē basileia, kai hē dynamis, kai hē doxa, eis tous aiōnas"*), although this isn't strictly necessary. For the divine names, you might use Monas, Barbelo, Christos, and Sophia. For the archangels, use the Four Lights of the Apocryphon of John: Eleleth, Daveithai, Oriel, and Harmozel, in that order. (In a similar context, the Aurum Solis uses Sōtēr, Alastōr, Asphaleios, and Amyntōr.)

On the other hand, in line with the Gnostic approach, any opening protective and purificatory ritual that you normally use—or one of your own extemporaneous devising, with or without words—might be appropriate.

Standing behind the altar facing East, recite as follows:

> *O divine Sophia, source of all true knowledge, guide to the fullness, redeemer of the highest soul of every person, look with favor upon my endeavors here today (tonight). Silence the insistent chaos of this my prison, my mind and body, that I may know my true Self and attain to the divine gnosis.*
>
> *I know that there is one God, the pre-existent, unknowable*

Monad, about whom one may say nothing. And I know that the consort of this invisible spirit is Barbelo, She who is the glory of the Aeons, whose light shineth like unto that of the All. And that Sophia, lowest of the Aeons but exalted beyond all creation, looked with pity upon the divine sparks of Light held within the prison of Samael, fell from the Pleroma into the sufferings of the world of the Archons, and was rescued and redeemed; She remains in Her person as Achamoth to guide us to the Light.

Now you are to visit each planetary image in turn, beginning with the Moon. Always move clockwise from one image to the next, and it wouldn't hurt to make a complete circumambulation before returning to the next image. You may wish to dance these circum-ambulations, which you may do either "free-form" or by using the steps described by Ted Andrews in *Imagick* (Llewellyn, 1989).

In the following speeches, the names of the Archons and the Demiurge (Ialdabaoth) are not to be vibrated, for that would empower the opposition. These names are to be "announced," as it were, in an authoritative voice of command, but only the names of Sophia and Barbelo are to be vibrated in the usual manner. Before making the address to each Archon, visualize a hostile entity of the appropriate planetary character. As his name and the name Ialda-baoth are spoken, let the image grow smaller and less regal, the colors fading, the clothing being revealed as rags. Let the image begin to fade when the name *Sophia* is vibrated and pop out of existence altogether when you vibrate the name *Barbelo*. If you know how to make the banishing hexagrams or heptagrams of the planets, do so. You may use either a dagger, a sword, the lower end of a wand, or your index finger, according to your preference. (Banishing hexagrams are shown in *The Golden Dawn* and in *Modern Magick*—and in many other places besides. Banishing heptagrams are given in *Mysteria Magica* by Denning and Phillips.) If you are using candles, extinguish the appropriate candle with your fingers or candle snuffer as soon as the image has vanished.

Moon—Sabbade may be visualized as a man in a dark purple jumpsuit with a head of flame—something like "the dread Dor-mammu" from the Doctor Strange comic books, if your reading has been that inclusive. Sabbade represents the negative side of change—fleeting and purposeless (the dancing flame emits no heat)—and the inability to concentrate on the object of attention because of distractions.

Say:

> *I know who I am. I know where I came from. I know where I am going. I know thy name and the name of thy creator. Fall back, thou Archon of the Sphere of the Moon, for I know thee for what thou art. Have done with thy vacillation! Thou shalt hinder me no longer! Step aside and let me pass! Sabbade! Ialdabaoth! SOPHIA! BARBELO!*

When you vibrate the name "Barbelo," make the banishing figure of the Moon with your magical weapon, if you know how, and then immediately extinguish the candle, if you are using candles. Then make one complete circumambulation and return to the image you have set up for Mercury.

Mercury—Adonin is essentially an ape, perhaps with an orange tunic or loincloth. As he fades, he becomes more and more like a little monkey chittering away in frustration, or perhaps an organ-grinder's monkey. He represents the intellect that disdains intuition and feeling. Speak as follows.

> *I know who I am. I know where I came from. I know where I am going. I know thy name and the name of thy creator. Fall back, thou Archon of the Sphere of Mercury, for I know thee for what thou art. Have done with thy sophistry! Thou shalt hinder me no longer! Step aside and let me pass! Adonin! Ialdabaoth! SOPHIA! BARBELO!*

Venus—Sabaoth, although a holy name in some branches of Gnosticism, is here the Archon of Venus. The image should be nude, male or female in accordance with your sexual preference and, at first, very attractive—albeit with a stern, angular countenance. A forked serpent's tongue flicks out, and small flames suddenly appear and vanish at the corners of the mouth. Closer examination reveals that the skin is covered with scales. Sabaoth here represents the less wholesome aspects of sexual desire, including violence, unrequited lust, power games, and exploitation. Address this entity as follows:

I know who I am. I know where I came from. I know where I am going. I know thy name and the name of thy creator. Fall back, thou Archon of the Sphere of Venus, for I know thee for what thou art. Have done with thy lubricity! Thou shalt hinder me no longer! Step aside and let me pass! Sabaoth! Ialdabaoth! SOPHIA! BARBELO!

Sun—Iao, in this context, represents false and unworthy authority—specifically, your own ego, although here he is external-ized and objectified. He has no head as such, but seven hissing serpents sprouting from his neck, an apt analogy for the usual fragmentation of the conscious mind. Otherwise, he starts out as a slim young man clad in yellow.

I know who I am. I know where I came from. I know where I am going. I know thy name and the name of thy creator. Fall back, thou Archon of the Sphere of the Sun, for I know thee for what thou art. Have done with thy arrogance! Thou shalt hinder me no longer! Step aside and let me pass! Iao! Ialdabaoth! SOPHIA! BARBELO!

Mars—Astaphaios is dressed in Roman armor over a red tunic, and he has the head of a hyena—rather like the "gnolls" in the Dungeon & Dragons game. Naturally, he represents wrath, ill-considered and hasty anger and hostility.

I know who I am. I know where I came from. I know where I am going. I know thy name and the name of thy creator. Fall back, thou Archon of the Sphere of Mars, for I know thee for what thou art. Have done with thy fury! Thou shalt hinder me no longer! Step aside and let me pass! Astaphaios! Ialdabaoth! SOPHIA! BARBELO!

Jupiter—Eloaiou is dressed in a royal blue robe and sits on a silver throne—which, upon closer examination, is made of shiny tin. His most distinguishing characteristic is that he has the head of a donkey. He represents the abuse of power and the desire to dominate others.

*I know who I am. I know where I came from. I know where I am
going. I know thy name and the name of thy creator. Fall back,
thou Archon of the Sphere of Jupiter, for I know thee for what thou
art. Have done with thy tyranny! Thou shalt hinder me no longer!
Step aside and let me pass! Eloaiou! Ialdabaoth! SOPHIA!
BARBELO!*

Saturn—Athoth is an old man dressed in an off-the-shoulder
indigo tunic. He bears a scythe and has the head of a sheep. He
represents sloth, inertia, sluggishness, laziness, and depression.

*I know who I am. I know where I came from. I know where I am
going. I know thy name and the name of thy creator. Fall back,
thou Archon of the Sphere of Saturn, for I know thee for what thou
art. Have done with thy morbidity! Thou shalt hinder me no
longer! Step aside and let me pass! Athoth! Ialdabaoth! SOPHIA!
BARBELO!*

Now return to a position behind the altar, facing East, lay your
magical implement (if any) on the altar, and extend your arms in the
form of a cross. Say the following, feeling free to improvise as the
Spirit moves you.

*I have cast aside the cloak of soma! I have cast aside the cloak of
psyche! I have cast aside the blinding garments of the Archons by
the power of the gnosis of Sophia, by the illumination of the
dazzling light of Barbelo! Purified, I stand as my True Self, the
undefiled pneuma, and the glory of the Pleroma is open before me!
Lo, I am enfolded by the Light, and the Light is God, and I am the
Light, and the Light is Glory, and the Light is All—and I have
come home!*

Conclude by intoning "Amen" or "So mote it be," according to
preference. If you don't feel anything, you haven't done it correctly.
The idea is to "enflame yourself with prayer," and you will not get
anything if you don't invest anything. At any rate, once the feeling
has been held for a while, quietly close with a repetition of the
opening ritual.

A simple group ritual that would be entirely faithful to the spirit
of Gnosticism and that could be easily re-enacted would be the

round dance described in the *Acts of John* and widely reprinted elsewhere (for example, in the works by G.R.S. Mead and Stephan A. Hoeller that are cited in the bibliography). In addition, the text of a Gnostic document entitled *The Thunder, Perfect Mind*, or a part of it, would be ideal for a ritual of invocation. This is Gnosticism. You are the Pneumatic. Do what thou wilt shall be the whole of the Law.

IX

The Greek New Testament

Hellenism also influenced the Jews, of course, and not just Philo. Palestine was very much a part of Alexander's empire. There came to be a certain amount of conflict between Hellenized Jews and traditional Jews who preferred the old ways. Christianity started out as a Jewish cult, but it, too, rapidly became Hellenized as well. It became Hellenized to the extent that all its sacred literature was written in Greek. All the books of the New Testament were written in Greek (or, conceivably, in Aramaic in one or two instances; but the earliest surviving versions are Greek), and many of them were written in that language with the specific purpose of appealing to a Hellenized world.

Many people have the idea that the Apostles Matthew and John must have carried around scrolls and inkpots in their backpacks in order to write down the words and deeds of Jesus every night by the light of a campfire. Others suppose that they just wrote from memory after the Crucifixion. Actually, in the opinion of Biblical scholars, none of the gospels was written down for the first time until several years after the death of Paul in about 67 A.D., although they may have been based in part on earlier oral traditions. The "Greekest" of the Greek New Testament is probably represented by Revelation and by the gospels of John and Luke, both written around the turn of the century—that is, around 100 A.D., with the

Gospel of John being written later than the Apocalypse. All the gospels were written after the Epistles of Paul. You'll note that this is well after Philo of Alexandria and after Neo-Pythagoreanism and Middle Platonism had gotten off the ground.

The original Christian church was, of course, a Jewish sect that considered Jesus to be the rightful king of the Jews by right of direct descent from David and Solomon. As the Anointed One, the *Messiach* or Christos, he was expected to establish a new sovereign nation and drive out the Romans. Since he hadn't done it during his lifetime, he was expected to come back from the dead and do it sometime in the near future. Indeed, he had already risen from the dead and ascended into heaven, whence he would come to make Palestine hot for the Romans.

To be a Christian, you had to be a Jew and follow the Mosaic law, including being circumcised (if you were a man) and following the dietary code. This was the earliest church, headed by the apostle Peter. Peter's authority derived from the fact that he had been the first, or among the first, to see the risen Christ in the flesh and thus had one of the last contacts with The Authority—although, according to two of the four gospels, Mary Magdalene was the first to see the risen Christ. The orthodox position was that Mary didn't count. She was a woman. The Twelve Apostles were all men.

That's why all priests were supposed to be men, a custom and doctrine followed to this day by most Christian churches. It's worth noting, however, that the practice is not universal. In an effort to get back to the roots of the early church, the Christian Church (Disciples of Christ) has had women in the clergy since the late 19th century.

Peter evidently thought you had to be a Jew to be a Christian, but Saul of Tarsus (again, in Asia Minor) had other ideas. In a syndrome often seen since, he suddenly went from being rabidly anti-Christian to being devoutly Christian. The reason for this sudden change of heart was the fact that an apparition of Jesus knocked Saul off his horse and hinted that he ought to get off His back. According to the Jerusalem Christians, this did not qualify Saul as an authority because, unlike Peter, he had not seen Jesus risen in the flesh.

Saul was not content to become an orthodox Christian, however. Inspired by Hellenistic ideas, he carried Christianity one step further with the doctrine of the redemption of sin by Christ on the cross and went around trying to convert the Gentiles—mostly Hellenes, but also the Romans. Saul understood, rightly or wrongly, that he had been personally appointed by Jesus to carry the word to the gentiles. In order to carry that off, he had to dispense, either through necessity or preference, with the Jewishness of the sect, and that meant dumping the Mosaic law and proclaiming that a new covenant had been established by Jesus. In Saul's view, Judaism had been superseded—just as, in the view of Muhammad, both Judaism and Christianity were superseded by Islam.

Accordingly, Saul quit using his Jewish name (which, incidentally, is spelled in Hebrew the same as *Sheol*—grave or hell) and started using his gentile name, Paulos. We know him as Paul.

There may conceivably have been a numerological reason for this name change as well. Saul/Paulos must have known that at least the more educated members of his audience would have some familiarity with Greek number mysticism in the form of *isopsephos* (see appendix), which had been in existence for at least 450 years, but it may be just a coincidence that "Paulos" has the same numerical value (781) as *sophia*—wisdom. Coincidence or not, that numerical identity must have convinced more than one devoted isopsephosian when he worked it out by the light of a lantern after having heard Paul preach that evening. It may have been a calculated effect.

As recorded in the Bible itself, Paul didn't get along all that well with the Jewish-Christian church at Jerusalem. When the Jews revolted and the Romans sacked Jerusalem in 70 A.D., shortly after Paul's death, the Jewish branch of Christianity ceased to exist. The Roman Empire thus inadvertently won the day for Paul and the Pauline "heresy." If things had turned out otherwise and the Jerusalem church had flourished, we might now be reading books that lumped Paul in with the Gnostics as the author of a demonstrably inferior system that was bound to fail.

Paul deliberately presented Christianity as a new mystery religion, saying such things as, "Behold! I shall tell you a mystery" and referring to Christian converts as *teleioi* ("perfect" or "mature"), a term used for full initiates of the Pagan mysteries. If you use certain of the original Greek words, which are also the terms of the mysteries and of the Gnostics, in the translation of I Corinthians 2:6-7, you get, "But we speak Sophia among the initiates, but not the Sophia of this Aion, nor of the Archons of this Aion, those being brought to nothing. But we speak the Sophia of Theos in a mystery having been hidden, which Theos determined before the Aions for our glory." That's as Gnostic a statement as I've ever heard—despite the fact that it seems to be fairly opaque. In that, however, it is not greatly different from many other mystical writings.

Of course, in speaking of the Archons of the Aion, Paul may really have meant no more than "the rulers of this age." Still, the consistent use of these particular terms seems a little fishy, particularly in view of the fact that Paul used Plato's term for the soul—*psyche*—to designate the unregenerate "natural man." The term he used for the immortal soul that would animate the resurrected faithful was pneuma—again, all very good Gnostic doctrine.

But Paul himself was definitely not a Gnostic. For him, the way to salvation lay not in Gnosis, in knowledge, but in faith and grace. Some of the groups or churches that he founded became infiltrated by Gnostic ideas, such as the fundamental difference between the heavenly Christ and the earthly Jesus, and Paul preached against them (as in his first Epistle to the Corinthians).

Paul has somewhat of a reputation as a rabid misogynist, forbidding women to speak in church and placing men between them and God. However, one thing in his favor is that these opinions are expressed mostly in his letters to Timothy, and there is considerable doubt that he actually wrote these particular epistles. The general opinion is that they were just attributed to him.

The Gospel of John, generally thought to have been directed primarily to a Hellenized audience and even accepted by Valentinian Gnostics, is the most mystically oriented of the four. It begins logically enough with the statement, "In the beginning was the Logos." The gospel's *En arche* (In the beginning) consciously echoes the first word *(Berashith)* of Genesis. Well, we already know all about the Logos from Greek philosophy, but here it is made equivalent with god *(Theos)*: "In the beginning *[En arche]* was the Logos, and the Logos was with the Theos, and Theos was the Logos. The same [or This One, *Outos]* was in the beginning *[en arche]* with the Theos."

The Gospel continues with a nice recapitulation of Greek philosophical ideas concerning the creative power of the Logos: "All things were made by [came into being through] him; and without him was not any thing made that was made [came into being]."

Then we pick up a Gnostic or Zoroastrian idea: God as Light.

St. Paul at Ephesus
(engraving by Gustave Doré)

I hope I am not being perverse in giving the Greek term in this verse that also happens to be the name of a Valentinian Aeon: "In him was Zoe [Life]; and the Zoe was the Light of Men [*Phos ton Anthropon*]. And the Light shineth in Darkness, and the Darkness comprehended it not [did not overtake it]. [*Kai to Phos en te Skotia phainei, kai he Skotia auto ou katelaben.*]"

It is only in this Gospel, out of the four, that we encounter the reference to Jesus as the "only begotten" son of God. (In reference to Jesus, the term also occurs in Paul's Epistle to the Hebrews and in the first Epistle of John, but not in the gospels of Matthew, Mark, or Luke.)

There has been some discussion from time to time concerning this designation. It is generally taken to mean that Jesus is the only son of God, and nanny-nanny-boo-boo to those who say we are all children of God. The Greek term is *monogenes*. It has been put forth by various writers that the meaning of this term is that the one so designated is "one-begotten," that is, has only one parent. In the case of Jesus, this only parent would be God the Father, and the possibility of other sons of God is not excluded. The term is also used to describe Christ in the *Apocryphon of John*—which also describes the origin of Barbelo and a number of Aeons besides Christ.

But if God the Father is the only parent of Jesus—an echo of the woman-hating Greek myths about the birth of Athene and Dionysos from the head and thigh of Zeus, respectively, without need for a mother—then what is the function of Mary? A plowed field that merely holds the seed, as Apollo says of all mothers in the *Eumenides* of Aeschylus?

Unfortunately for this "one parent" theory of the meaning of *monogenes*, the term is used for other people besides Jesus. All such references are in the Gospel according to Luke. In the seventh chapter, we hear about a widow with an only son. In the eighth chapter, there's a man named Jairus who has an only daughter. Then there's a man with an only son in the ninth chapter. Every one of these offspring is referred to as *monogenes*. The idea that any one of them was supposed to have only one parent is just a little improbable.

It would therefore appear that the New Testament in its present form does indeed mean to say that Jesus is the only son of God. Of course, these scriptures, and none that contradicted them, were accepted as canonical by people with axes to grind; that is, by the established church with its vested interest in a strictly graded hierarchy of male priests and no competition, thank you, from other religions claiming to worship a son of God other than Jesus.

In other words, there's no need to prove that "the Bible" says something it doesn't unless you insist on (a) taking it as the revealed Word of God and the final authority on everything and (b) disagreeing with what it is normally understood to say. If, like a good Pagan, you think "it ain't necessarily so," then that includes the bit about "only begotten" along with all the rest. Those who try to use orthodox Christian scripture to refute Christianity and support Paganism or Gnosticism are biting off quite a mouthful. It is the argument for the prosecution and cannot easily be interpreted as an argument for the defense.

The Gospel according to Luke, who was supposed to have been Paul's physician and faithful follower, is even more obviously addressed to Pagan Hellenes than John's. It might be safe to say that John was talking to Gnostics and perhaps followers of the mystery religions, whereas Luke was talking to the "Pagan in the street." Luke's slant shows up most obviously in his devoting so much of his narrative to the sayings and doings of Mary—a necessity if he hoped to convert goddess worshipers. It is from Luke that the Catholics derive much of their inspiration for their veneration of Mary—to the point that She was finally promoted to Queen of Heaven in our own century. She is not, however, recognized as a Goddess existing from eternity, much less as the primal God—yet.

The final major Greek document of the Christian canon is the Revelation (Apocalypse) of John the Divine ("Divine" means "theologian"—*theologos*—not that John was a god). In the early church, there was a lot of controversy about whether the Apocalypse should be considered canonical. The main argument against it was that nobody was any too sure about just what it was really supposed to be saying. Nobody is too sure even to this day, although there is no shortage of superhuman minds and scripture-jugglers who profess to find it all as clear as daylight. And, even though the book itself plainly explains some of its more outlandish images as allegorical (ten horns = ten kings, for example), there are still those who insist upon taking every word literally and fully expect a fantastic beast to rise from the surf—probably somewhere near Los Angeles.

Another fashion in Revelation interpretation is to take a passage literally if it suits you to do so but otherwise insist that it is allegorical. For example, Jesus will really and literally descend from heaven upon the Mount of Olives and the nations will make war against him, but the setting up of the "Abomination of Desolation" in the (non-extant) Temple at Jerusalem is a way of saying that European troops (from the Roman Empire in its seventh guise as the European Free Trade Association) will occupy the city. By the time you've reached this point, arbitrary interpretation and analysis of scripture and history has become the order of the day and the whole thing has become a game.

Manly P. Hall *(The Secret Teachings of All Ages)* stated that Revelation is plainly Gnostic and that it has to be either a presentation of the Greek mysteries, an attempt to reconcile Pagan philosophy with Christianity, or else a parody that was originally directed against Christianity.

Another popular game—also taken dead seriously—connected with the Apocalypse is "beasting." At the end of the 13th chapter, it says, "Here is wisdom *[Sophia]*. Let him that hath understanding *[Nous]* count the number of the beast *[Therion]*: for it is the number of a man *[Anthropos]*; and his number is Six hundred threescore and six."

This advice plainly has to do with Hebrew gematria or Greek *isopsephos,* and people since the 1st century have been adding up the letters of names by various methods to prove that this person or that was the beast of the Apocalypse. Most scholars nowadays think it was supposed to refer to Nero, although he was already dead by the time of the oldest copy that we have of the Apocalypse. (Yet he was rumored to be still alive.) There are a couple of ways of getting Nero to be 666—"Neron Caesar" spelled with Hebrew letters (NRVN QSR), or *trijon* (ThRYN, "little beast"), a Talmudic designation for Nero.

Another candidate is Domitian, who was emperor at the time of the Greek Apocalypse that we possess. In *The White Goddess,* Robert Graves has made out a case for taking the Roman numerals for 666—DCLXVI—as an acronym. A couple of possible phrases say that either Domitian or Domitius (Nero's pre-imperial "plebe" name) persecuted the Christians: *"Domitianus [or Domitius] Caesar legatos Xti viliter [or violenter] interfecit."*

But when the world failed to end in the first few centuries of the Christian era, other candidates were selected for "the Beast 666," usually this or that pope or king. In Nikolai Tolstoy's *War and Peace,* Pierre Bezuhov uses some rather contrived French "gematria" to get 666 out of "L'Empereur Napoleon." Napoleon was a popular beast. Most American presidents and Soviet premiers, at least in the last 50 years—not to mention such personalities as Khomeini, Khadafi, Saddam Hussein, and that obnoxious neighbor who throws loud, all-night parties—have managed to get their names added up to 666 somehow or another by somebody. At the moment, Mikhail Gorbachev is a popular candidate, largely because of a conspicuous birthmark—"the mark of the Beast." However, if you consult scripture rather than horror movies, you will find that the Beast puts this mark on other people; it is not something he possesses himself.

The magician/mystic/poet Aleister Crowley was exceptional in that he volunteered for the job. His method for getting his own name (in the form "Aleister E. Crowley") to add to 666 is likewise a trifle contrived. "I will deserve it if I can," he said in a little verse. "It is the number of a man."

It may after all turn out to be a colossal joke. The Greek phrase *to mega therion*—the Great Beast—adds up perfectly by *isopsephos* to 666.

The older versions of the Apocalypse use the Greek letters *chi-xi-stau* to designate the number 666. It has been suggested that these might also be somebody's initials, but that seems unlikely in view of the fact that the letter *stau* was no longer used for anything but the number 6, and even Hebrew has no letter to designate the sound "st." It would have to be Latin, as in Graves' example given above. Some Greek New Testaments now in print, however, spell the number out as *hexakosioi hexekonta hex,* the sum of which by *isopsephos* is 1025—another possible bestial number.

It has been pointed out that *Iesous Christos* (the Greek form of the name Jesus Christ) adds up perfectly to 888, and that 888 (besides containing six loops on the eights) may be taken as $8 + 8 + 8 = 24$ and $2 + 4 = 6$. The square of 6 is 36, and all the numbers from 1 through 36 add up to—ta da—666!

Numerological considerations abound in the Apocalypse. The number seven seems to predominate (seven churches, candlesticks, stars, angels, lamps, seals, spirits, horns, eyes, trumpets, thunders, plagues, heads, vials, etc., all corresponding to the seven planets, the seven Greek vowels—which constitute a powerful name of God— and the seven chakras). In correlating the seven churches to the seven planets, the natural thing to do is to take the traditional order (based on the apparent rapidity of motion)—Moon, Mercury, Venus, Sun, Mars, Jupiter, and Saturn—and assign the Moon to Ephesus on the basis of the fact that it was the site of the Temple of Artemis.

Jesus is quoted as chiding the church at Ephesus "because thou hast left thy first love." The first love of the Ephesians was, of course, the Goddess. Are we dealing here, as Hall suggests, with a sly Pagan author slipping in his own non-Christian messages? The tongue of Jesus is described as a two-edged sword, after all, and this could mean that there is a hidden message beneath the one that is obvious.

The four horsemen (chapter 6) are said to represent not only the four elements and the four stages of human life (youth, adulthood, maturity, and old age), but also, in connection with the elements, the Greek gods Zeus, Here, Poseidon, and Hestia.

There's a possible example of *isopsephos* in Rev. IX:11—Apollyon, the angel of the bottomless pit *(abyssos)*, has the same numerical value (1461) as *hypostasis,* meaning foundation or reality. The Gnostic implication would be either that this world is a bottomless pit of separation from the true God or that actual reality resides only in "the Deep," *Bythos,* the supernal God and crown of the Aeons. There's also a possible connection with the goddess Eurynome, which name has the same numerical value as *abyssos* (1073). Eurynome would thus be identified with Bythos as the supreme deity, which, as we have seen, She was in at least one pre-patriarchal goddess religion.

The "woman of the Apocalypse" in chapter 12, "clothed with the sun, and the moon under her feet, and upon her head a crown of twelve stars," is usually taken to be the Virgin Mary; as such, this passage provides inspiration and liturgy for those who venerate the Virgin. But the figure could just as well be Isis pregnant with Horus and confronted by Typhon (Set); the myth, after all, fits the description perfectly. The figure may be intended to be Isis, or it may represent an attempt to identify Mary with Isis in order to attract converts.

It's also possible that Christianity here improves upon Gnosticism in its veneration of the Goddess by making Sophia the mother of Her own redeemer rather than Her having to be rescued by someone from the Pleroma. In this, however, it merely replicates the mysteries of Isis. It's also possible that the woman is Sophia and the

The Woman of the Apocalypse
(*Woodcut by Albrecht Dürer*)

dragon is the Demiurge attempting to prevent her from bringing enlightenment to humanity.

It is probably no accident that there are 22 chapters, the same as the number of letters in the Hebrew alphabet. In places, the content seems to bear out this intention. For example, the first verse of chapter 4, corresponding to the Hebrew letter *daleth*, mentions a door opening in heaven. *Daleth*, of course, is also a Hebrew word meaning "door." Chapter 13, corresponding to the Hebrew letter *mem* (meaning also sea or waters), begins, "And I stood upon the sand of the sea...," and the beast comes out of the sea. I am obliged to Osborne Phillips for calling my attention to these points; he also speaks of purification by the tooth of Fire in the 21st chapter (the 21st letter being *shin*, meaning "tooth," which the *Sepher Yetzirah* associates with the element Fire).

The triumph of Christianity over Paganism and the Gnostic version of itself was far from complete with Constantine's Council of Nicea in 325. So many Pagan Greek ideas became incorporated into the new official religion that much of the original message became submerged. Doubters and some Christians are alike in pointing out some of the ways in which the beliefs of most Christians are more Hellenistic than biblical. Here's a list of just a few Pagan beliefs that can't really be justified too well on Biblical authority: the existence and immortality of the soul (as opposed to resurrection of the body), an immediate consignment to heaven or hell after death (as opposed to sleeping until Judgment Day), hell itself (as opposed to the fires of Gehenna—the Jerusalem garbage dump—or Sheol, the grave), the holidays of Christmas (the Roman Saturnalia, a solstice celebration) and Easter (named after the goddess Eostre, from the Mesopotamian Ishtar—an equinox celebration), and goddess worship in the form of reverence for Mary, Sophia, and the female saints. As far as some Christians are concerned, the religion needs to dump all this baggage and get back to basics. According to others, however, Christianity is much better off for it. The thing is, if Christianity had rigidly suppressed all these elements rather than incorporating them, it might not have survived the competition.

I know that I have come down pretty hard on Christianity in the pages of this book, and I may have aroused some indignation in so doing, but my criticisms, if you'll note, have been directed at the abuses of the man-made church much more than they have been at the religion itself. It's unrealistic to expect every professed Christian to be a saint, even when they are in positions of authority. If I may take a heretical stance, Christianity isn't about revival meetings and getting worked up into an emotional experience called being "born again." It isn't about an angry God who is ready to send most of humanity into an eternal fiery pit. It doesn't even have to be literally true in any historical sense. According to the understanding of many, Christ is the true, inner Self, which must be nurtured within the unconscious mind (Mary) after impregnation not by an earthly father (the ego) but by God. The lower vehicle, Jesus (the ego again), must be sacrificed so that Christ can arise. Or is this Gnosticism?

I have barely scratched the surface in this chapter, and I realize that the emphasis on Greek ideas at the expense of an overall viewpoint has tended to make it just a little rambling and discursive. That's just as well. It'll put you in the mood for one of the world's most rambling and discursive philosophers—Plotinus.

X

Neoplatonism

It wasn't only authoritarian Christianity that opposed Gnosticism. One of its greatest critics was a Pagan, Plotinus (204-270). His objection was not that it distorted traditional revelation but rather that it made a mess of Greek philosophy! The idea of throwing logic to the winds for the sake of intuited revealed truth was abhorrent to his philosophical mind. He was also less than fond of what the Gnostics did with the Demiurge of his hero, Plato. Plotinus and his followers—referred to historically as the "Neoplatonists"—regarded the writings of Plato as divinely inspired and not to be questioned—in much the same way that modern fundamentalist Christians regard the Bible or fundamentalist Communists regard the writings of Karl Marx.

But, of course, they can be interpreted. In the case of both Marx and the Bible, there are many people who claim that interpretation is a snare, that you just have to read "what it plainly says." The difficulty arises from the fact that wars have been fought over just exactly "what the Bible plainly says." The Neoplatonists didn't fight any actual wars among themselves, but they didn't all agree about everything, either. It was possible to have all due respect and reverence for Plato and Plotinus and still "develop" their teachings in ways they never thought of and probably would not have condoned.

Actually, the designation "Neoplatonism" is fairly arbitrary, inasmuch as it was a natural outgrowth of Middle Platonism and the Hellenistic world view in general. As far as they themselves were concerned, they were simply Platonists. However, the label is kept for convenience to indicate the philosophy of Plotinus and his followers.

The teacher of Plotinus was Ammonius Saccas, in Alexandria, but, since none of his writings survive, it is not known to what degree he was really a "Neoplatonist." Neoplatonism really starts with and depends upon Plotinus, who moved to Rome to establish his philosophical school. By all accounts, Plotinus was a "really nice guy," admired and praised for his virtue and unselfishness. He freed his slaves, gave away his wealth, became a vegetarian, and fasted every other day. He talked his pupil, Porphyry (232-305), out of committing suicide.

Plotinus was all but unique among philosophers because he somehow managed to combine the rational, reasoned approach— one of his main gripes against Gnosticism was that it abandoned logic for inspiration—and mysticism. He opposed Christianity because it had substituted faith for reason. Although many people consider him a mystic first and a philosopher second, Plotinus strove to apply traditional Greek rational philosophy to inner, mystical experience. In other words, he was in tune with the times— times of mysticism, mysteries, magic, and new religions popping up everywhere—and tried to fit all these phenomena into the classical philosophy of Plato. How well he succeeded is a matter of opinion, but he is best regarded as a thinker in his own right rather than the man who interpreted Plato in the light of 3rd-century mysticism.

Somehow, Plotinus's philosophical reasoning—and, apparently, meditation—led him into transcendental mystical experiences in which he achieved a direct perception of God, union with God, at one with the universe—nirvana, moksha, satori, union, enlightenment, the great work, the philosopher's stone, the pearl of great price, the knowledge and conversation of the holy guardian angel, cosmic consciousness, or something else, assuming that all these terms refer to the same thing or at least to degrees of the same thing.

The writings of Plotinus seem a little disconnected and wandering at times, and he doesn't always seem too sure about just where he stands on various minor issues. The reason for this is that he did not just sit down and write his major work, the *Enneads*. This collection, assembled by Porphyry, essentially represents his lecture notes.

As stated by Porphyry, one aim of Neoplatonic endeavor was the unification of the individual, a process later made the ultimate goal of analytical psychology and called "individuation" by Carl Jung. In saying that we must try to draw our own obscure ideas into the light, Porphyry seemed to be anticipating modern psychology and magic by saying that we have to be in touch with our unconscious minds—although, of course, nobody in the 3rd century had ever heard of such a thing as the "unconscious mind." Be that as it may, Plotinus described it accurately and at length; he just didn't use the modern term for it. The point is, Sigmund Freud, as he himself freely acknowledged, did not invent it or discover it for the first time. It's just that, like most other ideas that were irrelevant or inimical to Christianity as defined by the established church, it sort of got lost for 1500 years or so.

Like most other people of his type at the time, Plotinus was rumored to be a magician, a magus. Various sorcerers are said to have worked elaborate curses against him for one reason or another—to their great grief. Things like that had a nasty habit of bouncing right back if Plotinus was the object of them. He apparently didn't go to any great lengths to set up protections, either; it was just that his aura was impregnable to such petty efforts.

Although it may not have been entirely original, Plotinus expounded at length on his concept of the *hypostases* (foundations or realities)—a series of emanations from the One reminiscent of Gnosticism or the later cabalism, although it lacks the latter's concept of synthesis and balance. At the top of the ladder is the indescribable One *(En)*, the first God, *Protos Theos*, which Plotinus also called the Good *(Agathos)*. He had a hard time explaining how the One could be entirely without characteristics and still be Good, but he gave it a good try. Conceivably, he was attracted to this name because of its numerical identity (284, by isopsephos) with holy *(hagios)* and god *(theos)*. God's thought or mind, Nous—a term we've heard before in the contexts of philosophy and of Gnosticism—is the first emanation. Nous contains the Platonic forms or archetypes. From Nous comes Soul *(Psyche)*, which includes both individual souls and the World Soul or Soul of the All *(Pantos Psyche)* and which has a higher and a lower aspect, the lower being the archetype of nature, *Physis*. From that comes the material world as we know it. Normally, these are regarded as three hypostases—En, Nous, and Psyche. Individual souls are particularizations of the World Soul but exist separately in their own right and are equal to it.

If all this sounds vaguely familiar, it's probably because it looks very much like an early version of the Middle Pillar of the cabalistic Tree of Life, where the One is *Kether*, Nous is *Chokmah/Binah/Daath*, the higher World Soul is *Tiphareth*, Physis is *Yesod*, and the material world is *Malkuth*. Remember that the Tree itself was a later development; the idea of ten emanations was propounded in the *Sepher Yetzirah*, which was produced at about the time of Plotinus or a little later, but the Tree diagram as we know it didn't come along for another thousand years or so. The similarity of Plotinus's scheme is actually much closer to the cabalistic notion of the Four Worlds; that is, En corresponds to *Atziluth*, Nous to *Briah*, Psyche to *Yetzirah*, and the manifested world to *Assiah*. (If this sounds totally unfamiliar, read the next chapter for a little background.)

Incidentally, despite occasional superficial resemblances, Plotinus did not get any of his ideas from the Gnostics, at least not consciously. As far as he was concerned, they all came right out of Plato.

A notable element of the cabalistic Tree that is missing in both Gnosticism and Plotinus, however, is the Hegelian dialectic of thesis-antithesis-synthesis—a third thing arising from two opposites. Neoplatonists after Plotinus did come up with the idea that everything comes in threes, but the third term is an intermediary, not a result. In terms of the Tree, the third term of Neoplatonism is a path rather than a sephirah.

In line with certain Gnostic or Manichaean ideas, however, Plotinus considered emanation to be analogous to Light—Light considered not in any material sense but as pure incorporeal power.

Other concepts of Plotinus that proved to be very influential, then and now, included the idea that the goal of human existence should be a return to the One—in his case, through contemplation. Some of his followers put more emphasis on theurgy—invocation by magical ritual. In any event, all the hypostases—including the individual human soul—were said to be independent of such material constraints as space and time. They do not occupy space, yet they are everywhere present. The soul is not contained in the body; rather, the body is contained in the soul, which produces it.

The Soul of the World (Παντος Ψυχη)

All the hypostases and the soul are spheres whose centers are everywhere and whose circumferences are nowhere. They are separate, but not separated by space or in space. Furthermore, the soul is considered to be "impassible"—that is, incorruptible and immune to suffering, regardless of what the poor body and illusory ego have to go through or what sins they commit. Their existence in the first place depends on the soul looking outward instead of inward, back to its source.

One of the most important contributions of the thought of Plotinus is that this eternal state of things is mirrored in states of consciousness. Plotinus was just as interested in "altered states" as any modern psychologist, mystic, or pharmacist, although he did not recommend the use of drugs to achieve them. In fact, the whole concept that there might be different states of consciousness was more or less original with Plotinus. The way to achieve these states was by contemplation. One recommended technique was to visualize the universe and then mentally abolish its limitations.

To summarize some of the main points of Neoplatonism as formulated by Plotinus, he taught:

1. God is completely beyond human knowledge or definition.
2. The world is a result of progressive emanations from God.
3. The soul is incorruptible.
4. The goal of life is to return to God.
5. The way back lies in contemplation.

It may be seen that some of these ideas have certain resemblances to some of the doctrines of Gnosticism. The one outstanding feature that Neoplatonism lacks, however, is the idea that the world is being run by an evil Demiurge who wants to keep us all imprisoned in the gross and evil matter that constitutes the world.

Plotinus recommended contemplation as the path to take, but Iamblichus (d. 326), a pupil of Porphyry, concentrated on theurgy—communication with or union with God by means of ritual magic. One form of this was invoking a god or spirit into a statue or figure. Sometimes only one person, a medium, could hear the god speak, or the god would speak through the medium. Calling it "channeling" does not make it a new technique.

In modern ceremonial magic, where the technique is fairly common, theurgy normally consists of invoking a deity—that is,

Iamblichus

complete identification with or actual possession by the god. The goal is usually considered to be spiritual advancement. To unite with a deity is to awaken the "higher" (or inner, or true) self, the Jungian Self, or the "Holy Guardian Angel." Another frequent use of the technique is to balance your personality by taking on the characteristics of a god. Wimps should invoke Ares, for example. The absent-minded would do well to invoke clear-seeing Athene, who sees everything as it is and reacts immediately and appropriately.

A third possible aim of invocation is to invoke a deity for the sake of gaining the powers of that god for some specific purpose. This is the goal emphasized by critics who are hostile to magic and magicians, but in fact it is considered dangerous and ill-advised. It's also self-defeating and useless, because a successful invocation causes you to take on all the characteristics of the god, not just the powers. If, for example, you invoke the Hindu god Ganesha in order to obtain wealth, you may find yourself giving away all the money that you already have!

The Neoplatonists, however, seem to have practiced theurgy in the form previously described—rarely, if ever, in the form of invocation by the operator—for the purpose of divination or obtaining oracles. Plotinus himself favored contemplation and didn't think much of this procedure, but his successors, especially Iamblichus, thought it was the best technique available. Presumably, Iamblichus didn't use theurgy to find out how to bet on the chariot races but for the purpose of obtaining spiritual knowledge and the answers to philosophical questions, such as "What is the nature of Nous?"

Unfortunately, no examples of Neoplatonic theurgic rituals survive. Like the mysteries, they were kept secret and were never written down. We can gather enough from what was written, however, to see that the rituals must have been very, very similar to those used in ceremonial magic today. The basic principle was one of sympathy—using sounds, words, music, scents, colors, and so on that were harmonious with the nature of the god.

We do not know the particulars of these correspondences as used by the Neoplatonists, but modern versions have been worked out in great detail. Many of them were carefully indexed by Aleister Crowley in *Liber 777*, although his list of scents needs updating. It is no longer possible to pop down to the corner drugstore for Siamese benzoin, for example. Many of Crowley's incenses are available only from magic shops and other specialty stores, and some of them not even there.

The approved method for ceremonial magic is to burn incense over charcoal, but this may not be the best method for the small-time operator (like me). Here are a few seldom-mentioned pointers: if you keep feeding incense to the charcoal in order to keep it burning at all times and maintain a constant and lasting scent, you are going to use a lot of incense because of rapid burning. (The idea is for the scent to arise at appropriate and/or climactic moments.) The area has to be large and well ventilated—more so than most apartment living rooms—or you are liable to get carbon monoxide poisoning from the charcoal. In such an environment, you are also going to be constantly aware of the odors of burning charcoal and hot metal and/or sand when the incense is not actually burning, which it will do for less than a minute under the best of conditions unless it is constantly replenished. Burning charcoal is also very, very hot and must be well insulated, preferably by placing it in a bowl of sand. If you try burning it in a plastic, ceramic, or glass container, you will shatter the container.

For minor ceremonies such as "routine" daily rituals and all but the most elaborate occasions, stick or cone incense is a thousand times more convenient and practical. (Sticks last longer than cones but are not as pure.) Unfortunately, the emphasis with commercial stick and cone incense is on fruity and flowery scents. Sandalwood and jasmine are no problem; frankincense (galbanum) is available but harder to find. It is particularly difficult, if not impossible, to find Martian or earthy scents, and you can forget all about dittany of Crete, the incense favored by H. P. Blavatsky and Crowley. Anything like this is going to be harder to find and will require charcoal.

As for a scent appropriate to Mars (the god or the planet, or the sephirah Geburah), I do not recommend Crowley's citation of tobacco. In the time that has passed, tobacco has lost its specifically masculine associations and has been found to be distinctly unhealthy to boot. If you happen to be a smoker, you will not even be aware of it. Unfortunately (or fortunately), you can't buy stick or cone incense labeled "hot gun metal" or "sweaty khaki" that would be appropriate for the warlike aspects of Mars. A few grains of black gunpowder might suffice, but I cannot find it within myself to recommend such a dangerous solution. (If you attempt to burn gunpowder like incense, you will have plenty of time in the hospital to puzzle out what you did wrong.) Pine will do.

The solution to this problem for the beginner, who has been frantically scouring around trying to find onycha or dragon's blood, is provided by Ted Andrews in *Imagick* (Llewellyn Publications, 1989). He gives a list of scents that are usually available in stick or cone form. It's high time somebody did this instead of just copying Crowley's out-of-date list of hard-to-find scents—a sin to which I myself plead guilty.

The Neoplatonic divine names associated with the planets, according to Denning and Phillips in *Planetary Magick,* are:

Moon—Aigle Trisagia (Thrice-Holy Splendor)
Mercury—Alethes Logos (True Word)
Venus—Charis (Grace)
Sun—Theios Nous (Divine Intelligence)
Mars—Ischyros (Mighty One)
Jupiter—Pantokrator (All-Mover)
Saturn, Supernal—Hagios Athanatos (Holy Immortal One)
Saturn, Planetary—Aionos Kyrios (Lord of the Ages)

Needless to say, however, even though these names might well be used in ritual, they are not normally the deities who would be invoked. In actual practice, any god that appeals to you and who is associated with the planetary sphere in question would be appropriate. It is also entirely feasible to forget about planets and sephiroth and simply invoke the god according to known characteristics and associations particular to that god; you'd have to pay a certain amount of attention to those anyway.

Later Neoplatonists found Plato's *Cratylus* very useful for theurgic purposes, inasmuch as it explains (ironically) the etymology of the names of some of the gods. Thus Ares, for example, can be called Arren (manhood) or Arratis (hard and unchanging) in addition to his usual name. It's also difficult to imagine an effective invocation of a classical Greek god that does not take into account Homer's standard taglines—"bright-eyed *(glaukōpis)* Athene," "cow-eyed *(boōpis)* Hera," "cloud-gatherer *(nephelegereta)* Zeus," and so on. Poseidon is also called *Enosichthōn* (Earth-Shaker), and Hermes is sometimes referred to as *Argeiphontēs,* a term of uncertain meaning. The best guess is "Swift-Appearer." (Hint: *boōpis* is pronounced buh-OPE-iss—no relation to Betty Boop.)

Later Neoplatonists who took theurgy as the "easy way out" (as opposed to a life of contemplation as advocated by Plotinus or virtue as emphasized by Porphyry) made much of the so-called Chaldean Oracles of Zoroaster. These oracles survive only in fragments quoted by people such as Porphyry, but current opinion holds that they were channeled by a man named Julianus (or a medium employed by him) in the 2nd century when Marcus Aurelius was emperor. They don't really sound very Chaldean; they sound Neoplatonic, or perhaps Middle Platonic, perhaps with Gnostic overtones.

There's a lot of emphasis on triads in the Oracles—a development of later Neoplatonism, which had a predictable tendency to multiple the hypostases—and they use a lot of fire imagery (hence the connection with Zoroaster). Unfortunately, from the standpoint of both Neoplatonists and non-patriarchal religion, the supreme deity is identified as "the Father," with the highest triad consisting of His existence, power, and intelligence (hyparxis, dynamis, and nous). This went over real well with the Christians, and Porphyry identified the Father as the One of Plotinus. Hardly anyone agreed with him on that; most Neoplatonists put the One far above this triad, which they said was Nous.

William Wynn Westcott's edition of Thomas Taylor's translations of some of these fragments were and are used as a standard part of Golden Dawn rituals, including the "Opening by Watchtower," where they are tied in with Enochian magic. On the face of it, neither these little excerpts nor the Oracles as a whole make a great deal of sense without a good understanding of the philosophies involved. For example, "Stoop not down into that darkly splendid world" etc., used in connection with the element of Earth, is probably an admonition to the soul not to become involved in the concerns of physical existence but rather to turn back to its origin. The "darkly splendid world," in other words, is not hell nor the planes of the shells (demons, *qlippoth*) but rather the present material world of manifestation. The Neoplatonists did not regard the material world as downright evil, but they thought it was as far removed from God as possible and hopelessly imperfect.

The Chaldean Oracles also bring in the Greek goddess Hecate, who is identified with the World Soul—an image altogether at variance with the medieval Christian (and modern) conception of a hag goddess of witchcraft, black magic, and crossroads at night.

Even most modern Wiccans shy away from this name, but here She is identified as the highest aspect of Gaia. Porphyry identifies her with Zōē (Life), the middle term of the triad Being, Life, and Intelligence that was said to be the nature of Nous, the second hypostasis, and the World of Forms. If you really want to get confused, try correlating this fact with the Zōē of Gnosticism! The fact that the Neoplatonists and Gnostics were, in a manner of speaking, at each other's throats doesn't mean that they couldn't pick up and use each other's ideas and change them around to fit their own system.

The Oracles tie in with Hellenistic magic, by the way—and with theurgy as well—as is evidenced by the oft-quoted admonition, "Change not the barbarous Names of Evocation for there are Sacred Names in every language which are given by God, having in the Sacred Rites a Power Ineffable."

Getting back to Iamblichus, he solved the problem of how the unthinkable One could also be the Good by saying there was another hypostasis, the true One who is above the Good and is truly ineffable. The intelligible world (kosmos noētos), which is to say the world of Platonic forms or ideas, is an emanation of the One, and the next step is the intellectual world of intelligent beings (kosmos noeros) which contains Nous and the Demiurge. Finally we get down to at least three stages of Psyche. Gods, heroes, daimons, and so on are part of the world.

Neoplatonism reached its apex under the emperor Julian (322-363), who sought to undo the Christianizing of the Roman Empire that had taken place under Constantine and restore Paganism. That's why he's known to Christian historians as "Julian the Apostate."

Finally, Neoplatonism sort of split between Athens, where the school tended more toward theurgy and mysticism, and Alexandria, where it tended more toward scholasticism. The most important member of the Athenian school was Proclus (410-485), who tried to synthesize and reconcile Plato, Aristotle, Pythagoras, mysticism, magic, and all religions—not without some minor success. It was Proclus who really got into the idea of triads, all based on the idea of stasis or equilibrium (abiding, monē), proceeding forth (advance, proodos), and turning back (a military term, wheeling about, epistrophē). According to Proclus, the One (which he explains as being necessary as a First Cause) emanates the gods or Henads (unities), which administer providence, and from them the Nous. Nous is subdivided as per Iamblichus into *noētoi, noētoi* and *noeroi* mixed, and *noeroi*. After Nous, as usual, comes Psyche, which is formed of divine, daemonic, and human souls. The traditional gods are included among the divine souls.

Although she was perhaps not the most important of the Alexandrian Neoplatonists, the best known member of that school was probably Hypatia. We know very little about her except that she was into mathematics and that she was brutally and sadistically murdered by a Christian mob—the same one that burned the library—in 415. Hollywood (and evangelists) have made much of the tough times that the early Christians went through and how ruthlessly they were persecuted and martyred by the Pagan Romans—and how many converts they made by refusing to renounce their beliefs in spite of that persecution. When it came to persecution, the Pagan Romans were not nice people.

But, when the Christians ceased to be persecuted and achieved power of their own, they were no better. Their persecution of "heretics" was no less savage than the Roman persecution of the Christians had been, although at least it did not include being used as entertainment in the arena. Pagans were not thrown to the lions or even crucified—they were just scraped to death with clam shells or otherwise murdered in a civilized manner.

Before we condemn either the Pagans or the Christians of this era, however, perhaps we should keep in mind that people acted that way not so much because of their religious beliefs as because they were denizens of their times. You'd think that the teachings of Jesus would have tended to mitigate such savagery, but they didn't —no more than they have prevented wars in our own time. The aggravating thing about the Christians, I suppose, is that they seemed to think they were doing the really righteous thing. On the other hand, so did the Pagans.

In 529, the emperor Justinian closed the Platonic Academy at Athens. The one at Alexandria hung on, became Christianized, and did not achieve or contribute much of anything except commentaries on Aristotle until the city was conquered by the Muslims in 641. So much for Neoplatonism, you might think. That was indeed the end of the organized schools, but Neoplatonic thought continued to exert a terrific influence on Christians and philosophers right down to the present day.

A Neoplatonic Theurgic Ritual

For this one, you are going to need a seer or medium unless you yourself are sensitive to astral manifestations. A statue is going to speak, but it is—probably—not going to be audible, certainly not to a tape recorder. The words of the god, speaking from the image, must be heard mentally. That means that the voice in your head, or in the head of the seer—or, strictly speaking, the auditor—must not simply represent your own wandering thoughts. It should have a quality of "otherness" and, preferably, a numinosity not to be found in the usual astral chatter.

The auditor, whether it be yourself or another, is to repeat aloud the words of the god. These may be taken down by someone other than the auditor, or you can use a tape recorder. Note that the god is not being invoked into the auditor, but into an image. (Properly speaking, therefore, you are *evoking* the deity.) The auditor will be repeating the words, not channeling them directly. If the auditor begins to speak in an altered voice, you'd be best advised, I think, to dismiss and banish according to your skill and knowledge, for the ritual has gone awry.

Inasmuch as things can get out of control this way fairly easily, particularly with a medium who is accustomed to vacate his or her mental premises in favor of an astral entity, you should not attempt this ritual with another person as auditor unless you have a solid foundation of experience in ceremonial magic. If you are yourself acting as the auditor, then you will tend to be able to exercise greater control over the proceedings and will in any case be responsible only for your own welfare.

The danger is, of course, that, despite all precautions and protections, you cannot be a hundred percent sure of getting the god or a representative of the god. In almost all cases, whatever you *do* get will be relatively harmless and will "get out" on its own whenever it gets bored. In that case, the worst you have done is to waste your time. If, however, the entity is successfully evoked into the image rather than invoked into the auditor, then the concern about such astral transients is not so great.

For more on the whole subject of the use of another person as a seer, consult Kraig's *Modern Magick,* Part III of Lesson 9.

For this ritual, you will need first of all an image of the god. In this example, the deity involved is Hephaestos. (However, the basic procedure would be the same for any other god you might choose to evoke.) The difficulty, of course, is in finding an image of Hephaestos. It isn't difficult to find a drawing or a reproduction of a painting or even a photograph of a statue, and you can use these things in a pinch. Some of the statuettes of deities that are sold commercially are less than ideal. I have seen one that is supposed to be Athene, but you'd never know it without the label. The statuette lacks spear, helmet, aegis, owl, or any other attribute associated with the goddess. Let us assume for the present, though, that you have acquired or made a little statuette of the god.

Hephaestos is the blacksmith of the gods and is closely associated with the element of Fire. Therefore, you should use a red altar cloth, red candles (preferably three, arranged in a triangle with the vertex toward the East), and a brazier for the incense (that is, burning charcoal in a bowl of sand). The incense should be frankincense, sometimes called "olibanum." The image and brazier should be set up in the South. To complete the environment, it would help if the room were a bit overly warm. You might even try eating a few "red hots" beforehand to get in a "fiery" frame of mind. It also wouldn't hurt a thing if you were to place a smith's hammer and tongs beside the brazier.

Begin with the usual ritual of protection and purification, which is particularly necessary with a ritual of this sort in order to minimize the chance of getting random astral wayfarers. The Golden Dawn's Opening by Watchtower would not be entirely inappropriate, inasmuch as the Hellenes were already using Hebrew godnames in their rituals at the time when Neoplatonism flourished. (The Enochian system, however, had yet to be developed.) The "classical Greek" protection ritual included in this book might be sufficient, however, provided it has been well practiced and provided you put all you've got into it. If you are a practicing magician with some experience, you should have no problem designing something appropriate and customizing this ritual for your own requirements. If on the other hand you are relatively new to ceremonial magic, you will probably be safe enough with the basic ritual.

However, it would also be an excellent idea to purify by Water and consecrate by Fire (if not also Air and Earth). The procedure for such purification is fairly standard, although details vary. One method is to sprinkle (from a cup, preferably a consecrated magical item) in each of the four quarters (East, South, West, North), each time making an appropriate magical statement such as "So therefore first the priest who governeth the works of Fire must sprinkle with the lustral Water of the loud resounding sea" (from the Chaldean oracles) or *"Asperges me, Dominus, hyssopo, et mundabor; lavabis me, et super nivem dealbabor"* (from the Latin mass, meaning, "Sprinkle me, Lord, with hyssop, and I shall be clean. Wash me, and I shall be made whiter than snow"). Complete the circle back to the East, of course.

The consecration by Fire may be done with a thurible, a stick of incense, or a magical implement consecrated to Fire (such as the Golden Dawn Fire Wand). The statement this time will be "And when, after all the phantoms are banished, thou shalt see that holy and formless Fire, that Fire that darts and flashes through the hidden depths of the Universe, hear thou the voice of Fire" or *"Accendat in nobis, Dominus, ignem sui amoris et flammam aeternae caritatis"* ("Kindle in us, Lord, the fire of your love and the flame of eternal affection"). If the Latin forms are used, there is no reason in the world why you cannot substitute "Domina" (Lady) for "Dominus" (Lord)—and every reason why you should, if your main deity is a Goddess.

The auditor should be seated before the image, preferably in a cross-legged position on the floor. The use of a chair is to be preferred, however, if the auditor finds the other position uncomfortable. The auditor is to stare at the image and listen attentively, trying to sense any sound that might come from it.

You may note that the following evocation, which is to be recited at this point, is much different from that used in the Goetia. You are respectfully requesting an audience with a god rather than evoking a lesser spirit or "demon"; hence, there is no question of commanding or compelling. If He manifests, it will be as a special favor to a sincere seeker. You are a sincere seeker, aren't you? If not, forget it. You may get something, but it won't be Hephaestos.

Standing in the center facing the image, say:

O Hephaestos, Lord of Light, Lord of Fire, son of Zeus and Hera, husband of Aphrodite, smith, artificer, jeweler, god, who showeth

*forth Thy might in the thundering volcanoes, we supplicate Thee
this day to manifest Thyself in this unworthy image that we may
learn of Thee the secrets of Fire. Phaeos Histora, come to us in this
day and hour. O Thou who wert cast into the sea by Thy mother,
Hera; Thou who wert rescued and nurtured by Thetis and
Eurynome; Thou who wert returned to Olympus by Thy mother
and there didst 'stablish Thy great, magical forge—speak to us
through this image that we may learn of Thy wisdom.*

The idea is to carry on in this vein until the auditor signals that
the god had begun to speak. In all likelihood, you will need to
extemporize and repeat yourself until the god manifests. Naturally,
to carry this off with any degree of effectiveness, you should have
studied the myths of the god as thoroughly as possible beforehand.
That which is given here is really only an example. You can repeat it
word for word if you wish, but it may not be enough. The idea is to
get yourself and/or the auditor in the proper frame of mind or state
of consciousness to hear what the god has to say, if anything. Pause
briefly now and then to see if anything is happening, or is about to
happen. You might continue thus:

*O Hemera Phaistos, Light of Day, Lord of the Fiery Furnace,
Smith of the Gods, Mighty Craftsman, come to us here this day
and hour and grant us the glorious favor of Thy presence! Speak
unto us through this image! O Thou who didst catch the mighty
Ares and the errant Aphrodite in thy net that even the God of War
was the subject of divine laughter; Thou who didst dare the wrath
of Zeus when Thou didst defend Thy mother Hera and who wert
cast out upon the Isle of Lemnos by Zeus in His anger, but who
didst return to thy godly forge—speak with us this day and
impart unto us, Thy supplicants, the fiery wisdom of Thy glorious
Light! Hepahestos! Hephaestos! Hephaestos!*

It should go without saying, of course, that all divine names
(Hephaestos, Zeus, Hera, Aphrodite, Thetis, Eurynome, and so on)
should be vibrated rather than merely spoken.

At some point, the auditor should begin to hear something—
perhaps a mental voice saying merely, "I am here." Once this has
been repeated aloud by the auditor, you may begin your questions.
Naturally, you have not evoked a god for trivial purposes of

divination. You are supposed to be asking about spiritual concerns that you cannot possibly know in any other way. For example, "What is the nature of Fire?" "What are the different types of Fire?" "Was the world created through Fire?" Perhaps you could inquire about salamanders and djinn. The most mundane thing that it would be appropriate to ask would be something like "How can I increase my manual dexterity?" or "How can I enhance the quality of Fire within myself?"

Once you have received the god's answers, you should thank Him and politely end the interview. Something like this:

> *O great Hephaistos, Lord of Fire, Olympian smith, we thank Thee for Thy grace in speaking to us here this day. In our ignorance, we have naught more to ask at this time. We therefore bid Thee farewell until such time as Thou mayest again favor us with Thy presence.*

At this point, you might offer a grateful libation if you so choose, or throw in an extra pinch or two of incense by way of offering. The god should now depart the image, and the auditor at least should be able to sense when this happens. Then you may close the ritual appropriately, either with the standard Watchtower closing, if you have used that opening, or with a repetition of the protection ritual.

XI

The Renaissance and Beyond

Neoplatonic ideas remained throughout the Dark Ages, some being incorporated into official Christianity, some being declared heretical. Gnostic ideas remained also. The Bogomils, Cathars, and Albigensians paid the price for not adhering to the doctrines of the authoritarian church. The Albigensian crusade wiped out whole villages and devastated the countryside. And then there were the Knights Templar, about whose beliefs almost nothing is actually known—although the volumes of speculation and "revealed truth" published about them would fill a library. Perhaps they were just "good old boys," professional soldiers doing their job who were framed by the French king, who coveted their wealth. Perhaps they were the original Freemasons and Rosicrucians. Perhaps they had absorbed Sufi teachings from their time in Palestine. Perhaps they were Gnostics. Perhaps they were really extraterrestrials from Sirius or deros from inside the hollow earth. Perhaps anything. Any fabulous theory your brain can concoct has had a book written to prove it. Therefore, the less said about them here, the better.

Dionysius the Areopagite, about whom we know next to nothing except for his writings and that he was said to have been a disciple of Paul (although the actual writings are from a much later date and were simply attributed to the disciple), had passed on a Christian version of Neoplatonism complete with elaborate hierarchies of angels. In fact, his philosophy was so close to Pagan Neoplatonism that he tended to get in trouble with the church. In the 9th century, his ideas gained currency when his works were translated into Latin by John Scotus Erigena. Other Christian Neoplatonists included Michael Psellus (1018-1079) and George Gemistus Pletho (1360-1450). Meanwhile, the Neoplatonism of the Alexandrian school had been perpetuated within Islamic philosophy whence it made its way back to the West during the crusades.

Neoplatonism also influenced Thomas Aquinas, Dante, Meister Eckhart, and others. It was not a dead donkey, by any means. In fact, as far as medieval and Renaissance Europe were concerned, Neoplatonism was indistinguishable from pure Platonism.

Classical texts had been searched out and used by scholars and churchmen for centuries, but it was not until the 15th century or thereabouts that people really began to realize that civilization had decayed into darkness and barbarism from the heights that it had reached in classical Greece. They could scarcely exaggerate the wretched conditions of their own times, but, in reaction against these conditions, they tended to idealize antiquity and overlook its darker aspects.

Architecture turned to classical models. Buildings began to be based on human proportions. Today, the mental images that most people have of the Greek gods and heroes are based not on classical art but on Renaissance painting and sculpture. The Dukes of Burgundy even went so far as to claim descent from Herakles (Hercules).

Hidden wisdom and profound truths, it was thought—including the secret knowledge communicated by God to Moses—were to be found in Greek myth and legend, in Egyptian hieroglyphics, in Mesopotamian mythology, in the Orphic hymns, in Pythagoras, in Plato, in Neoplatonism, and in the Jewish cabala. All of these systems were supposed to be interconnected, all of them communicating the same mystic wisdom. Paganism was thought to be a disguised, prefiguring form of Christianity, or else both were thought to represent a true, primordial religion. In any event, efforts were made to reconcile everything about them. Interpreting the myths in allegorical terms—an old tradition indeed—was very helpful in this endeavor.

Thus Demeter's search for Persephone after her abduction by Hades was an allegory of the church seeking lost souls. The myth of

Pico della Mirandola

the homosexual rape of Ganymede by Zeus (followed by Ganymede's ascension to Olympus as cupbearer and catamite) illustrated a saying of Jesus: "Suffer the little children to come unto me." Neoplatonic triads fit right in with the Christian doctrine of the Trinity. The judgment of Paris among Here, Athene, and Aphrodite was said to be a choice among power, wisdom, or pleasure, or among active, contemplative, or passive lives.

Finally, Marsilio Ficino (1433-1499) re-established the Platonic Academy, this time at Florence. Ficino opened the gates with his translations of Plato, Plotinus, and the writings attributed to Hermes Trismegistus, but he nevertheless adhered to Christian orthodoxy.

But it was Giovanni Pico della Mirandola (1463-1494) who really started the ball rolling. Pico sought to reconcile and blend Neoplatonism, Chaldean systems, the cabala, and Christianity. By various ingenious devices, he thoroughly Christianized the cabala and thereby became very unpopular with orthodox Jews. In Pico's

Johann Reuchlin

Christian version, the Sephirah Chokmah is God the Father, Binah is
the Holy Ghost, Tiphareth (Beauty) in the center of the whole
diagram is Christ (or Adam, who is identified with Christ), and
Malkuth (Kingdom), the lowest Sephirah, is the soul (or the church,
or Eve) which is to be redeemed as the bride of Christ. That isn't
quite what the Jewish cabalists had in mind. However, Pico's ideas
became very widespread within the Western Hermetic Tradition
and are to be found today in such phenomena as Christian cabala of
the Golden Dawn and the eclecticism of the "perennial philosophy"
of Rene Guenon and Julius Evola.

Pico was less tied to orthodoxy than Ficino and lay more
emphasis on the mystical experience and the application of magic to
religion. Orthodox or not, however, the teachings of both Ficino and
Pico were condemned by the church.

Johann Reuchlin (1455-1522), a student of Pico, thought that
Pythagoras had been inspired by the cabala and Plato by Hermes
Trismegistus. He got into Pythagorean numerology and equated
the Pythagorean tetractys with the Hebrew tetragrammaton

(YHVH, commonly rendered as Yahweh or Jehovah).

The ideas of people such as Pythagoras and Plotinus were liable to crop up anywhere. Although no specific mention is made of the trumps of the Tarot until the 15th century (with ordinary playing cards mentioned only a century earlier), it would be surprising, in view of the climate of the times, if the trumps did not reflect a few classical and Neoplatonic ideas. In fact, variant packs of cards depicting the Greek gods were specially painted for various nobles.

The usual approach, at least since Court de Gebelin in the late 18th century, is to associate the 22 trumps of the Tarot with the 22 letters of the Hebrew alphabet and tie them in with cabalism and the Tree of Life. The mere coincidence of numbers is enough. The connection may be valid—or at least workable—but, at the same time, it ought to be remembered that every number below fifty is almost bound to crop up at least once in every fifty random instances. There were so many significant numbers floating around at this time that some sort of correlation had to occur somewhere.

The prominence of female figures on the trumps may point back to a religion in which goddesses were prominent—perhaps a primordial European religion (such as Wicca is supposed to be, according to the theories of Margaret Murray), but also perhaps the religion of classical Greece as it came to be understood in the Hellenistic age. If we must talk in terms of numbers, and assuming that the oldest forms of the Tarot did in fact have 22 trumps, we could consider the trumps as a triad of three sevens plus one unnumbered card (The Fool). (As Donald Tyson has so rightly pointed out, The Fool was originally unnumbered altogether and did not bear a zero that would tend to argue in favor of placing it at the beginning of the sequence.) There's a certain amount of medieval Christian symbolism, and common medieval figures such as The Juggler (or The Magician) are among the trumps, but the existence of the card entitled The High Priestess (or The Papess) would tend to argue against a Christian (or Islamic) origin. The legend of Pope Joan seems to me entirely inadequate to account for the inclusion of such a card among the trumps. The legend was simply not sufficiently well known or long lasting to be a popular subject for playing cards, and no other such legends (as far as we know) are depicted on the cards. Can we instead be looking at a priestess of the Greek mysteries?

Even without resorting to the mysteries, it has already been explained how priestesses were prominent even in patriarchal Greece. The fact that the earliest existing examples of this card show a female Pope doesn't prove much; in the art of the period, people from Biblical and classical times were always depicted as wearing contemporary dress. They just assumed that people had always dressed the same way. A Pagan priestess would be depicted as a contemporary cleric who happened to be female.

As for The Empress, there were certainly no Empresses in classical Greece; the idea was inconceivable. But there were queens—Cleopatra, for example—in Hellenistic Egypt, and there were goddesses. Some modern packs have the Empress and Emperor labeled Juno and Jupiter, the Roman names corresponding to Zeus and Here.

A detailed examination of the trumps and their possible (or probable) Hellenistic/Neoplatonic associations—without reference to cabalism—is a fairly ambitious undertaking and one that I am unprepared to present at this time, particularly since it would rightfully require a book to itself.

The Stoic/Neoplatonic doctrine of sympathies, whereby everything in the universe is connected in an ordered fashion (which provides an explanation for both magic and astrology) was enthusiastically used by Cornelius Agrippa (1486-1535), author of the *Three Books of Occult Philosophy*. Agrippa also apparently thought the Platonic/Neoplatonic idea of the World Soul was revealed truth. By his time, there were already a lot of books floating around that listed things by sympathies, usually keyed to the seven planets or twelve signs of the Zodiac. Aleister Crowley continued this tradition in the 20th century with his *Liber 777*.

Agrippa devotes something like 30 chapters of Book One of his *Three Books* to the question of sympathies. He begins by describing the "virtues" (qualities) of various stones, plants, and animals, taking his material mostly from the Roman natural historian Pliny the Younger (61-113). In this section, we have such quaint aphorisms as, "...the lion, if he be feverish, is recovered by eating of an ape" or "A snake is afraid of a man that is naked, but pursues a man that is clothed"—or my personal favorite, "Death is fatal to all." Eventually, Agrippa gets around to talking about the source of these qualities in the World Soul and from celestial influences. He explains it this way:

Hereunto may be added, that in the Soul of the World there be as many seminal forms of things, as Ideas in the mind of God, by which forms she did in the heavens above the stars frame to herself shapes also, and stamped upon all these some properties; on these stars therefore, shapes, and properties, all virtues of inferior species, as also their properties do depend; so that every species hath its celestial shape, or figure that is suitable to it, from which proceeds a wonderful power of operating, which proper gift it receives from its own Idea, through the seminal forms of the Soul of the World. (James Freake translation of 1651).

Heinrich Cornelius Agrippa

Giordano Bruno (1548-1600), who managed to get himself burned at the stake for his trouble, latched onto Neoplatonic and Gnostic ideas and said that all natural things (including, of course, people) contain the light of divinity which causes them to seek their source, just as the Neoplatonic soul "wheels about" to its origins or the Gnostic pneuma seeks its creator among the aeons and the primal Bythos.

Throughout these pages, I've attempted to call attention to apparent precursors of cabalistic doctrine. My reason for this is that cabalism constitutes such an enormous influence on modern magical and occultist thought, and yet the version that has achieved the widest circulation and popularity owes more to Pico, the Neoplatonists, and classical Greek ideas than it does to the *Zohar* of Moses de Leon in the 13th century.

Cabalism is not a simple subject, Christianized or otherwise. A good starting point, I suppose, is with the Four Worlds. These more or less correspond—though not exactly—with the hypostases of later Neoplatonism. First is the archetypal world, the World of Nobility, *Olam ha-Atziluth*. The Platonic ideas exist here, but only in their most rarefied form. Then come the World of Creation (*Olam ha-Briah*), the World of Formation (*Olam ha-Yetzirah*), and the material world, *Olam ha-Assiah*. God dwells in Atziluth, the archangels in Briah, the angels in Yetzirah (which is also the "astral plane"), and humanity in Assiah. These four worlds correspond to the four elements (Fire, Water, Air, and Earth, respectively) and, much more importantly, to the four letters of the Name—YHVH, Yahweh, Jehovah. They are also represented in Sufi thought as *'alamu 'l-'izzah, 'alamu 'l-jabbarut, 'alamu 'l-malakut,* and *'alamu 'l-mulk.*

Since "Jehovah" is an Elizabethan corruption and "Yahweh" is a doubtful guess—no one really knows how the name is supposed to be pronounced—this Name is commonly just called "Yod Heh Vav Heh," pronouncing each letter separately. (The *yod* corresponds to the Father and the *vav* to the Son. The two *heh*s are the Mother and the Daughter. Therefore, to avoid pronouncing the letters in an unconsciously sexist fashion, you should emphasize *heh* and *heh* just as strongly as *yod* and *vav*, avoiding such run-it-all-together pronunciations as "Yuddy-Vavvy"—which, in any case, is all too reminiscent of William Blake's "Nobodaddy.")

The "Four Worlds system" can be made to correlate to a diagram known as the Tree of Life. The Tree depicts ten circles (spheres, actually)—the Sephiroth—connected by 22 lines or "paths" that correspond to the 22 letters of the Hebrew alphabet. Each circle represents an emanation from God, the paths the relationships among them. The Tree therefore seems to be related to the Gnostic aeons and the later Neoplatonic hypostases—but I'd hate to try to make a one-for-one correlation.

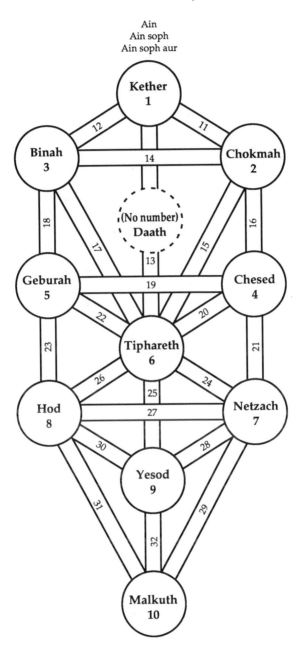

The Tree of Life

It needs to be emphasized that the Tree is not mentioned or described in the 3rd-century *Sepher Yetzirah*. That anonymous document describes the Sephiroth, but does not arrange them in any particular pattern. The Tree itself seems to be a second-generation version of a similar diagram, with eight emanations rather than ten, that was promulgated by the 10th-century Islamic Ikhwan El Safa (Brethren of Sincerity) in Basra, Iraq. Or so says Idries Shah *(The Sufis*, 1964).

Triads are important in the composition of the Tree, beginning with the "Supernal Triad," the numbers one, two, and three considered in their archetypal, Pythagorean sense—that is, Kether (Crown), Chokmah (Wisdom), and Binah (Understanding). Incidentally, it seems a bit odd that Chokmah, which is the Hebrew word corresponding to the Greek Sophia, is considered to be masculine—the Supernal Father, in fact. In cabalistic terms, however, Sophia might best correspond to Daath, Knowledge, a non-sephira that mediates between the Supernals and the rest of the Tree. Binah itself corresponds fairly well with Barbelo or Ennoia.

Beyond Kether is the inexpressible Ain Soph ("Without Limit"), which seems to be more or less identical with the One of Plotinus or the Bythos of Gnosticism. Of course, Iamblichus would say that Plotinus's One is Kether and that the highest hypostasis exists beyond that as Ain Soph.

The Tree itself is a triad inasmuch as it consists of three columns or "pillars"—the Pillar of Mercy, the Pillar of Severity, and the Pillar of Mildness or Middle Pillar mediating between them and balancing them.

The system of triads is yet further reflected in the fact that cabalism postulates a process of devolution or disintegration (creation by emanation via a descending Lightning Flash or Flashing Sword), equilibrium (the Middle Pillar and the balance of the Tree), and evolution or integration (the ascent of the soul of the mystic to God, symbolized by the Serpent of Wisdom climbing the Tree— with a supposed analog in the caduceus).

All of this triad business, actually, including that of the Neoplatonists, may very well originate in Hindu doctrines concerning Brahma the Creator, Vishnu the Preserver, and Shiva the Destroyer. It's things like this that point to the essential unity of all religions, or at least of all mysticism. Scholars look for mutual influences, but, as explained before, facts can be discovered independently. This is a hard thing to accept for most people when you start talking philosophy, religion, and mysticism, however, since the currently prevailing world view is to see this whole area as simply not true, wildly speculative at best, and an area where the word "fact" has no meaning.

Finally, there is the cabalistic doctrine of the soul and its parts—the animal soul *(Nephesh)*, the rational soul *(Ruach)*, and the three-part immortal soul *(Neshamah, Chiah, and Yechidah)*. Nephesh perishes with the body, Ruach may hang around for a little while as a "shell"—and in some cases may manifest as a ghost or start handing out worthless advice to a medium or channeler—and Neshamah goes on to better things (probably the next incarnation). I don't wish to burst anyone's esoteric bubble, but this is all straight out of Plato. Oh, well. He probably got it from the oral traditions of ancient cabalists who just didn't bother to write anything down for another 1500 years or so. Right. Nevertheless, the evidence would seem to suggest that the Jews of Plato's time had no belief at all in a soul that could exist apart from the body.

To recap some of the probable Greek influences on cabalism, Anaximander said the basic stuff of the universe was the Boundless *(apeiron)*, which is nothing more than a translation of the term *Ain Soph*. Heraclitus advocated stability through change and came up with a system of emanations based on the elements (Fire, Water, Earth). He also described the "first swirlings" *(Rashith ha-Gilgalim)* of the Nous. The Pythagorean Speusippus codified the sacredness of the number ten as per the ten Sephiroth. Posidonius said that the moon is the borderland between the upper and lower worlds, much as the Sephirah Yesod (the sphere of the Moon, in the World of Assiah) mediates between Malkuth and the rest of the Tree. And all that does not even consider the even more pervasive influence of Neoplatonism.

The Renaissance Christian Neoplatonists did not hesitate to change things 'round a bit to fit Christianity. It was probably sincere; certainly it was safer. Thus the triadic scheme of Proclus *(mone, proodos, epistrophe*—abiding, going forth, turning back) became procession, rapture, and reversion and was symbolized by the Three Graces, a common subject of the art of the time.

In England, John Dee (1527-1608), counselor to Queen Elizabeth, scientist, engineer, astrologer, and all-around Renaissance magus, was finding out from angels, through his seer Edward Kelly, all about the 30 "aires" of the heavens. It is probably more than coincidence that there are also 30 aeons in Valentinian Gnosticism; Dee had almost certainly read Irenaeus and/or Hippolytus and had probably talked about it to Kelly—although, of course, all this is only conjecture. Maybe the angels really did say there were 30 aires because, in fact, there are 30 aires (or aethers, or aeons). The only difficulty is that, in Gnosticism, there is considerable distance between the lowest aeon and the material world, whereas the lowest Enochian aire is more or less immediately accessible and contiguous to the material plane.

It was when some of the angels began to come out with other Gnostic and Pagan ideas that Dee and Kelly freaked. Dee suspected Kelly of losing his marbles or becoming possessed. The angels told Kelly that Jesus was not God and ought not to be prayed to and that there is no such thing as sin. They also affirmed reincarnation. Someone as sincerely Christian as Dee had no choice but to reject these ideas as monstrous heresies born of madness and deception. The chronology of these events is not clear, but they apparently occurred early in the workings before the system(s) of angelic magic had been revealed. Things calmed down somehow, and the scryings continued. However, this one "anomaly" argues more strongly than anything else for the objective existence of Dee's angels.

In 1610, two years after Dee's death, Rosicrucianism burst upon the scene with the publication of the anonymous *Fama Fraternitatis*. Although, on the face of it, this document is primarily concerned with Christian mysticism and has been made the foundation of various mystical and magical societies, its main thrust seems to have been altogether in line with the spirit of the Renaissance. Although it superficially seems to be an invitation to seek out and join the (apparently fictional) Rosicrucians, it is in fact primarily a call to men of intelligence and education to seek and disseminate knowledge. It has also been interpreted as an effort to reform the Catholic church and unite Christendom, although it lumps the Pope in with "Mahomet" as one of those who deserve rough handling.

The *Fama* speaks of Aristotle and Porphyry as authorities who are often appealed to but whose knowledge contained "erroneous Doctrines" that need amending in light of subsequent knowledge. Later, it credits Pythagoras, Plato, and Aristotle as being among those who "hit the mark," their knowledge along with that of Enoch, the Hebrew prophets, and the Bible forming a sphere about a hidden center. At the same time, it sounds almost like an appeal to abandon superstition and knowledge by reference to authority in favor of empirical science and investigation.

However, even though the impact of the Rosicrucian legend has been immense, any deep consideration of the subject is outside the limits of this book. Greek elements exist in Rosicrucianism—in fact, at least one modern organization using that name still talks about Nous—but they are by this time so watered down and mixed up with cabalism and everything else that they cannot be said to be the predominant factor. The dimensions of the tomb of Christian Rosenkreutz—seven sides, each measuring five by eight feet—can of course be related to Pythagorean number mysticism, but any concise correlation must remain mostly theoretical supposition.

Still in print is the MacGregor Mathers translation, edited by Aleister Crowley, of the 17th-century (or earlier) *Lesser Key of Solomon: Goetia*, listing 72 spirits or demons (daimons?) that can be summoned for one purpose or another. Besides having a Greek title (*Goeteia*), more than a third of these spirits have obviously Greek names. It has been observed that a good many of these "demons" are actually the gods of old religions—for example, Bael, Haures (Horus), Amon, Ashtaroth, and so on. I can find no instance in this catalog of any Greek gods, although the names of some of the spirits are actual Greek words. For example, the very first, Agares, also known as Agreas, is apparently derived from the Greek word *agreus*, meaning "hunter." It may be significant in this connection that "Agreas" carries a goshawk on his fist. The name Botis may be a corruption of Bootes, and Sallos of *salos*, meaning the swell of the sea. Purson may be related to the prefix *pyrso-*, which designates something having to do with fire. "Ipos" is a trap or the weight in a trap. "Stolas" is a cloak; the variant "Stolos" is an expedition or voyage. "Phoenix" is fairly obvious. Even more intriguing Greek names, though of unknown origin (to me) are Marchiosas, Andrealphus, Dantalion, and Malphas. There are more. The point is that the Greek influence was still very much around when this book was compiled.

It was definitely present in all of the magical manuals or grimoires floating around at this time. The first thing you see when you open one of them is long strings of "barbarous names of evocation" straight out of Hellenistic magic. Chances are some of the incantations, if not the spells themselves, were copied directly from Hellenistic magical papyri.

Painting before this time had usually concerned itself with Christian motifs, but themes from Greek mythology became common in the Renaissance. This trend has continued to a lesser extent right down to the present century (for example, Pablo Picasso's Minotaur series). The paintings of Sandro Botticelli (1444-1510)—who was a student at the Platonic Academy of Florence—possess an unequaled ethereal, lyrical charm. We can only regret that he was caught up in the "fundamentalist" anti-Pagan revival led by Girolamo Savonarola (1452-1498) and moved to destroy much of his work on this subject. Peter Paul Rubens (1577-1640) also dealt extensively with mythological themes, although, to the modern viewer, all of his figures seem unnecessarily obese. ("How on earth is he ever going to lift her onto that horse?") But perhaps the nadir of inappropriateness was reached by Francois Boucher (1703-1770). There is no scene from mythology, however tragic or dramatic, in which he did not include flocks of those "darling little Cupids." Boucher's gods and goddesses belong in 18th-century French drawing rooms, not in the wilds of Greece. Francisco Goya (1746-1828) probably came closer than any of his predecessors to catching the true, terrible numinosity of the Greek religion with his painting of "Saturn [Kronos] Devouring His Children."

Classical Greek patriarchal myth was preserved in part by an 18th-century romance telling of the conquest of the wicked Queen of the Night by the benevolent Sun King. This version was presented in 1791 in Vienna in Wolfgang A. Mozart's popular opera, *The Magic Flute*—a wonderful piece of work, but one that is—if you happen to understand sung German—offensively sexist right along with being vastly entertaining, magically enchanting, supernally inspirational, and spiritually stirring. It's a shame.

In defense of Mozart, it should be pointed out that he did not write the libretto. His input to the story and the words of the opera was limited to musical considerations. The libretto was nominally written by a fellow Freemason, Emanuel Schikaneder, although Carl Ludwig Giesecke, a notorious misogynist, had a large hand in it. Contrary to an opinion that has been expressed, Mozart did not write difficult coloratura arias for the Queen of the Night because he hated women but rather because 18th-century sopranos were in the habit of demanding opportunities to display their abilities. To give Mozart his due, I must say that it very much seems to me as if his music deliberately undercuts the more extreme sexist polemic that occasionally occurs in the libretto and turns it into a satire of male supremicists.

Music from *The Magic Flute* was used extensively, by the way, in the rituals of the German Fraternitas Saturni in the 20th century. This group used a number of Gnostic ideas as well, but belongs chronologically in the next chapter.

Having sort of slid past the Renaissance by this time, let us close this chapter by mentioning the attempted revival of Neoplatonism made by Thomas Taylor (1758-1835). He translated a good many Neoplatonic works into English; in many cases, his translations are the only ones available. Hence we find such figures as William Blake and Samuel Taylor Coleridge being influenced by the thought of Plotinus.

But it doesn't end there. Far from it.

A Renaissance Ritual in Quest of Knowledge

There were, of course, innumerable magical rituals of every description practiced during the Renaissance. The influence of Neoplatonic and cabalistic ideas must have been immense—and undoubtedly resulted in a certain amount of confusion.

One example of a somewhat later spell (the 17th or 18th century, or perhaps earlier) that might have modern applicability is the one entitled, "To hinder a sportsman from killing any game" in *The Key of Solomon the King,* one of the many grimoires of the period. The technique seems to have echoes of Hellenistic magic. The prescription itself—which apparently assumes the knowledge of how to charge the ritual object with power—calls for hollowing out both ends of a stick of green elder, placing pieces of inscribed parchment in both ends, and sealing them in again with the pith that has been removed. The stick is to be fumigated (again, no ceremonial details are given) on a Friday in February and buried under an elder tree. It is used by digging it up and leaving it in the path of the would-be sportsman.

Anyone experienced in magical practice should have little trouble formulating an effective ritual for charging this device. For those less experienced, I once again recommend Don Kraig's *Modern Magick,* which contains an excellent section on making and charging amulets and talismans.

The pieces of parchment were to be made from the skin of a hare and inscribed with the blood of a black hen, but there is no particular reason for this beyond the fact that the effect of an object of this sort, technically an "amulet," is directly proportional to the amount of care and trouble you take to prepare it. The inscription includes the word "ABIMEGH" and a figure that faintly resembles a horizontal Christmas tree with a penis sticking out of the base.

A. E. Waite considered this spell hopelessly trivial and thereby a good example of the general silliness of grimoires. But suppose . . .

Suppose such a stick were to be prepared (with the proper accompanying rituals) and thrown into the sea in the path of a Japanese whaling vessel. Greenpeace, take note. I am not attempting to be facetious; it might be worth a try.

The following ritual, however, is directed toward the search for knowledge—a major concern during the Renaissance. It is based on Dr. John Dee's angelic magic and is thus representative of the Renaissance in England, but Greek and eclectic elements have been added to the preliminary evocation as they might have been by a devoted Neoplatonist of a slightly earlier period in Italy.

Once again, you will need a seer. If that is not practical for some reason (that is, you can find no one qualified or your previous "auditor" is now gibbering in a corner because of a bungled evocation), the ritual may nevertheless have a delayed effect; that is, the sought-for knowledge may come to you unexpectedly within a few days in the form of a book or communication. You will also need a "shewstone" or crystal. This can be a black mirror (that is, a pane of glass painted flat black on its reverse side) or a hematite sphere. It need not be large. Aleister Crowley used a large, golden topaz for a similar purpose. The seer is to be seated in the East and is to concentrate upon gazing into the shewstone.

For this ritual, it would be entirely appropriate to use the Opening by Watchtower (given in *The Golden Dawn* and in Kraig's *Modern Magick*). Enochian magic had finally been discovered. On the other hand, if you wish something less elaborate, use the procedure outlined in the Neoplatonic ritual. You must do something in the way of protection, however; otherwise you may get spurious knowledge. I suppose there's no particular reason why, without protections, you couldn't get a lingering shell of Lee Harvey Oswald or Lincoln Rockwell. I don't think you'd really care for the sort of knowledge they would have to impart.

The ritual should be performed on a Sunday. Candles may be white, yellow, or gold. Frankincense is appropriate. Standing behind the altar, facing the East, say, vibrating the names:

In the name of Yod Heh Vav Heh Eloah va-Daath, Pallas Athene, Minerva, Sophia, and Odin who gave His eye, may my quest this day for knowledge be successful, and may the Spirits grant unto me that which I seek.

O puissant and noble King Bobogel, and by what name else soever thou art called, or mayest truly and duly be called, to whose peculiar government, charge, disposition, and kingly office doth appertain the distributing, giving, and bestowing of wisdom and science, the teaching of true philosophy, true understanding of all learning, grounded on wisdom, with the excellencies in nature, and of many other mysteries, marvelously available and necessary to the advancing of the glory of our God and Creator, therefore, in the name of the King of Kings, the Lord of Hosts, the Almighty God, Creator of Heaven and Earth and of all things visible and invisible, O right noble King Bobogel, come now and appear with thy Prince and his ministers and subjects, to my perfect and sensible eye's judgment, in a goodly and friendly manner, to my comfort and help, for the advancing of the honor and glory of our Almighty God, by my service, as much as by thy wisdom and power, in thy proper kingly office and government, I may be helped and enabled unto. Amen. Come! O right noble king, Bobogel, I say come! Amen.

Inasmuch as this last paragraph represents the words of John Dee, the Christian bias is fairly blatant. (This rendering is based on the rendition that appears in *The Enochian Invocation of Dr. John Dee*, Heptangle Books, Gillette, NJ, 1988, and is reproduced by permission of Geoffrey James.) Many people who wish to attempt this ritual will have no objection to that and may in fact feel safer with it than otherwise. Others will find it annoying or even offensive. If you fall into the latter category, there's nothing to keep you from altering the wording as necessary to accord with your own beliefs. No one need delude himself or herself that there is not also a Queen of Queens.

If the seer (which may be yourself) hasn't detected anything in the shewstone by this time, and still fails to do so after a reasonable pause, repeat the evocation ("O puissant and noble King...") from the beginning. You might even persist with a third repetition. After that, however, whether Bobogel appears or not, go ahead and ask your questions, but in the form of statements: "I wish to know..." For example, to stir up an already fairly vexed question, "I wish to know the true origin of the Tarot."

If the entity has not manifested and does not answer through the seer, proceed immediately to the closing. If you are answered, *then* go ahead and close. Dee apparently did not think it necessary to thank Bobogel personally. If you're maintaining Dee's Christian approach, say, "Glory be to the Father, to the Son, and to the Holy Ghost, as it was in the beginning, is now and ever shall be, world without end. Amen." Otherwise, you might use the Watchtower closing ("Unto thee, sole wise, sole eternal and sole merciful One, be the praise and glory forever, who has permitted me who now standeth humbly before Thee to enter this far into the sanctuary of the mysteries. Not unto me but unto Thy name be the glory. Let the influence of Thy Divine Ones descend upon my head, and teach me the value of self-sacrifice so that I shrink not in the hour of trial, but that thus my name may be written on high and my genius stand in the presence of the Holy Ones.") Note that this closing does not designate the "One" as either male or female. If you specifically wish to honor the Goddess, however, you might say something like, "Glory be to the Goddess, Great One of a thousand thousand names since before time was, as it was in the beginning, is now and ever shall be, world without end. So mote it be."

Then continue the closing in harmony with the opening you used.

If you want to follow Dee's methods faithfully, first of all observe that this ritual comes from his "heptarchical" system rather than from the later system based on the four angelic tablets and the keys. You would need a ring and a fairly elaborate sigil, the Sigil of Aemeth (truth), upon which you would place the shewstone. Further details on this system may be had from *The Enochian Evocation of Dr. John Dee* (edited and translated by Geoffrey James) and *The Heptarchia Mystica of John Dee* compiled by Robert Turner (Aquarian Press, 1986). I confess that I have been unable to find a copy of the latter work, although, judging from his *Elizabethan Magic* (Element Books, 1989), he may be the most reliable authority. The above evocation is based upon James's reproduction, but I have modernized the spelling and punctuation.

Incidentally, "shew" is merely an old spelling for "show" and is not pronounced any differently. It's not a shoe-stone.

You may be puzzled at this point by the fact that, aside from my very minor additions, there's not a whole lot about this ritual that seems particularly Greek. None of it is in the language, and no Greek divine names are used. But consider: who was it that first advocated in print the invocation of gods and daimons as a means of spiritual development? Yes, it was Iamblichus, the Neoplatonist, in the 4th century. Dee's angel magic was merely the latest development of this continuing theurgy, and there can be no doubt that he was familiar with *On the Mysteries*, written by Iamblichus. Don't think that he didn't take the Neoplatonist into consideration when constructing his own rituals.

If that's not enough, then by all means feel free to Paganize Dee's ritual and substitute Pagan or Gnostic names for the Christian ones. The ritual will not thus be rendered any less effective.

Even though you might or might not get a direct contact with Bobogel, Dee's angel of Sunday, in charge of wisdom and knowledge, the ritual may not therefore be without effect. Knowledge of this kind can come in many ways. As mentioned above, you might find what you're looking for in a book you just happen to pick up (although probably not, if you've asked that question about the Tarot). There are also such things as communications in dreams, during meditation, and in hypnagogic states. Perhaps the meaning of an obscure divination will become clear to you. But magic works.

Yes, that's right. Magic works. It's true that you can't get much in the way of results if you buy a book of spells, pick one out, and rush through it. There are techniques involved that the average book of spells doesn't go into very much, if at all. Kraig's book, cited above, is an excellent guide for beginners. (If I'd had that book 20 years ago, I could have saved an incalculable amount of wasted effort.) The ideal way to learn, of course, is to have a competent and reliable personal teacher, preferably someone who is or has been associated with a known and legitimate group.

What skeptics and debunkers completely fail to understand is that magic (or, if you prefer, magick) is not a matter of turning princes into toads or summoning demons to hunt down your enemies. Neither is it a quest for personal power on a par with God; such a quest is bound to fail, in any event. Magic is a question of affecting probabilities. If something has zero chance of happening, then no magic spell is going to make it happen. If the chances are even slightly in favor of its happening even without a spell, then it will almost certainly happen if you do carry out a ritual to bring it about. At a rough guess, I would hazard that a proper spell cast by a competent magician or witch increases probability by approximately twenty percent.

There's also the question of how you look at things. No spell effect ever occurs that cannot be explained by coincidence. Sometimes the coincidences are fairly unlikely, but the explanation is still available. Naturally, from the viewpoint of the skeptic, it *must* be chance coincidence because the idea that magic does not and cannot work is taken as absolute truth beyond question. Then, too, the magical personality is much more apt to notice effects that would be overlooked or dismissed by the skeptic.

If nothing else, magic affects the consciousness and therefore the behavior of the magician. If someone casts a spell to find a job, the mere fact that he has concentrated his attention on job finding may lead him to spend more time looking at want ads and filling out applications. Many times, however, the effects of a spell are rather striking and are not easily explained by any possible change in behavior on the part of the spell-caster.

Magic works in mysterious ways.

John Dee

XII

Modern Manifestations

It should be apparent by now that Greek magic and occult philosophy are far from being a thing of the past. In this chapter, we will examine some modern phenomena with emphasis on their Greek elements. We will also look at a few survivals or modern versions of rituals that are overtly Greek, including Neo-Gnostic.

Of course, it all goes back to Plato and Aristotle—Plato the metaphysician and Aristotle the empirical scientist. European Hermeticists of the school of perennial philosophy might wish to push things farther back, to Heraclitus, saying that degeneration set in with Socrates, but what we are concerned with here is the situation as it currently exists. We are still experiencing this same split between the spiritual outlook and the scientific/materialistic viewpoint that so permeated the Hellenistic world.

In 1801, *The Magus* of Francis Barrett appeared. Though largely pirated verbatim from Agrippa, the book contained supplementary biographies of Hermes Trismegistus, Apollonius of Tyana, Apuleius, and Aristotle. The Greek and Roman influence on cultural life in general was so pervasive in the 19th century that, when Richard Wagner came to write *The Ring of the Nibelung,* a series of four operas based on Germanic mythology, the Teutonic elements were all but swallowed up. This isn't really Wotan and Fricka bickering over Wotan's infidelity—it's recognizably the Zeus and Here of late classical myth. I've already hinted that the relationship between Wotan and his valkyrie daughter Brünnhilde, the warrior maiden, is identical to that between Zeus and Athene in classical myth. Brünnhilde is at least the daughter of Erda, the earth goddess, rather than having sprung from Wotan's head, but Fricka/Here is still not involved. The hero Siegfried has more in common with Perseus— and the Parzival of Arthurian legend—than with the Teutonic/ Danish hero who helped the Burgundians fight Attila/Alberich.

H. P. Blavatsky (1831-1891) based the bulk of her Theosophy on Hindu and Buddhist religion and philosophy, but she freely acknowledged that a great many of the same ideas had been expressed by Plato and Pythagoras. Of course, she assumed that they owed their ideas to India rather than to a common source such as Siberian shamanism, but she praised "the boundless sublimity of their views of the Unknown Deity." She also had a good deal to say about the Greek mysteries and about Gnosticism, in every case pointing out their superiority to official Christianity. "Theosophy" itself is a close synonym for "Gnosticism," and it has in fact been called a form of Neo-Gnosticism.

The Hermetic Order of the Golden Dawn, founded in 1887 by William Wynn Westcott, W. R. Woodman, and S. L. MacGregor Mathers, was based primarily on Rosicrucian, cabalistic, and Egyptian concepts (the latter within the limits of late-19th-century Egyptology). Nevertheless, Greek elements were not missing from their rituals and curricula. In their initiation ceremonies, they were in some respects attempting to duplicate the mysteries of Eleusis. The initiation ritual for the grade of Practicus incorporated elements of the mysteries of the Kabeiroi, although the ritual as it was written probably represents a considerable distortion of the original. Every Neophyte initiation, equinox ceremony, and vault consecration opened with what was supposed to be a duplication of the opening of the Eleusinian mysteries—the Greek words, "Hekas! Hekas! Este bebeloi!" And, of course, they relied heavily upon the Greek concept of five elements (the fifth element being Spirit or aether). When selecting accounts of experiences of "skrying in the spirit vision"—a technique which would now be subsumed under the term "pathworking"—to present to the membership as examples, Moina Mathers' vision of Hermes was chosen.

The 19th-century romanticism that became attached to classical Greek myth may have reached its peak as late as 1920 with the publication in the amateur press of a story called "Poetry and the Gods," written by a rather starry-eyed young lady named Anna Helen Crofts in collaboration with—surprise, surprise—H. P. Lovecraft, progenitor of cosmic horrors in the magazine *Weird Tales*. Lovecraft had not forgotten the infatuations of his youth.

Aleister Crowley (1875-1947), whom we've had occasion to mention before in these pages, was sufficiently impressed with Greek ideas to cast at least one ritual (the Star Ruby) in that language. He also wrote a Gnostic mass. His "Hymn to Pan" was read at his funeral.

Pan gets around. Hymns to Pan were also written by such diverse figures as Lovecraft and Percy Bysshe Shelley.

The Star Ruby ritual is patterned after the Golden Dawn's Lesser Banishing Ritual of the Pentagram. A sincere performance of this ritual (which is reproduced in *Magick in Theory and Practice*) requires that the operator be a Thelemite; that is, adhere to the teachings of *The Book of the Law*—although there is some question in my mind as to whether Crowley was intentionally injecting his weird sense of humor into the ritual.

The Star Ruby begins with the words, *Apo pantos kako-daimonos* —"Away, all evil spirits!" This is immediately followed by a Greek version of the cabalistic cross, normally accompanied by the words *Ateh Malkuth ve Geburah ve Gedulah le-Olam. Amen.* This is Hebrew for the well-known phrase "For thine is the kingdom and the power and the glory for ever and ever. Amen." Crowley substitutes *Soi O phalle, ischyros, eucharistos. Iao!* In the version of *Magick* annotated by John Symonds and Kenneth Grant (Samuel Weiser, Inc., 1973), this is translated "To Thee, O Phallus, Power, Thanksgiving, IAO." The difficulty arises from the fact that *ischyros* and *eucharistos* are not nouns meaning "power" and "thanksgiving." That would be *ischys* and *eucharistia*. *Ischyros* and *eucharistos* are adjectives meaning "powerful" or "mighty" and "thankful" or "grateful." The phrase now translates, "To you, O phallus, mighty thankful. IAO."

Crowley says, "The secret sense of these words is to be sought in the numeration thereof." That really doesn't get us very far, though, unless we happen to know what he had in mind. *Phalle* is 566, 100 short of the number of the Beast; i.e., Crowley. It is numerically equivalent to the Greek word *mathetes*, "disciple." *Eucharistos* is 1886, the same as "The Lord is with thee." It is doubtful that Crowley intended these particular meanings, however. Perhaps he meant

O phalle to indicate masculinity and femininity conjoined, inasmuch as O is a female symbol and the enumeration of *O phalle*, 1366, is equal to *phallos* plus *kteis*. But who knows?

The formulation of the pentagrams in the quarters (which, unlike the Golden Dawn ritual, involves mental images rather than figures that are actually traced in the air) is accompanied not by the Hebrew divine names Yod Heh Vav Heh, Adonai, Eheieh, and Agla, but by the names Therion, Nuit, Babalon, and Hadit. These are all names from *The Book of the Law*. *Therion* (Beast) is Crowley himself in his persona as Logos of the Aeon.

The circumambulation that is involved in this part of the ritual is counterclockwise (widdershins) rather than clockwise (deosil) as in the Golden Dawn ritual. Dion Fortune saw this as a trap for the unwary, but it's more likely that it simply represents Crowley's preferred method of working. Logically, a counterclockwise circumambulation is more appropriate for a banishing ritual, but traditional thinking connects it with evil and black magic. Crowley did not have an excessive respect for traditional ways of doing things. Nevertheless, the very un-Crowleyan and respectable Aurum Solis to this day uses widdershins circumambulations for banishing.

After returning to the center and crying "Io Pan," one evokes the guardians by the usual formula, but, instead of the archangels of the Golden Dawn ritual (Raphael, Michael, Gabriel, and Uriel), Crowley uses Iunges, Teletarchai, Synoches ("Chunoches" is a misprint), and Daimonos. The last name simply means "spirits."

Crowley's Gnostic mass isn't really very Gnostic. It is essentially a Thelemite ritual of sex magick. It includes a repetition of the "Apostles' Creed" altered to fit the new religion. Instead of Father, Son, and Holy Ghost, belief is asserted in Chaos, Babalon, and Baphomet. Chaos is just what it sounds like. Babalon is part of Crowley's mythology, and Baphomet is the idol that was supposed to have been worshiped by the Templars—no particular connection with Gnosticism in any case out of the three. A few Gnostic names do enter into one incantation of the priest: "Io Io Io Iao Sabao, Kyrie [Lord] Abrasax, Kyrie Meithras, Kyrie Phalle. Io Pan, Io Pan Pan Io Ischuron, Io Athanaton, Io Abroton Io Iao. Chaire [hail] phalle chaire pamphage [All-Devourer] chaire pangenetor [All-Begetter]. Hagios [holy], hagios, hagios Iao."

The Fraternitas Saturni, active in Germany from 1928 until

(presumably) the present day, being extremely eclectic in nature, not only adhered to Crowley's Law of Thelema (though not to his authority), but also used many Gnostic concepts. If recently published material is accurate and correct, there seems to have been a certain amount of confusion involved in modernizing these ideas. Not only were the Gnostic Aeons thought of in terms of periods of time (as, for example, the Aeon of Horus) rather than eternally existing divine emanations (Logos, Anthropos, Ecclesia, and so on), but the lodge ended up virtually worshiping Saturnus, the Archon of Saturn, as Demiurge. In classical Gnosticism, of course, the Demiurge was considered to be the enemy, not the leading spirit or an object of reverence.

In any case, the Fraternitas Saturni did use the Greek language in its rites—along with Latin and many "barbarous names"—usually with some reference to Gnosticism. For reputed examples of F.S. rituals and something about their general approach, consult *Fire & Ice* by S. Edred Flowers (Llewellyn, 1990).

The greatest modern exponent of Gnostic ideas was undoubtedly Carl Gustav Jung, the Swiss psychologist and rival of Sigmund Freud. Although hard pressed at times to keep the scientific approach required by his profession separate from his interest in Gnosticism and alchemy—which, in his opinion, represented highly significant psychological insights—Jung wrote at least two Gnostic works himself: *Seven Sermons to the Dead* and *Answer to Job*.

In the latter piece, Job is shown to be morally superior to God, who can reply to Job's legitimate questions only by bragging and throwing his weight around. God thereupon repents and tries to do better. His incarnation and crucifixion as Christ are not to redeem humanity, but Himself. This document was not too popular with orthodox Christians. He also wrote *Aion*, a textbook exploration of spirituality from an essentially Gnostic viewpoint with reference to its significance for an understanding of the human mind.

A somewhat more representative format than Aleister Crowley's for Greek, Hellenistic, Gnostic, and Neoplatonic magical ideas is a modern, currently operational society known as the Aurum Solis (Gold of the Sun) headed by Melita Denning as Grand Master and Osborne Phillips as Grand Preceptor. We are told that the Aurum Solis is based on the "Ogdoadic Tradition." But what is this tradition? It's not Rosicrucianism; that much is certain. The Aurum Solis is not just another Golden Dawn clone.

Egyptian pantheons normally came in sets of nine (enneads) or ten (decads). The Greeks got it up to a dodecad with the Olympian twelve, although the so-called Pelasgian system does constitute a double ogdoad (Eurynome, Ophis, and a pair for each of the seven planets). The first clear-cut ogdoad we have encountered in this survey, however, is that of Valentinian Gnosticism. Indeed, the Aurum Solis does incorporate many features of Gnosticism, although it does not adhere to the idea of an inferior Demiurge and all creation as the result of a gross mistake on the part of Sophia.

In fact, Denning and Phillips, in *The Sword and the Serpent*, speaking of the reflection of the Goddess of Binah in Malkuth, say:

> The descent of the Divine Force of the Third Sephirah to the Tenth is presented in the Greco-Judaic cosmogonies of the Eastern Mediterranean as the descent of the Sophia, Holy Wisdom, into the material world. This was in fact to declare her the formative principle of the material world, so that this involution should have been regarded as an essential part of the cosmic process. Unfortunately, however, by a not uncommon confusion of ideas, the early Christian Gnostics regarded the material world as a pre-existing and corrupt condition into which the Sophia descended, and more unfortunately still they therefore declared her descent to be a sin.
>
> This interpretation was not only false, it was pernicious. Followed to its logical conclusions, it would have closed the Way of Return to all incarnate beings.

Also in the Ogdoadic Tradition might be counted the eightfold Tree of Life of the Brethren of Sincerity and the eightfold path of Buddha, although these are not mentioned in the teachings of the order. In their recently published *Foundations of High Magick*, Denning and Phillips describe it this way:

> The name *Ogdoadic* means "pertaining to the number eight." As distinct from the use of the adjective in defining our tradition, the noun *ogdoad* also occurs in the history of philosophy, with regard to the number of Aeons in certain Gnostic systems. There is no connection between the philosophies, save that the Gnostics undoubtedly chose the number eight because of the nature of its associations: those same associations which give eight rays to the Glorious Star of Regeneration, the distinguishing symbol of the

Ogdoadic Tradition and hence of the Aurum Solis.

In ancient Mesopotamian texts the eight-pointed star, sometimes adapted to the cuneiform script, is juxtaposed to the name of a deity as a determinative sign to indicate the divine nature. In Pythagorean lore, eight is the number of perfection, and in Christian usage it was very quickly adopted—if indeed there was not a simple continuity of symbolism from faith to faith—to indicate regeneration, *theosis,* **palingenesis.** There is a somewhat obscure reference in the second epistle of Peter (2:5) to the saving from the flood of "Noah, the eighth person" without further amplification, as if the author expected his readers to be familiar with the ideas involved. The eight-pointed star, or eight-petaled flower, frequently adorns the veil of the Theotokos (the Virgin Mary) in Byzantine ikons, and to this day the eight-pointed star is a familiar symbol on Greek greeting cards for Easter. Outside of Christian symbolism, it appears to be no accident that the Arabic numeral 8 is essentially the same as our symbol for infinity.

The Aurum Solis was founded in 1897 and was based, not on Rosicrucianism or Freemasonry, but on alchemy, Gnosticism, and medieval and Celtic motifs. Whereas the Golden Dawn traced its origins to a German quasi-Masonic Rosicrucian order, the Aurum Solis follows a different line of descent. It looks back to an organization known as the Order of the Helmet, which flourished in Elizabethan England and included Francis Bacon, Edmund Spenser, and Christopher Marlowe among its members. Beyond that, this particular tradition reaches back to the Fideli d'Amore (apparently related to and/or inspired by the Ismaili organization known as the Faithful Ones of Love) and Careggi of Renaissance Italy.

And like these Neoplatonists and mystics of the Italian Renaissance, the Aurum Solis also concerns itself with the cabala—with the praiseworthy and vital purpose "of detaching the timeless teachings of the Qabalah from the limitations of historical and theological particularity, and re-stating them for the modern student of high magick."

The founders of the Aurum Solis were all members of the inner body (the Societas Rotae Fulgentis) of the same antiquarian society, much as the founders of the Golden Dawn had been members of the Societas Rosicruciana in Anglia. The first head of the order, or warden, was George Stanton (who, unlike so many spiritually minded individuals of that era, does not seem to have been a member of the Golden Dawn).

Although there is some superficial similarity between certain lesser rituals of the Golden Dawn and a few of the minor rituals currently used by the Aurum Solis, the fact remains that the two organizations originated independently and have entirely different histories, approaches, and philosophies.

The order ceased official activities in 1939 due to the war but resumed normal functioning in 1949. (There had been a similar but briefer hiatus during the First World War.) In 1957, a disagreement over emphasis led to a split out of which arose the Order of the Sacred Word (OSV) on the one hand and the Aurum Solis on the other. The split was healed in 1971, and the Sacred Word was reabsorbed at that time.

Most of the lesser rituals of the Aurum Solis come in three versions—Hebrew, Greek, and Latin. Naturally, it is the Greek versions which concern us here. In order to give the flavor of an Aurum Solis Greek-language ritual, the Greek version of the Calyx and the Setting of the Wards of Power is reproduced at the end of this chapter.

Triads make their appearance with the gods of the Aurum Solis "Constellation of the Worshipped," which was established with the inception of the order. Leukothea (the White Goddess) and Melanotheos (the Dark God) produce (or, in another sense, are produced by) Agathodaimon (the Benign Spirit).

The order also provides lists of Greek divine and angelic names for each of the cabalistic 32 paths in Atziluth (divine names), Briah (archons), and Yetzirah. Three sets of names are given for Yetzirah: ruling, intermediate, and servient. The selection of these names has been mostly a matter of experience. Most of them originated with the founders of the order, but—in the best traditions of operational Gnosticism—some of them have been purposely altered or modified over time.

To give you an idea, the first ten divine names in Atziluth are En-to-Pan, Ieeooua, Turana (supernal) or Ialdabaoth (planetary), Zaraietos, Sabao, Onophis, Albaphalana, Azoth, Iao, and Bath-Menin-Hekastou. The complete lists are given in Denning and Phillips' *Mysteria Magica* (Llewellyn, 1986). Almost the whole system of the order—as well as a wealth of wisdom and good advice—is presented in this book and in *The Foundations of High Magick* (1991) and *The Sword and the Serpent* (1988).

The Aurum Solis is not the only organization that concerns itself with Greek and Gnostic ideas. Dr. Stephan A. Hoeller is head of the Gnostic Society of Los Angeles and a regionary bishop of the Ecclesia Gnostica (Gnostic church). He has written a number of books relating Gnosticism to Jungian psychology (e.g., *Jung and the Lost Gospels*, Quest Books, 1989) and is a regular contributor to the magazines *Gnosis* and *Quest*.

According to Hoeller, the Gnostic view is—and probably was—that it isn't the world that's imperfect, it's our distorted perceptions and ideas of it that are imperfect. This imperfect image of the world—which, not only through the limited nature of our perceptions, but also through choice and social conditioning, emphasizes certain phenomena and excludes others; sees things and events in a particularized, slanted way; and excludes the whole (or the fullness, *pleroma*) in its frequently necessary tendency to focus on the particular—is largely the creation of the ego (that is, the Demiurge). If you see the world through rose-colored glasses or become involved in the petty details of daily living, that is your Eden; the Archons have succeeded; their created world of illusion has seduced you away from your true destiny. The whole elaborate mythology of Gnosticism is an objectification or projection of events within the individual psyche (i.e., the mind). Of course, the same can be said for any mythology, including the Christian. It's just that some objectifications are more efficient or appropriate than others.

This imperfect way of seeing things also applies to the body. The flesh may be "evil," but it can also be sanctified and redeemed through Gnosis.

It is said in some of the Gnostic manuscripts that gnosis, when achieved, destroys the world created by the Demiurge. If you balk at the idea of the entire universe being snuffed out by mere knowledge, consider the idea that a false way of seeing the world—and therefore, the world in which you previously existed—can in fact be extinguished in an instant of illuminated understanding.

The ultimate goal of Jungian psychotherapy is integration of the whole personality or "individuation." This process includes coming to terms with your feminine or masculine side (if you are a man or a woman, respectively), the darker parts of yourself that you've banished as "not you," and the integrating, directive principle of your essential being—that is, your anima/animus, shadow, and Self. The ideal situation is identification with the Self, a goal identical to that of much mysticism, and realizing that the Self is the archetype of God—or, in mystical terms, that it is the spark of divinity with you—in Gnostic terms, the pneumatic soul. In Christian Gnosticism, Jesus Christ signifies the individuated person.

Interfering with this process or endeavor is not only the ego, the temporarily dominant part of your mind that thinks it's in charge, but also complexes and constellated but (usually) suppressed subpersonalities, not to mention the various faces you put on for various situations (at home, on the job, in a social situation, and so on). Such a face, or persona, is sometimes assumed consciously and sometimes automatically, unconsciously. In any event, identification with it certainly stands in the way of integration and identification with your true Self.

The correspondence between the Demiurge and the ego—particularly the inflated ego that denies the value of the subconscious mind and of intuition—and between the Archons and these other facets of the mind is fairly obvious. In order to enter the the fullness of the Pleroma, they must be defeated or circumvented by the experience of gnosis.

Greek ideas other than Gnosticism persist everywhere as well. Take a look at the trump entitled "The World" in the popular Rider-Waite Tarot deck. What do you see right away? *Mone* (the dancer balanced on one foot) and *Proodos* and *Epistrophe* (the two wands). This aspect is emphasized even more clearly in some other versions of this card. Of course, those who undertake to explain the symbolism don't use the Greek terms; they usually resort to something like "involution and evolution, the descent and ascent of the Tree of Life," but it's the same thing and it's a Neoplatonic idea. Aside from the question of the survival of Greek ideas in modern Tarot decks, Juliet Sharman-Burke, Liz Greene, and Tricia Newell go back to the roots with *The Mythic Tarot*—a deck based entirely on classical Greek mythology. In this deck, The Emperor is Zeus, Justice is Athene, and so on. The four suits (Wands, Swords, Cups, and Pentacles) are based on four classical Greek myth cycles—Jason and the Argonauts (Wands), Eros and Psyche (Cups), Orestes and the House of Atreus (Swords), and Daedalus, the architect and technician of Crete (Pentacles). Those who have studied the Tarot within the Western Hermetic Tradition may find some of their interpretations and symbolism somewhat askew—although the

Tarot Trump The World

selection of Pan as the Devil, as they explain it, is entirely appropriate. In any case, there is no Council of Nicea to say that only one set of ideas about the Tarot is correct and all others heretical. The authors do show an exceptional understanding of Greek myth.

Periodicals dealing with Greek Neo-Paganism include *Scroll of Oplontis* (P.O. Box 1036, Beloit, WI 53511), which, however, appears to emphasize the Roman aspect. *Gnosis* (P.O. Box 14217, San Francisco, CA 94114) frequently features articles on Gnosticism and Greek spirituality, although it covers the entire western esoteric tradition. Back issues are available. Greek rituals, or at least rituals dedicated to the Greek gods, frequently turn up in Pagan publications such as *Circle Network News* (Box 219, Mt. Horeb, WI 53572). The Holy Order of Wisdom (P.O. Box 7084, Santa Cruz, CA 95061-7084) is "dedicated to communicating and spreading the wisdom of the Spirit of Holy Sophia for the enlightenment, enrichment, peace and prosperity of all."

The western esoteric tradition is often referred to as hermetic. This term refers to Hermes, usually considered to be Hermes

Trismegistus, the Egyptian Thoth—but Hermes is a Greek god and even "Thoth" is the Greek version of the Egyptian god-name Tehuti or Djehuti.

Greek thought (classical, Hellenistic, Gnostic, and Neoplatonic) is thus plainly the major formative principle in modern occultist philosophy. Yes, the emphasis is usually on the cabala and often on Rosicrucianism, but you can scarcely read any book on the subject without seeing Plato and Plotinus on every page.

One frequently comes across ideas that were publicly presented by Plato purveyed as Great Secrets handed down through an oral tradition and only now proclaimed by the Hidden Masters as fit for dissemination (for example, that the planets are conscious beings). Gurus establish their reputations on little-known items of Greek philosophy that are perceived as their own unique and original thoughts. This is not to say, of course, that authentic guides resort to such divine deception.

Alternative spirituality has this in common with Christianity: It suffers from a poor reputation because of the confidence artists and lunatics that have associated themselves with it. However, an old Sufi saying states that counterfeit implies the existence of real gold. In this book, I hope I have provided at least a sketch of a map to the gold mines.

An Aurum Solis Ritual
The Setting of the Wards of Power

(Stand in the centre of the place of working, or as nearly the centre as the arrangement of the chamber will allow.)

i. Facing East, assume the Wand Posture. Vibrate EI

ii. Raise the arms at the sides, vibrate 'Η ΒΑΣΙΛΕΙΑ

iii. Touch the right shoulder with the left hand, vibrate ΚΑΙ 'Η ΔΥΝΑΜΙΣ

iv. Touch the left shoulder with the right hand, vibrate ΚΑΙ 'Η ΔΟΞΑ

v. Keeping the arms crossed, bow the head and vibrate ΕΙΣ ΤΟΥΣ ΑΙΟΝΑΣ

vi. Advance to the East. Trace the circle, returning to the East.

vii. Return to the centre. Facing East, vibrate:—
'Η ΠΕΛΕΙΑ ΚΑΙ 'Η 'ΥΓΡΑ
'Ο ΟΦΙΣ ΚΑΙ ΤΟ ΩΙΟΝ

viii. Facing East, make the Gesture *Cervus:* at the first point vibrate ΑΘΑΝΤΟΣ, at the second ΣΕΛΑΕ–ΓΕΝΕΤΗΣ.

ix. Turn to face North: make the Gesture, vibrating ΙΣΧΥΡΟΣ at the first point, and ΚΥΡΙΟΣ at the second point. [Note that *ischyros* is here used properly as an adjective—*ischyros kyrios* = "Mighty Lord."]

x. Face West: make the Gesture, vibrating ΙΣΧΥΡΟΣ then ΠΑΝΚΡΑΤΗΣ.

xi. Turn to face South. Make the Gesture, vibrating ΑΘΑΝΤΟΣ and ΘΕΟΣ.

xii. Face East. Assume the Wand Posture. Vibrate:—
ΓΑΙΑ ΚΑΙ 'Ο ΙΧΩΡ ΤΟΥ ΟΥΡΑΝΟΥ
Raise the arms to form a Tau, vibrate:—
TO THE EAST ΣΩΤΗΡ
TO THE SOUTH ΑΛΑΣΤΩΡ
TO THE WEST ΑΣΦΑΛΕΙΟΣ
TO THE NORTH ΑΜΥΝΤΩΡ

xiii. Repeat the Calyx, i to v.

(Commentary)

The Calyx is performed:

EI—*Thou Art* [not "Thine is"]
HE BASILEIA—*The Kingdom*
KAI HE DYNAMIS—*And the Power.*
KAI HE DOXA—*And the Glory.*
EIS TOUS AIONAS—*To the Ages.*

The operator advances to the East. He moves widdershins round the place of working, tracing the circle with his outstretched right hand. As he proceeds, he visualizes a silver mist which he is thus drawing round the limits of the chamber: when he links the circle in the East, the place of working is completely encompassed by this shimmering wall.

The operator returns to the centre. Facing East, he vibrates:—

HE PELEIA KAI HE HUGRA—*The Dove and the Waters*
HO OPHIS KAI TO OION—*The Serpent and the Egg*

He makes the Gesture Cervus: at the completion of the first point he visualizes a pentagram of brilliant light on his brow, framed by his hands.

Holding this in mind he vibrates **ATHANATOS.** The pentagram is flung forth with the second point of the Gesture, the operator vibrating **SELAE-GENETES:** as the pentagram is flung forth it is seen to diffuse as a burst of light into the shimmering mist-wall.

This procedure is repeated with the paired names **ISCHYROS** and **KYRIOS, ISCHYROS** and **PANKRATES, ATHANATOS** and **THEOS,** for the North, West, and South respectively.

The operator faces East. He assumes the Wand Posture and vibrates:—

GAIA KAI HO ICHOR TOU OURANOU
Earth and the Blood of Heaven.

He raises his arms to form a Tau, remaining thus throughout the fourfold invocation:—

Before him he visualizes a tall and slender form clad in a voluminous and billowing robe of yellow, heightened with traces of violet. While this figure is contemplated, a cool rushing of wind is to be felt as emanating from the East. (It awakens the hidden aspirations and wordless hopes which have lain dormant in the toils of sloth and of habitude. It sings to the inner ear of the potentialities of a life which reaches forth to spiritual heights.) When this image has been formulated, the operator vibrates **TO THE EAST SOTER.**

To the south he visualizes a lean muscular figure with an appearance of great strength, clad in a robe of brilliant red with changeful sparks of green, and standing amid flames. This figure holds in his right hand a wand of burnished copper. While this figure is contemplated, a sensation of powerful heat is to be felt as emanating from the South. (The fire from which this heat is generated is the fire of inspiration: there is in its power a kernel of inebriation too, as may be understood by recalling that Dionysus took birth from the all-consuming fire of Zeus. Nevertheless, although the nature of the Element is to be acknowledged, it is not to receive in this rite our inner submission to its power; but we salute its great Regent with veneration.) When this image has been formulated, the operator vibrates **TO THE SOUTH ALASTOR.**

To the West he visualizes a tall and powerful figure standing amid foaming turbulent waters, clad in a robe of blue merging into highlights of orange, and holding in his left hand a silver cup. While this figure is contemplated, the mighty surge of the sea-tides is imagined, pouring in successive waves from the West. (These waves are of the cold and shining waters which purify the intellect in their flood, healing it of unreason's fever and tempering it as steel is tempered.) When this image has been formulated, the operator vibrates **TO THE WEST ASPHALEIOS.**

To his left he visualizes a broad-shouldered placid figure, robed in indigo gleaming with flashes of pale gold, and standing upon wild grass studded with yellow flowers. In one hand the figure bears a golden orb, in the other a golden sickle. While this figure is contemplated, a feeling of great peace and stability is to be imagined. (The succession of the seasons wipes out or mitigates past errors, the innocence of the Golden Age ever await us in earth's renewal. Elemental Earth itself is the medium of nature's work: and the instinctual faculties of man find repose therein.) When this image has been formulated, the operator vibrates **TO THE NORTH AMYNTOR,**

The Calyx is repeated.

That is the conclusion of the ritual and commentary by Denning and Phillips, but a few words remain to be said. The Wand Posture is described thus:

The Wand Posture is a normal and well-balanced standing

position. The head is held erect, the shoulders are dropped back so that they are neither drooping nor held rigidly square. The arms hang by the sides with a slight natural curve at the elbow; the feet are placed side by side, the toes being turned neither in nor out.

If this posture is correctly maintained, it should be possible to take a step forward with either foot as required, without shifting the weight.

And the Gesture Cervus?

1. The Wand Posture is assumed.

2. Both hands are raised to the brow, so as to frame the center of the forehead in the space formed by conjoining thumb with thumb, forefinger with forefinger, palms facing forwards. (The two middle fingers will also touch.) This constitutes the first point of the Gesture; while this position is held, the first Word of Power is vibrated.

3. In one vigorous movement the hands are separated and flung forward, slightly apart and upward: the elbows should be straightened and the fingers slightly spread. The palms are still facing forwards. This position constitutes the second point of the Gesture. The second Word of Power should be forcefully uttered while this movement is being made. The arms are then lowered.

To round things out, *calyx* is the Greek word for cup or chalice; *cervus* is Latin and means a stag or deer.

Appendix

Isopsephos
The Enumeration of the Greek Alphabet

Actually, the Greek alphabet has been numbered in several ways. The simplest method was to number the letters consecutively, and this may have been intended by Homer when he headed his chapters with the letters of the Greek alphabet. On the other hand, this isn't very useful; the numbers don't go high enough. The 119th Psalm is "numbered" in this way by using Hebrew letters, but it is doubtful if the letters of the Hebrew alphabet were ever numbered 1 through 22 and used as numbers in this form. Even in Hebrew scripture, letters used as numbers go 1-9, 10-90, and 100-900 (using terminal forms of the letters to get beyond 400). Another Greek system was like Roman numerals—not really of much use to either the Greeks or the Romans.

The most useful and widely used system, which seems to have originated around 400 B.C., more or less copies the Hebrew/Phoenician system. Euclid, among others, made use of it in his mathematical writings around 300 B.C.

Greek ισοψηφος (isopsephos—literally, "equal stones," here meaning the calculation and comparison of the numerical values of words) was similar to the Hebrew gematria in that words that added up to the same number were thought to be related. This may sound like a fairly time-wasting game on the order of anagrams, but this game was played by many mystical writers—including those

197

who wrote the New Testament—and is therefore of some importance in understanding their writings.

Here, then, are the numerical values of the Greek letters
according to the so-called Pythagorean system:

α	alpha (a)—1	ν	nu (n)—50
β	beta (b)—2	ξ	xi (x)—60
γ	gamma (g)—3	ο	omicron (short o)—70
δ	delta (d)—4	π	pi (p)—80
ε	epsilon (short e)—5	ρ	rho (r, rh)—100
ζ	zeta (z)—7	σ, ς	sigma (s)—200
η	eta (long ē)—8	τ	tau (t)—300
θ	theta (th)—9	υ	upsilon (u)—400
ι	iota (i)—10	φ	phi (ph)—500
κ	kappa (k)—20	χ	chi (ch)—600
λ	lambda (l)—30	ψ	psi (ps)—700
μ	mu (m)—40	ω	omega (long ō)—800

Early Letters Later Used Only for Numbers:

F or ς Digamma (w) or Stau (st)—6
ϙ Qoppa (q)—90
ϡ Sampi (s)—900

Stau is sometimes called *stigma,* although, properly speaking,
stigma just means "a mark."

The following list of Greek names and words is by no means
comprehensive and does not take into account dialectical spelling
variations or case endings other than the nominative. The most
disappointing thing about it may be that there are in fact so few
actual correspondences. This phenomenon, which possibly occurs
because of the greater numerical range of Greek as opposed to
Hebrew (wherein correspondences abound), may be the reason that
Aleister Crowley regarded "the Greek qabalah" as essentially
"unsatisfactory." Those few correspondences that do crop up,
however, do tend to be meaningful. This listing is therefore
intended merely to form a basis for further study and investigation.

If you're interested in this phase of Greek mysticism, you will
probably want to add to this list from your own investigations. A
technique commonly used by those trying to "prove something" by

isopsephos is to use alternate case endings for a word, usually the genitive. Using this approach, any word ending in "os," for example, can be altered to the genitive case by changing the ending to "ou" and adding 200 to the enumeration of the word. Or you can change the ending to "on" for the accusative case and subtract 150. I don't recommend this sort of "fudging" in most instances, but it may have some validity in special cases—as, for example, when investigating a text.

Crowley planned a comprehensive dictionary of this sort (*Liber MCCLXIV: The Greek Qabalah*), but he never completed it nor got around to publishing it. Some of his notes for the book were published by the caliphate O.T.O. some time ago ("An. LXXIV e.n."), under the full title, but this publication was inscribed "The short form. Reconstructed from surviving index slips—with an Introduction and technical notes." However, this "book" is very incomplete and in some cases inaccurate.

The Thelemite implications of isopsephos, otherwise called "Greek gematria," have been and continue to be thoroughly explored by G. M. Kelly in *The Newaeon Newsletter* (P.O. Box 19210, Pittsburgh, PA 15213). Reading a few back numbers of this newsletter will enable you to expand this dictionary considerably, and not just as regards *The Book of the Law* and Thelema. Kelly has done invaluable work in this area—as, for example, with *The Odyssey*—and he knows what he's doing. He is a little unpopular with groups calling themselves the O.T.O. or A.A., primarily because he shows them little mercy in exposing their failings and pretensions.

In this list, there are a number of words beginning with the letter "h." There is no such letter in Greek, but some words beginning with vowels are designated with a diacritical mark to be preceded by "heavy breathing"—that is, the sound of "h." These words are usually transliterated with an initial h. The letter "h" also sometimes occurs after the letter "r" in transliteration, but it is not a separate letter; it's just that the letter "rho" is sometimes rendered as "rh." Greek also has no letter "y," but "y" is a standard transliteration the letter upsilon (υ).

Other conventions of Greek-English transliteration involve the substitution of "ae" for alpha iota (αι) and a simple "i" for the diphthong epsilon iota (ει), neither of which I have done here because they tend to confuse things. There's also the use of "oe" for omicron iota (οι) and "u" for omicron upsilon (ου). This practice seems to have been inherited from Latin, where there was some attempt to spell the words and names as they sounded in that language.

There's also the practice—which makes a lot better sense—of the phonetic rendering of a double gamma (γγ) as "ng," gamma xi (γξ) as "nx," and gamma kappa (γκ) as "nc" or "nk." Oh, yes—whenever you see a "c," it represents "k" (kappa)—another Latinism—except that "ch" represents the letter chi (χ). Of course, "ph" represents the letter phi (φ) and "ps" is psi (ψ). To further confuse matters, a terminal omicron sigma (ος) or even omicron upsilon sigma (ους) is often given in the Latin form "us," as, for example, in "Dionysus." This practice, however, no longer seems to be standard and I have accordingly avoided it.

In the first section of this list, where terms are listed alphabetically in transliterated Greek, every item is also spelled with the Greek letters so that you can detect variations from the English spelling and also verify the enumeration.

For purposes of isopsephos, by the way, an apparently acceptable practice is to substitute a value of 6 (stau) for the sigma-tau combination, normally 500. Words containing "st" are therefore given two values.

A note on pronunciation: Greek letters are pronounced more or less like their English equivalents, except that chi has the sound of the German or Scottish "ch" (as in "loch"). It's the vowels that are different, and the diphthongs aren't too obvious. The problem is complicated by the fact that classical Greek and modern Greek are very different on this score. Generally, alpha is ah, like a in father; epsilon is eh like e in pen; eta is like the English long a as in pair (although, in modern Greek, it's like long e as in Pete); iota can be either long or short (long, it's ee as in feet; short, it's like i in fit); omicron is like o in "not"; upsilon can also be either long or short and is pronounced like the German umlaut u or like the French u (try saying "eh" and "oo" at the same time; or, for the long upsilon, it's "ee" and "oo"); omega is o as in gnome.

Things really get involved when you get to diphthongs, so I am presenting a table of alternative pronunciations for these. Each diphthong is shown as it is (or was) pronounced in classical Greek, in modern-day Greek, and in the modern British pronunciation of classical Greek. For magical purposes, I recommend the classical pronunciation—however, this is ultimately a matter of personal preference.

Diphthong	Classical	Modern Greek	British
αι (ai)	*air*	*said*	*aisle*
ευ (au)	*sauerkraut*	*av* as in *have*	*sauerkraut*
ει (ei)	*veil*	*receive*	*height*
ευ (eu)	*feud*	*ev* as in *never*	*euphoria*
οι (oi)	*oil*	*ee* as in *feed*	*oil*
ου (ou)	*group*	*couple*	*out*
υι (ui)	*ew* as in *Dewey*	*suite*	*ew* as in *Dewey*

The list on the following pages contains three sections: Greek, English, and numerical to facilitate reference by any one of the three methods.

A List of Greek Words and Names
Along With Their Numerical Values

a-e-ē-i-o-u-ō (α-ε-η-ι-ο-υ-ω)—the seven vowels of the Greek alphabet, sometimes considered to be the true name of God—1294

Abaddon (Αβαδδων)—the angel of the abyss—862

Aberamentho (Αβεραμενθω)—mystery name of Jesus in the *Pistis Sophia*—1013

Abraam (Αβρααμ)—Abraham—145

Abraxas (Αβραξας)—a Gnostic name—365

abyssos (αβυσσος)—abyss, bottomless pit—1073

Achamoth (Αχαμωθ)—the fallen Sophia—1451

Achilles (Αχιλλευς)—1276

Adam (Αδαμ)—46

Adamas (Αδαμας)—a Gnostic entity ruling six aeons—247

adelphe (αδελφη)—sister—545

adelphos (αδελφος)—brother—810

aer (αηρ)—air—109

aetos (αετος)—eagle—576

Agamemnon (Αγαμεμνων)—990

agape (αγαπη)—love, "charity"—93

agape sou he prote (αγαπη σου 'η πρωτη)—your first love (Rev. 2:4)— 2059

Agathodaimon (Αγαθοδαιμων)—good spirit—989

agathos (αγαθος)—the Good—284

Ageratos (Αγηρατος)—unaging—the third aeon of the decad—683

Aglaia (Αγλαια)—an aspect of Leukothea—46

agoge (αγωγη)—spell; conduct, lifestyle—815

agreus (αγρευς)—hunter—709

Aiana (Αιανα)—an aspect of Leukothea—63

aigle (αιγλη)—brightness, splendor—52

Aigle Trisagia (Αιγλη Τρισαγια)—thrice–holy splendor—677

aigoceros (αιγοκερως)—goat-horned, Capricorn—1209

Aigyptos (Αιγυπτος)—Egypt—1064

aion (αιων)—aeon—861

aionios (αιωνιος)—eternal—1141

aionos (αιωνος)—aeons—1131

Aionos Kyrios (Αιωνος Κυριος)—lord of the ages—1931

aither (αιθηρ)—ether, the upper air—128

aitherios (αιθεριος)—heavenly, ethereal—405

aitherios sophia (αιθεριος σοφια)—ethereal wisdom (Philo); the heavenly Sophia —1186

Akephalos (Ακεφαλος)—the Bornless One—827

Akinetos (Ακινητος)—immovable—the 7th aeon of the decad—659

akrides (ακριδες)—locusts—340

akris (ακρις)—locust—331

Alastor (Αλαστωρ)—avenger, tormentor; He who forgets not, an avenging daemon; a protective entity in Aurum Solis rituals—1432 (or 938)

Albaphalara (Αλβαφαλαρα)—divine name associated with Venus by Aurum Solis —667

Aletheia (Αληθεια)—truth, the fourth aeon—64

alethes (αληθης)—true—256

Alethes Logos (Αληθης Λογος)—true word—629

algos (αλγος)—pain—304

alpha (αλφα)—the first letter of the alphabet (name spelled out)—532

ambrosia (αμβροσια)—the food of the gods—424

amen (αμην)—Hebrew, "so be it"—99

Amyntor (Αμυντωρ)—defender, avenger—1691

anastasis (αναστασις)—resurrection—963 (or 469)

Andromeda (Ανδρομεδη)—282

aner (ανηρ)—man (as opposed to woman)—159

angelos (αγγελος)—angel—312

Anthesterion (Ανθεστηριων)—the 8th month, around February—1533 (or 1039)

Anthropos (Ανθρωπος)—man, human being, the seventh aeon—1310

apeiron (απειρον)—boundless—316

to apeiron (το απειρον)—The Boundless (Ain Soph)—686

Aphrodite (Αφροδιτη)—goddess of love—993

aphron (αφρων)—fool—1451

aphros (αφρος)—foam—871

apocalypsis (αποκαλυψις)—apocalypse, revelation—1512

apolytrosis (απολυτρωσις)—redemption—2191

Apo pantos kakodaimonos (Απο παντος κακοδαιμονος)—Away, all evil spirits! —1408

Apollo (Απολλων)—god of music, poetry, and the sun—1061

Apollyon (Απολλυων)—1461

aporia (απορια)—bewilderment—262

apsinthos (αψινθος)—wormwood—1040

arche (αρχη)—beginning; government; empire—709

archon (αρχων)—leader, ruler, chief—1551

archiereia (αρχιερεια)—high priestess—832

archiereus (αρχιερευς)—high priest—1421

Ares (Αρης)—god of war—309

arete (αρετη)—virtue, excellence—414

Argeiphontes (Αργειφοντης)—swift-appearer or slayer of Argus (Hermes)—1247 arithmos (αριθμος)—number—430

arma (αρμα)—chariot—142

arnion (αρνιον)—lamb—281

arretos (αρρητος)—ineffable, unspeakable, a name of the first aeon—779

Artemis (Αρτεμις)—goddess of the moon and the hunt—656

aselgeia (ασελγεια)—lasciviousness—255

Asia (Ασια)—212

asphaleia (ασφαλεια)—steadiness, safety, security, truth—748

Asphaleios (Ασφαλειος)—The Securer; a protective entity in Aurum Solis rituals —1017

aster (αστηρ)—star—609 (or 115)

asteres (αστερες)—stars—811 (or 317)

athanatos (αθανατος)—undying—632

Athene (Αθηνη)—goddess of wisdom and warfare—76

Atlas (Ατλας)—a Titan; Pelasgian Moon god—532

atrapos (ατραπος)—path—752

Atropos (Ατραπος)—one of the three Fates—821

auge (αυγη)—bright light—412

augoeides (αυγοειδης)—higher genius—701

Autophytos (αυτοφυτος)—self-begotten—the 5th aeon of the decad—2241

Azoth (Αζωθ)—an alchemical term; divine name associated with Mercury by the Aurum Solis—817

Babylon (Βαβυλων)—1285

Babylon he megale (Βαβυλων 'η μεγαλη)—Babylon the great—1380

Bacchos (Βακχος)—893

Barbelo (Βαρβηλω)—a Gnostic goddess, regarded as the first emanation in the Apocryphon of John—943

basileia (βασιλεια)—kingdom—259

he basileia ('η βασιλεια)—the kingdom—267

basileia ton ouranon (βασιλεια των ουρανων)—kingdom of heaven—2880

he basileia ton ouranon ('η βασιλεια των ουρανων)—the kingdom of heaven—2888

Basilides (Βασιλειδες)—467

basileus (βασιλευς)—king—848

basileus basileon (βασιλευς βασιλεων)—King of Kings—1946

basilissa (βασιλισσα)—queen—654

Bath-Menin-Hekastou (Βαθ-Μενιν-'Εκαστου)—"universal Deep Mind," a divine name used by the Aurum Solis—1163 (or 669)

bdelugma (βδελυγμα)—abomination—485

bdelugma tes eremoseos (βδελυγμα τησ ερημωσεως)—abomination of desolation —3151

bebeloi (βεβηλοι)—profane (plural noun)—127

bebelos (βεβηλος)—profane, unholy—317

Beelzeboul (Βεελζεβουl)—Beelzebub—556

beta (βητα)—the second letter of the alphabet (name spelled out)—311

Bethle'em (Βηθλεεμ)—Bethlehem—99

biblios (βιβλιος)—book—324

bios (βιος)—life—282

Boedromion (Βοηδρομιων)—the 3rd month, around September—1154

bomos (βωμος)—altar, step, pedestal—1112

boopis (βοωπις)—ox-eyed—1162

boopis Hera (βοωπις 'Ηρα)—ox-eyed Hera—1271

boule (βουλη)—will, determination—510

Bythos (Βυθος)—depth, abyss, the first aeon—681

Calliope (Καλλιοπη)—Muse of Heroic Poetry—249

Calypso (Καλυψω)—1951

calyx (καλυξ)—cup, bud, shell—511

carcinos (καρκινος)—crab—471

Cerberus (Κερβερος)—502

chaos (χαος)—871

chaire (χαιρε)—hail!—716

chaire kecharitomene (χαιρε κεχαριτωμενη)—"Hail, thou that art highly favored"
  or "Hail, one full of grace" (Luke 1:28)—2655

chalix (χαλιξ)—pebble, small stone—701

charis (χαρις)—grace—911

Charites (Χαριτες)—Graces—1216

Charon (Χαρων)—ferryman of the dead—1551

chi (χι)—22nd letter of the alphabet (name spelled out)—610

cheimon (χειμων)—winter—1505

choros (χορος)—dance—1040

Chrestos (Χρηστος)—kind, propitious; the Great Just One, ruler of the 14th aeon in
  the *Book of the Great Logos*—1478 (or 984)

Christ (Χριστος)—1480 (or 986)

Christe eleison (Χριστε ελεισον)—Christ have mercy upon us—1585

chronos (χρονος)—time—1090

chthon (χθων)—earth—1459

Circe (Κιρκη)—158

Clio (Κλειω)—Muse of History—865

Clotho (Κλωθω)—one of the three Fates—1659

Coeus (Κοιος)—Pelasgian god of the planet Mercury—370

Cypris (Κυπρις)—the Cyprian (i.e., Aphrodite)—810

Dabid (Δαβιδ)—David—21

dadouchos (δαδουχος)—torch-bearer—1349

daimon (δαιμων)—divine being, lesser deity, spirit—905

Damater (Δαματηρ)—original Doric spelling of Demeter—454

Dauid (Δαυιδ)—David—419

deca (δεκα)—ten—30

deisidaimonia (δεισιδαιμονια)—superstition—415

delta (δελτα)—fourth letter of alphabet (name spelled out)—340

Demeter (Δημητηρ)—goddess of agriculture—468

Destaphiton (Δεσταφιτον)—a divine name used by the Aurum Solis—1440

diabolos (διαβολος)—devil—387

didymoi (διδυμοι)—twins—538

digamma (διγαμμα)—early letter of Greek alphabet later used only for numerical purposes (name spelled out)—99

dikaiosyne (δικαιοσυνη)—justice—773

Dione (Διονη or Διωνη)—Pelasgian goddess of the planet Mars; mother of Aphrodite—142 or 872

Dionysos (Διονυσος)—god of wine and divine intoxication—1004

Dios (Διος)—Zeus—284

dodeca (δωδεκα)—twelve—834

doxa (δοξα)—glory—135

drakon (δρακων)—dragon—975

dryas (δρυας)—dryad—705

dryades (δρυαδες)—dryads—714

duo (δυο)—two—474

dynamis (δυναμις)—power—705

ear (εαρ)—spring—106

ecclesia (εκκλησια)—church, assembly, the eighth aeon—294

ecclesiai (εκκλησιαι)—churches—304

ecstasis (εκστασις)—astonishment, trance—936 (or 442)

ego (εγω)—I—808

ego eimi (εγω ειμι)—I am—873

Ego eimi he hodos kai he aletheia kai he zoe (Εγω ειμι 'η 'οδος και 'η αληθεια και 'η ζωη)—I am the way and the truth and the life (John 14:6)—2182

ego tas kleis tou hadou kai tou thanatou (εγω τας κλεις του 'αδου και του θανατου)—I hold the keys of hell and death (Rev. 1:18)— 4451

eidos (ειδος)—form, idea—289

eis (εις)—one; in—215

Elaphebolion (Ελαφηβολιων)—the 9th month, around March—1506

Eleleth (Ελεληθ)—a luminary in Sethian Gnosticism—87

Eleusin (Ελευσιν)—another name for Eleusis—700

Eleusis (Ελευσις)—850

elpis (ελπις)—hope—325

Emmanuel (Ημμανουελ)—644

En (Εν)—the One—55

en arche (εν αρχη)—in the beginning—764

En arche en ho logos (Εν αρχη ην 'ο λογος)—In the beginning was the Word—1265

ennea (εννεα)—nine—111

Ennoia (Εννοια)—idea, a name of the second aeon—186

Enosichthon (Ενοσιχθων)—earth-shaker (Poseidon)—1794

En-To-Pan (Εν–Το–Παν)—"within the all," a divine name used in the Aurum Solis —556

eos (ηως)—dawn—1008

Ephesus (Εφεσος)—980

epistrophe (επιστροφη)—turning back, wheeling about—1273 or 779

epsilon (ε ψιλον)—fifth letter of the alphabet (spelled out)—865

Erato (Ερατω)—Muse of Lyric and Love Poetry—1206

Eris (Ερις)—goddess of discord—315

Eros (Ερως)—love—1105

este (εστε)—until, even to—510 (or 16)

eta (ητα)—seventh letter of the alphabet (name spelled out)—309

etos (ετος)—year—575

Eua (Ευα)—Eve—406

eucharis (ευχαρις)—graceful, lovely—1316

eucharistos (ευχαριστος)—thankful, pleasant, witty—1886 (or 1392)

eulogemene su en gynaizin (ευλογημενη συ εν γυναιζιν)—"Blessed art thou among women" (Luke 1:28)—1805

eulogemenos ho karpos tes koilias sou (ευλογημενος 'ο καρπος της κοιλιας σου) —"Blessed is the fruit of thy womb." (Luke 1:42)—2941

eulogia (ευλογια)—praise—519

Eurydice (Ευρυδικη)—947

Eurymedon (Ευρυμεδων)—Pelasgian god of the planet Jupiter—1804

Eurynome (Ευρυνομη)—supreme deity in Pelasgian system—1073

Euterpe (Ευτερπη)—Muse of Music—898

evangelon (ευαγγελον)—gospel—567

Gabriel (Γαβριηλ)—154

Gaia (Γαια)—the earth—15

Galilaia (Γαλιλαια)—Galilee—86

Gamelion (Γαμηλιων)—the 7th month, around January—942

gamma (γαμμα)—the third letter of the alphabet (name spelled out)—85

Ganymede (Γανυμηδης)—714

ge (γη)—earth, soil—11

Geenna (Γεεννα)—Gehenna (Valley of Hinnom)—114

glaukopis (γλαυκωπις)—bright-eyed—1544

glaukopis Athene (γλαυκωπις Αθηνη)—bright-eyed Athena—1620

glaux (γλαυξ)—owl—494

gnome (γνωμη)—thought, judgment, intelligence—901

gnosis (γνωσις)—knowledge—1263

gnostikos (γνωστικος)—gnostic—1653 (or 1159)

goes (γοης)—a howling; enchanter, wizard, juggler—281

goetia (γοητεια)—sorcery, witchcraft, delusion—397

Golgotha (Γολγοθα)—186

grammateis (γραμματεις)—Scribes—700

grammateus (γραμματευς)—scribe—1090

gyne (γυνη)—woman, wife—461

Hades ('Αδης)—god of the underworld—213

hagion pneuma ('αγιον πνευμα)—Holy Spirit—710

hagios ('αγιος)—holy—284

Hagios Athanatos ('Αγιος Αθανατος)—holy undying one—916

hai ('αι)—the (feminine plural nominative)—11

he ('η)—the (feminine singular nominative)—8

Hecate ('Εκατη)—334

hecatombe ('εκατομβη)—hecatomb, a sacrifice of 100 oxen—446

Hecatombion ('Εκατομβαιων)—the first month, about July, supposed to begin at the summer solstice—1299

hecaton ('εκατον)—a hundred—446

Hector ('Εκτωρ)—1225

Hedone ('Ηδονη)—joy, pleasure—the sixth aeon of the decad—140

hegemon ('ηγεμων)—guide, leader—906

heimarmene ('ειμαρμενη)—fate—259

hekas ('εκας)—far off, far from—226

Hekas! Hekas! Este bebeloi! ('Εκας! 'Εκας! Εστε βεβηλοι!)—Far off! Far off! Even to the profane!—1089 (or 595)

helios ('Ηλιος)—sun—318

hemera ('ημερα)—day—154

Henad ('Εναδ)—unity—60

hendeca ('ενδεκα)—eleven—85

henotes ('ενοτης)—unity—633

Hephaistos ('Ηφαιστος)—god of the forge—1289 (or 795)

hepta ('επτα)—seven—386

hepta ecclesiai ('επτα εκκλησιαι)—seven churches—690

Hera or Here ('Ηρα or 'Ηρη)—queen of Olympus—109 or 116

Heraklees ('Ηρακλεης)—Hercules—372

heremias ('ερημιας)—hermit—364

Hermes ('Ερμης()—353

Hermes Trismegistos ('Ερμης Τρισμεγιστος)—Thrice-Greatest Hermes—1791 (or 1297)

Herodes ('Ερωδης)—Herod—1120

heroes ('ηρωες)—heroes—1113

heros ('ηρως)—hero—1108

Hestia ('εστια)—goddess of home and hearth—516 (or 22)

hex ('εξ)—six—65

hierax ('ιεραξ)—hawk—176

hiereia ('ιερεια)—priestess—131

hiereus ('ιερευς)—priest—720

hieron ('ιερον)—temple—235

hierophantes ('ιεροφαντης)—initiating priest—1244

hieros ('ιερος)—holy, strong—385

hippos ('ιππος)—horse—440

ho ('ο)—the (masculine singular nominative)—70

hodos ('οδος)—way—344

he hodos kai he aletheia kai he zoe ('η 'οδος και 'η αληθεια και 'η ζωη)—the way and the truth and the life (John 14:6)—1309

hoi ('οι)—the (masculine plural nominative)—80

hora ('ωρα)—hour—901

Horaia ('Οραια)—also called Norea, daughter of Adam and Eve, a Gnostic redemptive figure—182

horos ('ορος)—limit—440

hubris ('υβρις)—pride—712

huios ('υιος)—son—680

huios tou anthropou ('υιος του ανθρωπου)—Son of Man—2960

huios tou theou ('υιος του θεου)—Son of God—1934

hyalos ('υαλος)—crystal, glass—701

hydor ('υδωρ)—water—1304

hydrochoos ('υδροχοος)—water carrier, Aquarius—1514

hypsistos ('υψιστος)—most high (noun)—1880

hyetos ('υετος)—rain—975

hygra ('υγρα)—waters—504

hyle ('υλη)—matter; forest—438

hyparxis ('υπαρξις)—subsistence, existence—851

Hyperion ('Υπεριον)—Pelasgian sun god; a name of Apollo—715

hypostasis ('υποστασις)—foundation, reality—1461

Iabraoth (Ιαβραωθ)—a Gnostic entity ruling six aeons—923

Iacchus (Ιακχος)—mystic name of Bacchus—901

Ialdabaoth (Ιαλδαβαωθ)—the demiurge—858

Iamblichus (Ιαμβλιχος)—963

Iao (Ιαω)—a divine name in Gnosticism, associated by Aurum Solis with the Moon —811

ichor (ιχωρ)—divine blood—1510

ichthyes (ιχθυες)—fishes—1224

ichthys (ιχθυς)—fish—1219

Ieou (Ιεου)—a Gnostic entity—485

io (ιω)—Oh!—810

Ioannes (Ιωαννης)—John—1119

Ioannes ho Baptistes (Ιωαννης 'ο Βαπτιστης)—John the Baptist—2290

Iordanes (Ιορδανης)—Jordan—443

Ioseph (Ιωσηφ)—Joseph—1518

iota (ιωτα)—ninth letter of the alphabet (name spelled out)—1111

Ioudas (Ιουδας)—Judas—685

ischyros (ισχυρος)—strong, mighty—1580

Isis (Ισις)—420

isopsephos (ισοψηφος)—equal numerical values of words—1758

Iunges (Ιυγγες)—a Gnostic name used by Aleister Crowley in the Star Ruby ritual —621

Jezebel (Ιεζαβηλ)—63

Jesus (Ιησους)—888

Jesus Christ (Ιησους Χριστος)—2368 (or 1874)

Kabiroi (Καβιροι)—the central figures of the Samothracian mysteries—213

kai (και)—and—31

kakodaimon (κακοδαιμων)—evil spirit; unhappy, wretched—1016

kakos (κακος)—evil—311

kallos (καλλος)—beauty—351

kalon (καλον)—beauty; wood; ship—171

kalos (καλος)—beautiful—321

kappa (καππα)—tenth letter of the alphabet (name spelled out)—182

karpos (καρπος)—fruit—471

keleusma (κελευσμα)—order, command—701

kerux (κηρυξ)—herald—588

kiloi (κιλοι)—thousand—140

kleides tou hadou kai tou thanatou (κλειδες του 'αδου και του θανατου)—keys of hell and death (Rev. 1:18)—3151 (plus "the," hai 'αι = 3162)

kleis (κλεις)—key—265

kleos (κλεος)—glory—325

koilia (κοιλια)—womb—141

Konx Om Pax (Κογξ Ομ Παξ)—Light in Extension—404

korax (κοραξ)—raven—251

kosmokrator (κοσμοκρατωρ)—ruler of the world—1721

kosmos (κοσμος)—world—600

kosmos noeros (κοσμος νοερος)—intellectual world—1095

kosmos noetos (κοσμος νοητος)—intelligible world—1298

kratos (κρατος)—strength, power, force—691

kreion (κρειων)—lord, master, ruler—985

krios (κριος)—ram—400

krisis (κρισις)—judgment—540

Kronos (Κρονος)—510

kteis (κτεις)—female pudenda—535

kyria (κυρια)—lady, mistress—531

kyrie eleison (κυριε ελεισον)—Lord have mercy upon us—905

kyrios (κυριος)—lord, master—800

ho kyrios meta sou ('ο κυριος μετα σου)—"The Lord is with thee" (Luke 1:28)—1886

Lachesis (Λαχεσις)—one of the three Fates—1046

lambda (λαμβδα)—eleventh letter of the alphabet (name spelled out)—78

lampros (λαμπρος)—bright, shining, splendid—521

lamprotes (λαμπροτης)—splendor—829

Lamprotesis (Λαμπροτησις)—Aurum Solis name for the eighth Sephira—1039

Laodicea (Λαοδικεια)—151

leon (λεων)—lion—885

Leucothea (Λευκοθεα)—the white goddess—540

lithos (λιθος)—stone—319

Logos (Λογος)—word, the fifth aeon—373

Loukas (Λουκας)—Luke—721

mageia (μαγεια)—magic—60

magos (μαγος)—magician—314

Maimakterion (Μαιμακτηριων)—the 5th month, around November—1380

Makaira (Μακαιρα)—blessed, happy—the tenth aeon of the decad—173

makarios (μακαριος)—blessed, happy—442

margarites (μαργαριτης)—pearl—763

Maria (Μαρια)—Mary—152

Maria he Magdalene (Μαρια 'η Μαγδαληνη)—Mary the Magdalene—305

Markos (Μαρκος)—Mark—431

mathetes (μαθητης)—disciple—566

Maththaios (Μαθθαιος)—Matthew—340

Matthaios (Ματθαιος)—Matthew—631

Melanotheos (Μελανοθεος)—the dark god; one of the chief deities of the Aurum Solis—480

Melchisedek (Μελχισεδεκ)—919

Melpomene (Μελπομενη)—Muse of Tragedy—328

men (μην)—month—98

Metageitnion (Μεταγειτνιων)—the 2nd month, around August—1574

metanoia (μετανοια)—repentance—477

meter (μητηρ)—mother—456

he meter ton pornon ('η μητηρ των πορνων)—the mother of harlots (Babylon) —2764

Metis (Μητις)—wisdom, skill; Pelasgian goddess of the planet Mercury; mother of Athene—558

Mithras (Μειθρας)—365

Mixis (Μιξις)—mixing, mingling—the second aeon of the decad—320

moly (μωλυ)—the herb given by Hermes to Odysseus to protect him from the magic of Circe—1270

monachoi (μοναχοι)—solitary ones, unified ones, pneumatics—841

mone (μονη)—abiding, remaining—168

Monogenes (Μονογενης)—only-begotten—the ninth aeon of the decad—496

morphe (μορφη)—shape, form—718

Mounichion (Μουνιχιων)—the 10th month, around April—2030

Mousa (Μουσα)—Muse—711

Mousai (Μουσαι)—Muses—721

mu (μυ)—twelfth letter of the alphabet (name spelled out)—440

myrioi (μυριοι)—ten thousand—630

mystagogos (μυσταγωγος)—priest of the mysteries—2017 (or 1523)

mysteria (μυστηρια)—mysteries—1059 (or 565)

mysterion (μυστηριον)—mystery—1178 (or 684)

mythos (μυθος)—talk, story—719

naias (ναιας)—naiad (water nymph)—262

naiades (ναιαδες)—naiads—271

naos (ναος)—temple, sanctuary, divine dwelling—321

Nazareth (Ναζαρεθ)—173

nephele (νεφελη)—cloud—598

nephelegereta (νεφεληγερετα)—cloud-gatherer—1012

nephelegereta Zeus (νεφεληγερετα Ζευς)—cloud-gatherer Zeus—1624

nereid (νηρηις)—376

nereids (νηρηιδος)—450

nike (νικη)—victory—88

nikos (νικος)—victory—350

noeros (νοερος)—intellectual—495

noetos (νοητος)—intelligible, perceptible—698

nomos (νομος)—law—430

Nous (Νους)—thought or mind, the third aeon—720

nu (νυ)—13th letter of the alphabet (name spelled out)—450

nymphe (νυμφη)—nymph—998

nyx (νυξ)—night—510

Oceanos (Ωκεανος)—ocean; Pelasgian god of the planet Venus—1146

octo (οκτω)—eight—1190

Odysseus (Οδυσσευς)—1479

Oedipus (Οιδιπους)—844

oion (ωιον)—egg—930

Olympus (Ολυμπος)—890

omega (ω μεγα)—24th and last letter of the alphabet (name spelled out)—849 omicron (ο μικρον)—15th letter of the alphabet (name spelled out)—360

omphalos (ομφαλος)—navel—911

Onnophris (Οννοφρις)—1780

Onophis (Ονοφις)—a divine name used by the Aurum Solis—900

Ophion (Οφιον)—consort of Eurynome—700

ophis (οφις)—serpent—780

opora (οπωρα)—autumn—1051

oros (ορος)—mountain, hill—440

Oros ton Elaion (Ορος των Ελαιων)—Mount of Olives—2486

Orpheus (Ορφευς)—1275

Oudeis erchetai pros ton Patera ei me di emou (Ουδεις ερχεται προς τον Πατερα ει μη δι εμου)—"No one cometh unto the Father, but by me" (John 14:6)—3659

Pallas (Παλλας)—342

Pallas Athene (Παλλας Αθηνη)—418

Pamphagos (Παμφαγος)—All-Devourer—895

Pan (Παν)—131

Pangenetira (Παγγενετειρα)—All-Mother—563

Pangenetes (Παγγενετης)—All-Begetter, All-Father—655

Pankrates (Πανκρατης)—an Aurum Solis divine name—760

Pantokrator (Παντοκρατωρ)—the almighty—1822

pantos psyche (παντος ψυχη)—Soul of the All, World Soul—2409

parakletos (παρακλητος)—Comforter, paraclete—810

parthenos (παρθενος)—maiden, virgin—515

pater (πατηρ)—father—489

pater humon ho en tois ouranois (πατηρ 'υμον 'ο εν τοις ουρανοις)—your father in the heavens—2655

pater mou ho en tois ouranois (πατηρ μου 'ο εν τοις ουρανοις) —my father in the heavens—2605

pater ho en tois ouranois (πατηρ 'ο εν τοις ουρανοις)—father in the heavens (i.e., father in heaven)—2095

patroos (πατρωος)—paternal—1551

Paulos (Παυλος)—Paul—781

pax (παξ)—hush!—141

Pelasgos (Πελασγος)—Pelasgians—589

peleia (πελεια)—dove—131

pente (πεντε)—five—440

Pergamos (Περγαμος)—499

peristera (περιστερα)—dove—801

Persephone (Περσεφονη)—goddess of spring and the underworld—1018

Perseus (Περσευς)—990

Petros (Πετρος)—Peter—755

phainolis (φαινολις)—light-bringing—871

phallos (φαλλος)—ritual image of creative force of nature—831

phanos (φανος)—light—821

phantasia (φαντασια)—appearance, imagination—1063

phantasma (φαντασμα)—phantom, apparition—1093

Pharisaioi (Φαρισαιοι)—Pharisees—902

phaos (φαος)—light—771

phi (φι)—21st letter of the alphabet (name spelled out)—510

Philadelphia (Φιλαδελφεια)—1096

philetor (φιλητωρ)—lover—1748

philetores (φιλητωρες)—lovers—1953

philia (φιλια)—love—551

phobos (φοβος)—fear—842

Phoebe (Φοιβη)—Pelasgian Moon goddess; a name of Artemis—590

Phoebus (Φοιβος)—bright, pure—852

Phoebus Apollo (Φοιβος Απολλων)—1913

phoenix (φοινιξ)—a Phoenician; purple—700

phos (φως)—light—1500

to phos en te skotia phainei (το φως εν τη σκοτια φαινει)—the light shineth in darkness (John 1:5)—3410

phos tes zoes (φως της ζωης)—light of life (John 8:12)—3023

phos to alethinon (φως το αληθινον)—the true light (John 1:9)—2098

phos tou kosmou (φως του κοσμου)—light of the world (John 8:12)—3070

phosphoros (φωσφορος)—bringing light, morning star—2440

photismos (φωτισμος)—enlightening—2120

phrenos (φρενος)—mind, soul, heart, or reason—925

physis (φυσις)—nature—1310

pi (πι)—16th letter of the alphabet (name spelled out)—90

Pilatos (Πιλατος)—Pilate—691

pistis (πιστις)—faith—800 (or 306)

Pistis Sophia (Πιστις Σοφια)—"faith-wisdom," a Gnostic document; also another name for Sophia—1581

plane (πλανη)—wandering, error—169

plasma (πλασμα)—image—352

pleroma (πληρωμα)—fullness—1059

Plotinus (Πλωτινος)—1540

pneuma (πνευμα)—spirit, breath—576

pneuma tes aletheias (πνευμα της αληθειας)—spirit of truth—1348 (plus "the," το—1718)

pneumaton (πνευματον)—spirits—996

poimen (ποιμην)—shepherd—258

Polyhymnia or Polymnia (Πολυ῾υμνια or Πολυμνια)—Muse of Sacred Lyric—1081 or 681 polymetis (πολυμητις)—of many counsels, of many wiles—1138

polymetis Odysseus (πολυμητις Οδυσσευς)—Odysseus of many counsels—2617

polytimos (πολυτιμος)—precious—1200

polytimos margarites (πολυτιμος μαργαριτης)—pearl of great price—1963

porne (πορνη)—prostitute, fornicatrix—308

Porphyry (Πορφυριος)—1530

Poseidon (Ποσειδων)—god of the sea—1219

Poseideon (Ποσειδεων)—the 6th month, around December—1224

Poseideon deuteros (Ποσειδεων δευτερος)—second Poseideon, an intercalary month used every eight years between Poseideon and Gamelion—2308

presbyteroi (πρεσβυτεροι)—elders—1272

presbyteros (πρεσβυτερος)—elder—1462

Priapus (Πριαπος)—541

proarche (προαρχη)—"before-beginning," a name of the first aeon—959

probaton (προβατον)—sheep—673

pronoia (προνοια)—foresight, providence—381

proodos (προοδος)—advance—594

propater (προπατηρ)—"before-father," a name of the first aeon—739

proton (πρωτον)—first (n.)—1440

to proton (το πρωτον)—The First—1770

protos (πρωτος)—first (adj.)—1550

protos theos (πρωτος θεος)—first God, "the one," the unmanifest (Plotinus)—1834

psephos (ψηφος)—stone, pebble—1478

psephos leukes (ψηφος λευκης)—white stone (Rev. 2:17)—2141

psi (ψι)—23rd letter of the alphabet (name spelled out)—710

psychopompos (ψυχοπομπος)—psychopomp, Hermes as guide of the dead—2310

Pyanopsion (Πυανοψιων)—the 4th month, around October—2161

pyr (πυρ)—fire—580

Pythagoras (Πυθαγορας)—864

qoppa (κοππα)—early letter of Greek alphabet later used only for numerical purposes (name spelled out)—251

rhabdos (ραβδος)—wand—377

Rhea (Ρεα)—Pelasgian goddess of the planet Saturn; wife of Kronos; mother of Zeus—106

Rheia (Ρεια) = Rhea—116

rho (ρω)—17th letter of the alphabet (name spelled out)—900

rhododactylos Eos (ροδοδακτυλοσ Ηως)—rosy-fingered dawn— 2277

rhomsaia (ρομσαια)—sword—422

rhomsaia distomos (ρομσαια διστομος)—two-edged sword—1316 (or 822)

Sabao (Σαβαω)—divine name associated with Mars by Aurum Solis—1004

Sabaoth (Σαβαωθ)—a Gnostic enity, styled "the Good"—1013

sampi (σαμπι)—early letter of Greek alphabet later used only for numerical purposes (name spelled out)—331

Sardis (Σαρδεις)—520

Satan (Σαταν)—552

Satanas (Σατανας)—753

Saul (Σαυλος)—901 (Hebrew ShAWL, 337)

scorpios (σκορπιος)—scorpion—750

seiriokautos (σειριοκαυτος)—scorched by the heat of Sirius—1386

ho Seirios ('ο Σειριος)—the scorching one, Sirius—665

Selae-Genetes (Σελαη-Γενετης)—Father of Light—815

selas (σελας)—brightness, light; fire, flame—436

Selene (Σεληνη)—the moon; goddess of the Moon—301

Seth (Σηθ)—217

Sige (Σιγη)—silence, stillness, the second aeon—221

sigma (σιγμα)—18th letter of the alphabet (name spelled out)—254

Simon (Σιμον)—370

Skirophorion (Σκιροφοριων)—the 12th month, around June—1930

skotia (σκοτια)—darkness—601

skotos (σκοτος)—darkness—860

Smyrna (Σμυρνα)—myrrh—791

Solomon (Σολομων)—1260

soma (σωμα)—body—1041

Sophia (Σοφια)—wisdom, a goddess or aeon—781

Sophia Achamoth (Σοφια Αχαμωθ)—the fallen Sophia—2232

soter (σωτηρ)—savior—1408

soteira (σωτειρα)—savior (feminine)—1416

sphragizo (σφραγιζω)—seal—1621

stau (σταυ)—early letter of Greek alphabet later used only for numerical purposes (name spelled out)—901 (or 407)

stauros (σταυρος)—cross—1271 (or 777)

stephanos (στεφανος)—crown—1326 (or 832)

stephanos asteron (στεφανος αστερων)—a crown of stars—2782 (or 2288)

stigma (στιγμα)—mark—554 (or 60)

sukea (συκεα)—fig tree—626 [contracted form = suke, συκη = 628]

symbola (συμβολα)—symbols—743

Synoches (Συνοχες)—a Chaldean name used by Aleister Crowley in the Star Ruby ritual—1525

synthemata (συνθηματα)—sympathetic objects—1009

ta (τα)—the (neuter plural nominative)—301

Tartarus (Ταρταρος)—hell—1072

tau (ταυ)—19th letter of the alphabet (name spelled out)—701

tauros (ταυρος)—bull—1071

telesmata (τελεσματα)—talismans—882

telesterion (τελεστηριov)—place of initiation—1078 (or 584)

telestike (τελεστικη)—invoking a god into an image—878 (or 384)

Teletarchai (Τελεταρχαι)—a Gnostic name used by Aleister Crowley in the Star Ruby ritual—1352

telete (τελετη)—initiation, celebration—648

Terpsichore (Τερψιχορη)—Muse of Dance and Choral Song—1893

tessara zoa (τεσσαρα ζωα)—four living creatures—1615

tessera (τεσσερα)—the holy symbol of the Aurum Solis—811

tettera (τεττερα)—four—1011

tesseres (τεσσερες)—four—1015

Tethys (Τηθυς)—Pelasgian goddess of the planet Venus—917

thalassa (θαλασσα)—sea—442

Thalia (Θαλεια)—Muse of Comedy and Pastoral Poetry—56

thanatos (θανατος)—death—631

Thargelion (Θαργηλιων)—the 11th month, around May—1011

thaumatourgia (θαυματουργια)—thaumaturgy; conjuring, juggling—1335

thea (θεα)—goddess—15

Theia (Θεια)—Pelasgian Sun goddess—25

theios (θειος)—divine—294

theios aner (θειος ανηρ)—"divine man"; i.e., a theurgist—453

Theios Nous (Θειος Νους)—divine mind—1014

thelema (θελημα)—will—93

themelios (θεμελιος)—foundation—369

Themis (Θεμις)—law, right; Pelasgian goddess of the planet Jupiter; goddess of justice—264

theologos (θεολογος)—theologian—457

theomantis (θεομαντις)—diviner, soothsayer—685

theos (θεος)—god—284

theos phos esti (θεος φως εστι)—God is light (I John 1:5)—2299 (or 1805)

theourgia (θεουργια)—theurgy; divine work, sacramental rite—598

therion (θηριov)—beast—247

theros (θερος)—summer—384

Theseus (Θησευς)—822

theta (θητα)—eighth letter of the alphabet (name spelled out)—318

thronos (θρονος)—throne—499

thumos (θυμος)—soul, thought, will, courage—719

Thyatira (Θυατειρα)—826

thygater (θυγατηρ)—daughter—821

thyra (θυρα)—door—510

thyrsos (θυρσος)—staff entwined with ivy and tipped with a pine cone, sacred to Dionysos—979

to (το)—the (neuter singular nominative)—370

to A kai to O (το Α και το Ω)—the Alpha and the Omega—1572

To Mega Therion (Το Μεγα Θηριον)—The Great Beast—666

toxon (τοξον)—bow—550

toxotes (τοξοτης)—bowman—1008

tragos (τραγος)—goat—674

tria (τρια)—three—411

trigonon (τριγωνον)—triangle—1383

tris (τρεις)—three—615

trismegistos (τρισμεγιστος)—thrice-greatest—1438 (or 944)

Troia (Τροια)—Troy—481

Typhon (Τυφων)—2050

Tyrana (Τυρανα)—a divine name used by the Aurum Solis—852

tyrannos (τυραννος)—tyrant—1171

upsilon (υ ψιλον)—20th letter of the alphabet (name spelled out)—1260

Urania (Ουρανια)—Muse of Astronomy; also a title of Aphrodite—632

Uranus (Ουρανος)—heaven—891

xi (ξι)—14th letter of the alphabet (name spelled out)—70

Zaraietos (Ζαραιητος)—divine name associated with Jupiter by Aurum Solis—697

zeta (ζητα)—sixth letter of the alphabet (name spelled out)—316

Zeus (Ζευς)—612

Zion (Ζιων)—867

zoa (ζωα)—living creatures—808

Zoe (Ζωη)—life, the sixth aeon, or the middle term of the triad of Nous—815

zygon (ζυγον)—yoke, balance—530

Index of English Words

For the way in which these words are spelled with Greek letters, see the previous section.

Calypso—Kalypso—1951
Capricorn—aigokeros—1209
chaos—871
chariot—arma—142
charity—agape—93
chief—archon—1551
church—ecclesia—294
churches—ecclesiai—304
Circe—158
cloud—nephele—598
cloud-gatherer—nephelegereta—1012
Comforter—parakletos—810
command (n.)—keleusma—701
cross—stauros—1271 (or 777)
crown—stephanos—1326 (or 832)
a crown of stars—stephanos asteron—2782 (2288)
crystal—hyalos—701
cup—calyx—511
dance—choros—1040
darkness—skotia—601; skotos—860
daughter—thygater—821
dawn—eos—1008
day—hemera—154
death—thanatos—631
defender—amyntor—1691
depth—bythos—681
devil—diabolos—387
disciple—mathetes—566
divine—theios—294
diviner—theomantis—685
door—thyra—510
dove—peleia—131; peristera—801
dragon—drakon—975
eagle—aetos—576
earth—chthon—1459; Gaia—15; ge—11
earth-shaker (Poseidon)—Enosichthon—1794
egg—oion—930
Egypt—Aigyptos—1064
eight—octo—1190
elder—presbyteros—1462
elders—presbyteroi—1272
eleven—hendeka—85

error—plane—169

eternal—aionios—1141

ether—aither—128

evil—kakos—311

evil spirit—kakodaimon—1016

fantasy—phantasia—1063

fate—haimarmene—255

father—pater—489

father in heaven—pater ho en tois ouranois—2095 [my father in heaven—pater mou ho...—2665] [your father in heaven—pater humon ho...—2655]

fear—phobos—842

fig tree—sukea—626 (contracted form = suke = 628)

fire—pyr—580; selas—436

first (adj.)—protos—1550

first (n.)—proton—1400

fish—ichthys—1219

fishes—ichthyes—1224

foam—aphros—871

fool—aphron—1451

form—eidos—289; morphe—718

foundation—hypostasis—1461; themelios—369

four—tesseres—1015; tettera—1011

four living creatures—tessara zoa—1615

fruit—karpos—471

fullness—pleroma—1059

glory—doxa—135; kleos—325

goat—tragos—674

goat-horned—aigokeros—1209

god—theos—284

God is light (I John 1:5)—theos phos esti—2299 (or 1805)

the Good—agathos—284

gospel—evangelon—567

grace—charis—911

graceful—eucharis—1316

Graces—Charites—1216

The Great Beast—to mega therion—666

guide—hegemon—906

hail!—chaire—716

"Hail, one full of grace" (or "Hail, thou that art highly favored")—chaire kecharitomene—2655

happy—makaira—173; makarios—442

hawk—hierax—176

heaven—ouranos—891
heavenly—aitherios—405
herald—kerux—588
hermit—heremias—364
hero—heros—1108
heroes—heroes—1113
high priest—archiereus—1421
high priestess—archiereia—832
holy—hagios—284; hieros—385
Holy Spirit—hagion pneuma—710
hope—elpis—325
horse—hippos—440
hour—hora—901
hundred—hekaton—446
hunter—agreus—709
I—ego—808
I am—ego eimi—873
I am the way and the truth and the life (John 14:6)—Ego eimi he hodos kai he aletheia kai he zoe—2182
I hold the keys of hell and death (Rev. 1:18)—ego tas kleis tou hadou kai tou thanatou—4451
idea—eidos—289; ennoia—186
image—plasma—352
imagination—phantasia—1063
in the beginning—en arche—764
In the beginning was the Word—en arche en ho Logos—1265
ineffable—arretos—779
initiation—telete—648
intellectual—noeros—495
intellectual world—kosmos noeros—1095
intelligible—noetos—698
intelligible world—kosmos noetos—1298
intelligence—gnome—901
John—Ioannes—1119
John the Baptist—Ioannes ho Baptistes—2290
joy—hedone—140
Judas—Ioudas—685
judgment—gnome—901; krisis—540
justice—dikaiosyne—773
key—kleis—265
keys of hell and death—kleidos tou hadou kai tou thanatou—3151 (plus "the," hai = 3162)

king—basileus—848
King of Kings—basileus basileon—1946
kingdom—basileia—259 [plus "the" (he) = 267]
kingdom of heaven—basileia ton ouranon—2880 [plus "the" (he) = 2888]
lady (fem. of lord)—kyria—531
lamb—arnion—281
lasciviousness—aselgeia—255
law—nomos—430; themis—264
leader—archon—1551
life—bios—282; zoe—815
light—phanos—821; phaos—771; phos—1500; selas—436
light of life (John 8:12)—phos tes zoes—3023
light of the world (John 8:12)—phos tou kosmou—3070
light shineth in darkness, the (John 1:5)—to phos en te skotia phainei—3410
light, the true (John 1:9)—phos to alethinon—2098
light–bringing—phainolis—871
limit—horos—440
limitless—apeiron—316
lion—leon—885
living creatures—zoa—808
locust—akris—331
locusts—akrides—340
lord—kreion—985; kyrios—800
"The Lord is with thee"—ho kyrios meta sou—1886
love—agape—93; eros—1105; philia—551
lover—philetor—1748
lovers—philetores—1953
lovely—eucharis—1316
magic—goetia—397; mageia—60
magician—goes—281; magos—314; theios aner—453
maiden—parthenos—515
man (human being)—anthropos—1310
man (as opposed to woman)—aner—159
mark—stigma—554 (or 60)
master—kreion—985
matter—hyle—438
mind—nous—720
month—men—98
moon—Selene—301
most high (n.)—hypsistos—1880
mother—meter—456
Mount of Olives—Oros ton Elaion—2486

mountain—oros—440
Muse—Mousa—711
Muses—Mousai—721
mystery—mysterion—1178 (or 684)
mysteries—mysteria—1059 (or 565)
nature—physis—1310
navel—omphalos—911
night—nyx—510
nine—ennea—111
No one cometh unto the Father, but by me (John 14:6)—Oudeis erchetai pros ton
    Patera ei me di emou—3659
one—eis—215; en—55
only–begotten—monogenes—496
owl—glaux—494
ox–eyed—boopis—1162
pain—algos—304
path—atrapos—752
pearl—margarites—763
pearl beyond price—margarites polytimos—1963
phantom—phantasma—1093
power—dynamis—705; kratos—691
praise—eulogia—519
pride—hybris—712
priest—hiereus—720; mystagogos—2017 (or 1523)
priestess—hiereia—131
profane—bebelos—317
prostitute—porne—308
providence—pronoea—381
psychopomp—psychopompos—2310
queen—basilissa—654
rain—hyetos—975
raven—korax—251
redemption—apolytrosis—2191
repentance—metanoia—477
resurrection—anastasis—963 (or 469)
ruler—archon—1551; kreion—985
savior—soter—1408
savior (feminine)—soteira—1416
scorpion—skorpios—750
scribe—grammateus—1090
Scribes—grammateis—700
sea—thalassa—442

seal—sphragizo—1621
security—asphaleia—748
serpent—ophis—780
seven—hepta—386
seven churches—hepta ecclesiai—690
shape—morphe—718
sheep—probaton—673
shepherd—poimen—258
ship—kalon—171
silence—sige—221
Sirius—ho Seirios—665
sister—adelphe—548
six—hex—65
son—huios—680
Son of God—huios tou theou—1934
Son of Man—huios tou anthropou—2960
spell—agoge—815
spirit—daimon—905; pneuma—576
spirit of truth—pneuma tes alethaias—1348 (plus "the"—to—1718)
spirits—pneumaton—996
spring—ear—106
star—aster—609 (or 115)
stars—asteres—811 (or 317)
stone—chalix—701; lithos—319; psephos—1478
story—mythos—719
strength—kratos—691
strong—ischyros—1580
summer—theros—384
sun—helios—318
superstition—deisidaimonia—415
sword—rhomsaia—752
temple—hieron—235; naos—321
ten—deka—30
ten thousand—myrioi—630
thankful—eucharistos—1886 (or 1392)
thaumaturgy—thaymatourgia—1335
the (nominative case) –

	Masculine	**Feminine**	**Neuter**
Singular	ho—70	he—8	to—370
Plural	hoi—80	hai—11	ta—301

theologian—theologos—457

theurgist—theios aner—453
theurgy—theourgia—598
throne—thronos—499
thought—ennoia—186; gnome—901; nous—720
thousand—kiloi—140
three—tris—615; tria—411
time—chronos—1090
torch-bearer—dadouchos—1349
tormentor—alastoros—972 (or 478)
trance—ekstatis—936 (or 442)
triangle—trigonon—1383
true—alethes—256
truth—alethia—64; asphaleia—748
twelve—dodeka—834
two—duo—474
tyrant—tyrannos—1171
undying—athanatos—632
unity—Henad—60; henotes—633
unspeakable—arretos—779
victory—nike—88; nikos—350
virgin—parthenos—515
virtue—arete—414
wand—rhabdos—377
water—hydor—1304
water carrier—hydrochoos—1514
waters—hygra—504
way—hodos—344
the way and the truth and the life (John 14:6)—he hodos kai he aletheia kai he
    zoe—1309
wife—gyne—461
will—boule, 510; thelema—93
winter—cheimon—1505
wisdom—sophia—781
woman—gyne—461
womb—koilia—141
word—logos—373
wormwood—apsinthos—1040
world—kosmos—600
World Soul—pantos psyche—2409
year—etos—575

Numerical Listing

For the Greek spelling of these words and names, see the first section of this appendix, "A List of Greek Words and Names."

1—a (alpha)
2—b (beta)
3—g (gamma)
4—d (delta)
5—short e (epsilon)
6—st (stau) or w (digamma)—early letters of Greek alphabet later used only for numerical purposes
7—z (zeta)
8—long e (eta); he—the (fem. sing. nom.)
9—th (theta)
10—i (iota)
11—ge—earth, soil; hai—the (fem. pl. nom.)
15—Gaia—the earth; thea—goddess
16—este (st = 6)—until, even to
20—k (kappa)
21—Dabid (David)
22—Hestia (st = 6)
25—Theia
30—deca—ten; kai—and; l (lambda)
40—m (mu)
46—Adam; Aglaia—an aspect of Leukothea
50—n (nu)
52—aigle—brightness
53—Aiama—an aspect of Leukothea
55—En—the One
56—Thalia—Muse of Comedy
60—Henad—unity; mageia—magic; stigma (st = 6)—mark; x (xi)
63—Aiana; Iezabel (Jezebel)
64—Aletheia—truth
65—hex—six
70—ho—the (masc. sing. nom.); short o (omicron); xi (name spelled out)
76—Athene
78—lambda (name spelled out)
80—hoi—the (masc. pl. nom.); p (pi)
85—gamma (name spelled out); hendeca—eleven

86—Galilaia—Galilee

87—Eleleth

88—nike—victory

90—pi (name spelled out); q (qoppa)—early letter of Greek alphabet later used only for numerical purposes

93—agape—love; thelema—will

98—men—month

99—amen; Bethleem—Bethlehem; digamma—early letter of Greek alphabet later used only for numerical purposes (name spelled out)

100—r (rho)

106—ear—spring; Rhea

109—Hera; aer—air

111—ennea—nine

114—Geenna—Gehenna

115—aster (st = 6)—star

116—Here (Hera); Rheia (Rhea)

127—bebeloi—profane (pl.)

128—aither—ether

131—hiereia—priestess; Pan; peleia—dove

135—doxa—glory

140—Hedone—joy, pleasure—the sixth aeon of the decade; kiloi—thousand

141—koilia—womb; pax—hush!

142—arma—chariot; Dione

145—Abraam—Abraham

151—Laodicea

152—Mary (Maria)

154—Gabriel; hemera—day

158—Circe

159—aner—man

168—mone—abiding

169—plane—error

171—kalon—beauty; ship; wood

173—Makaira—blessed, happy—the tenth aeon of the decad; Nazareth

176—hierax—hawk

182—Horaia; kappa (name spelled out)

186—ennoia—idea; Golgotha

200—s (sigma)

212—Asia

213—Hades; Kabiroi (in the Samothracian mysteries)

215—eis—one

217—Seth

221—Sige—silence, stillness

226—hekas—far off, far from

235—hieron—temple

247—Adamas; therion—beast

249—Calliope—Muse of Heroic Poetry

251—korax—raven; qoppa—early letter of Greek alphabet later used only for numerical urposes (name spelled out)

254—sigma (name spelled out)

255—aselgeia—lasciviousness

256—alethes—true

258—poimen—shepherd

259—basileia—kingdom; heimarmene—fate

262—aporia—bewilderment; naias—naiad

264—Themis—law, right

265—kleis—key

267—he basileia—the kingdom

271—naiades—naiads

281—arnion—lamb; goes—enchanter, wizard, juggler

282—Andromede; bios—life

284—agathos—the Good; Dios—Zeus; hagios—holy; theos—god

289—eidos—form, idea

294—ecclesia—church, assembly; theios—divine

300—t (tau)

301—Selene—moon; ta—the (neu. pl. nom.)

304—algos—pain; ecclesiai—churches

305—Maria he Magdalene

306—pistis (st = 6)—faith

308—porne—prostitute

309—Ares; eta (name spelled out)

311—beta (name spelled out); kakos—evil

312—angelos—angel

314—magos—magician

315—Eris, goddess of discord

316—apeiron—boundless; zeta (name spelled out)

317—asteres (st = 6)—stars; bebelos—profane

318—helios—sun; theta (name spelled out)

319—lithos—stone

320—Mixis—mixing, mingling—the second aeon of the decad

321—kalos—beautiful; naos—temple, sanctuary

324—biblios—book

325—elpis—hope; kleos—glory

328—Melpomene—Muse of Tragedy

331—akris—locust; sampi—early letter of Greek alphabet later used only for numerical purposes (name spelled out)

334—Hecate

340—akrides—locusts; delta (name spelled out); Maththaios (Matthew)

342—Pallas

344—hodos—way

350—nikos—victory

351—kallos—beauty

352—plasma—image

353—Hermes

360—omicron (name spelled out)

364—heremias—hermit

365—Abraxas; Mithras

369—themelios—foundation

370—Koios; Simon; to—the (neu. sing. nom.)

372—Heraklees

373—Logos—word

376—nereid (nereis)

377—rhabdos—wand

381—pronoea—providence

384—theros—summer; telestike (st = 6)—invoking a god into an image

385—hieros—holy, strong

386—hepta—seven

387—diabolos—devil

397—goetia—sorcery, witchcraft, delusion

400—Krios—ram; u (upsilon)

404—Konx Om Pax—Light in Extension

405—aitherios—heavenly, ethereal

406—Eua—Eve

407—stau (st—6)—early letter of Greek alphabet later used only for numerical purposes (name spelled out)

411—tria—three

412—auge—bright light

414—arete—virtue, excellence

415—deisidaimonia—superstition

418—Pallas Athene

419—Dauid (David)

420—Isis

422—rhomsaia—sword

424—ambrosia

430—nomos—law

431—Markos (Mark)

436—selas—brightness, light; fire, flame

438—hyle—matter

440—hippos—horse; horos—limit; oros—mountain; pente—five; mu (name spelled out)

442—ecstasis (st = 6)—trance; makarios—blessed, happy; thalassa—sea

443—Iordanes—Jordan

446—hectaombe—hecatomb; hecaton—a hundred

450—nereids (nereidos); nu (name spelled out)

453—theios aner—divine man, theurgist

454—Damater—original Doric spelling of Demeter

456—meter—mother

457—theologos—theologian

461—gyne—woman

467—Basilides

468—Demeter

469—anastatis (st = 6)—resurrection

471—carcinos—crab; karpos—fruit

474—duo—two

477—metanoia—repentance

478—alastoros (st = 6)—avenger, tormenter

480—Melanotheos—the dark god

481—Troia—Troy

485—bdelugma—abomination; Ieou

489—pater—father

494—glaux—owl

495—noeros—intellectual

496—Monogenes—only-begotten—the eighth aeon of the decad

499—Pergamos; thronos—throne

500—ph (phi)

502—Cerberus

504—hygra—waters

510—boule—will; este—until, even to; Kronos; nyx—night; phi (name spelled out); thyra—door

511—calyx—cup, bud, shell

515—parthenos—maiden, virgin

516—Hestia

519—eulogia—praise

520—Sardis

521—lampros—bright, shining, splendid

530—zygon—yoke, balance

531—kyria—lady, mistress

532—alpha (name spelled out); Atlas

535—kteis—female pudenda
538—didymoi—twins
540—krisis—judgment; Leukothea—the white goddess
541—Priapus
545—adelphe—sister
550—toxon—bow
551—philia—love
552—Satan
554—stigma—mark
556—Beelzeboul—Beelzebub; En-To-Pan—"within the all" or "One, the All," a divine name
558—Metis—wisdom, skill
563—Pangenetira—All-Mother
565—mysteria (st = 6)—mysteries
566—mathetes—disciple
567—evangelon—gospel
575—etos—year
576—aetos—eagle; pneuma—spirit
580—pyr—fire
584—telesterion (st = 6)—place of initiation
588—kerux—herald
589—Pelasgos—Pelasgians
590—Phoebe (Artemis)
594—proodos—advance, going forth
595—Hekas! Hekas! Este bebeloi! (st = 6)
598—nephele—cloud; theourgia—theurgy
600—ch (chi); kosmos—world
601—skotia—darkness
609—aster—star
610—chi (name spelled out)
612—Zeus
615—tris—three
621—Iunges
626—sukea—fig tree
628—suke—fig tree
629—Alethes Logos—true word
630—myrioi—ten thousand
631—Matthaios (Matthew); thanatos—death
632—athanatos—undying; Ourania—Muse of Astronomy; Aphrodite
633—henotes—union
644—Emmanuel
648—telete—initiation

654—basilissa—queen
655—Pangenetes—All-Begetter
656—Artemis
659—Akinetos—immovable—the seventh aeon of the decad
665—ho Seirios—Sirius
666—to mega therion—The Great Beast
667—Albaphalara
669—Bath-Menin-Hekastou
673—probaton—sheep
674—tragos—goat
677—Aigle Trisagia—thrice-holy splendor
680—huios—son
681—Bythos—depth, abyss; Polymnia—Muse of Sacred Lyric
683—Ageratos—unaging—the third aeon of the decad
684—mysterion (st = 6)—mystery
685—Ioudas—Judas; theomantis—diviner, soothsayer
686—to apeiron—The Boundless
690—hepta ecclesiai—seven churches
691—kratos—strength, power, force; Pilatos—Pilate
697—Zaraietos, divine name associated with Jupiter
698—noetos—intelligible, perceptible
700—Eleusin—Eleusis; grammateis—Scribes; Ophion; phoenix; ps (psi)
701—augoeides—higher genius; chalix—pebble; hyalos—crystal, glass; keleusma
    —command; tau (name spelled out)
705—dryad (dryas); dynamis—power
709—agreus—hunter; arche—beginning
710—hagios pneuma—Holy Spirit; psi (name spelled out)
711—Mousa—Muse
712—hybris—pride
714—dryads (dryades); Ganymedes
715—Hyperion
716—chaire—hail!
718—morphe—shape, form
719—mythos—talk, story; thumos—soul, thought, will, courage
720—hiereus—priest; Nous—thought or mind
721—Lukas (Luke); Mousai—Muses
739—propater—"before-father"
743—symbola—symbols
748—asphaleia—security
750—scorpios—scorpion
752—atrapos—path
753—Satanas

755—Petros—Peter

760—Pankrates

763—margarites—pearl

764—en arche—in the beginning

771—phaos—light

773—dikaiosyne—justice

777—stauros (st = 6)—cross

779—arretos—ineffable, unspeakable; epistrophe (st = 6)—wheeling about, turning back

780—ophis—serpent

781—Paulos (Paul); Sophia—wisdom

791—Smyrna

795—Hephaistos (st = 6)

800—kyrios—lord, master; o (omega); pistis—faith

801—α + ω (alpha and omega); peristera—dove

808—ego—I; zoa—living creatures

810—adelphos—brother; Io—oh!; Kypris—the Cyprian (Aphrodite); parakletos —Comforter

811—Iao; tessera (holy symbol in Aurum Solis); asteres—stars

815—agoge—spell; Selae-Genetes—father of light; Zoe—life

817—Azoth

821—Atropos; phanos—light; thygater—daughter

822—rhomsaia distomos (st = 6)—two-edged sword; Theseus

826—Thyatira

827—Akephalos—the Bornless One

829—lamprotes—splendor

831—phallos—ritual image of generation

832—archiereia—high priestess; stephanos (st = 6)—crown

834—dodeca—twelve

841—monachoi—solitary ones

842—phobos—fear

844—Oedipus

848—basileus—king

849—omega (name spelled out)

850—Eleusis

851—hyparxis—subsistence, existence

852—Phoebus—bright, pure; Tyrana—a divine name used by the Aurum Solis

858—Ialdabaoth—the demiurge

860—skotos—darkness

861—aion—aeon

862—Abaddon—the angel of the abyss

864—Pythagoras

865—epsilon (name spelled out); Clio—Muse of History

867—Zion

871—aphros—foam; chaos; phainolis—light-bringing

872—Dione

873—ego eimi—I am

878—telestike—invoking a god into an image

882—telesmata—telesmans

885—leon—lion

888—Iesous—Jesus

890—Olympus

891—Uranus—heaven

893—Bacchos

895—Pamphagos—All-Devourer

898—Euterpe—Muse of Music

900—Onophis—divine name used by the Aurum Solis; rho (name spelled out); s (sampi)—early letter of Greek alphabet later used only for numerical purposes

901—gnome—thought, judgment, intelligence; hora—hour; Iacchos; Saulos (Saul); stau—early letter of Greek alphabet later used only for numerical purposes (name spelled out)

902—Pharisaioi—Pharisees

905—daimon—divine being, lesser deity, spirit; kyrie eleison—Lord have mercy upon us

906—hegemon—guide, leader

911—charis—grace; omphalos—navel

916—Hagios Athanatos—holy undying one

917—Tethys

919—Melchisedek

923—Iabraoth—a Gnostic entity

925—phrenos—mind, soul, heart, reason

930—oion—egg

936—ecstasis—astonishment, trance

938—Alastor (st = 6)

942—Gamelion—the 7th month

943—Barbelo—a Gnostic entity

944—trismegistos (st = 6)—thrice-greatest

946—Destaphiton

947—Eurydice

959—proarche—"before-beginning"

963—anastasis—resurrection

967—Iamblichus

972—alastoros—avenger, tormentor

975—drakon—dragon; hyetos—rain

979—thyrsos
980—Ephesus
984—Chrestos (st = 6)—the Great Just One
985—kreion—lord, master, ruler
986—Christos (st = 6)—Christ, useful, serviceable
989—Agathodaimon—good spirit
990—Agamemnon; Perseus
993—Aphrodite
996—pneumaton—spirits
998—nymphe—nymph
1004—Dionysos; Sabao—divine name associated with Mars by Aurum Solis
1008—eos—dawn; toxotes—bowman
1009—synthemata—sympathetic objects
1011—tettera—four; Thargelion—the 11th month
1012—nephelegereta—cloud-gatherer
1013—Aberamentho—mystery name of Jesus; Sabaoth (the Good)—a Gnostic entity
1014—Theios Nous—divine mind
1015—tessares—four
1016—kakodaimon—evil spirit; unhappy, wretched
1017—Asphaleios—the securer
1018—Persephone
1039—Anthesterion (st = 6)—the 8th month; Lamprotesis
1040—apsinthos—wormwood; choros—dance
1041—soma—body
1046—Lachesis
1051—opora—autumn
1059—mysteria—mysteries; pleroma—fullness
1061—Apollon (Apollo)
1063—phantasia—appearance, imagination
1064—Aigyptos—Egypt
1071—tauros—bull
1072—Tartaros—Tartarus (hell)
1073—abyssos—abyss, bottomless pit; Eurynome
1078—telesterion
1081—Polyhymnia—Muse of Sacred Lyric
1087—Pistis-Sophia (st = 6)—faith-wisdom
1089—Hekas! Hekas! Este bebeloi!
1090—chronos—time; grammateus—scribe
1093—phantasma—phantom
1095—kosmos noeros—intellectual world
1096—Philadelphia

1105—eros—love

1108—heros—hero

1111—iota (name spelled out)

1112—bomos—altar

1113—heroes—heroes

1119—Ioannes—John

1120—Herodes—Herod

1131—aionos—aeons

1138—polymetis—of many counsels

1141—aionios—eternal

1146—Oceanos

1154—Boedromion—the 3rd month

1159—gnostikos (st = 6)—gnostic

1162—boopis—ox-eyed

1163—Bath-Menin-Hekastou—"universal Deep Mind," a divine name used by the Aurum Solis

1171—tyrannos—tyrant

1178—mysterion—mystery

1186—aitherios sophia—heavenly wisdom

1190—octo—eight

1200—polytimos—precious, beyond price

1206—Erato—Muse of Love Poetry

1209—aigoceros—goat-horned (Capricorn)

1216—Charites—Graces

1219—ichthys—fish; Poseidon

1224—icthyes—fishes; Poseideon—the 6th month

1225—Hector

1244—hierophantes—initiating priest

1247—Argeiphontes—swift-appearer (Hermes)

1260—Solomon; upsilon (name spelled out); the number of days the woman of the Apocalypse was to be nourished in the wilderness

1263—gnosis—knowledge

1264—the number of Crowley's proposed book on "Greek qabala"

1265—En arche en ho Logos—"In the beginning was the Word" (John 1:1)

1270—moly—a magical herb

1271—boopis Hera—ox-eyed Hera; stauros—cross

1272—presbyteroi—elders

1273—epistrophe—wheeling about, turning back

1275—Orpheus

1276—Achilleus (Achilles)

1285—Babylon

1289—Hephaistos

1294—the seven vowels of the Greek alphabet

1297—Hermes Trismegistos (st = 6)

1298—kosmos noetos—intelligible world

1299—Hecatombion—the 1st month of the Greek calendar

1304—hydor—water

1309—he hodos kai he aletheia kai he zoe—the way and the truth and the life (John 14:6)

1310—Anthropos—man, human being; physis—nature

1316—eucharis—graceful, lovely; rhomsaia distomos—two-edged sword

1326—stephanos—crown

1335—thaumatourgia—thaumaturgy

1348—pneuma tes alethaias—spirit of truth

1349—dadouchos—torch-bearer

1352—Teletarchai

1366—O phalle—O phallus; phallus + kteis—penis + vagina

1380—Babylon he megale—Babylon the great; Maimacterion—the 5th month

1383—trigonon—triangle

1386—hypsistos (st=6)—most high; seiriokautos—scorched by the heat of Sirius

1392—eucharistos (st = 6)—thankful

1400—proton—first

1408—Apo pantos kakodaimonos—Away, all evil spirits; soter—savior

1416—soteira—savior (feminine)

1421—archiereus—high priest

1432—Alastor

1438—trismegistos—thrice-greatest

1440—Destaphiton—divine name used by Aurum Solis

1451—Achamoth—the fallen Sophia; aphron—fool

1459—chthon—earth

1461—Apollyon, the angel of the bottomless pit; hypostasis—foundation, reality

1462—presbyteros—elder

1478—Chrestos—the Great Just One; psephos—stone, pebble

1479—Odysseus

1480—Christos

1500—phos—light

1505—cheimon—winter

1506—Elaphebolion—the 9th month

1510—ichor—divine blood

1512—apocalypsis—apocalypse

1514—hydrochoos—water carrier (Aquarius)

1518—Ioseph—Joseph

1523—mystagogos (st = 6)—priest of the mysteries

1525—Synoches

1530—Porphyry

1533—Anthesterion—the 8th month

1540—Plotinus

1544—glaukopis—bright-eyed

1550—protos—first

1551—archon—leader, ruler, chief; Charon; patroos—paternal

1572—to A kai to O—the Alpha and the Omega

1574—Metageitnion—the 2nd month

1580—ischyros—strong, mighty

1581—Pistis Sophia—"faith-wisdom"

1585—Christe eleison—Christ have mercy upon us

1615—tessara zoa—four living creatures

1620—glaukopis Athene—bright-eyed Athena

1621—sphragizo—seal

1624—nephelegereta Zeus—cloud-gatherer Zeus

1653—gnostikos—gnostic

1659—Klotho

1691—Amyntor—defender, avenger

1718—to pneuma tes alethaias—the spirit of truth

1721—kosmokrator—ruler of the world

1748—philetor—lover

1758—isopsephos—equal numerical values of words

1770—to proton—The First

1780—Onnophris

1791—Hermes Trismegistos

1794—Enosichthon—earth-shaker (Poseidon)

1804—Eurymedon

1805—eulogemene su en gynaizin—"Blessed art thou among women" (Luke 1:28); theos phos esti (st = 6)—God is light (I John 1:5)

1822—Pantokrator—the almighty

1834—protos theos—first god

1874—Iesous Christos (st = 6)—Jesus Christ

1880—hypsistos—most high

1886—eucharistos—thankful; ho kyrios meta sou—"The Lord is with thee" (Luke 1:28)

1893—Terpsichore—Muse of Dance

1913—Phoebus Apollo (Phoibos Apollon)

1930—Scirophorion—the 12th month

1931—Aionos Kyrios—lord of the ages

1934—huios tou theou—Son of God

1946—basileus basileon—King of Kings

1951—Kalypso—Calypso

1953—philetores—lovers

1963—polytimos margarites—pearl beyond price

2017—mystagogos—priest of the mysteries

2030—Mounichion—the 10th month

2050—Typhon

2059—agape sou he prote—your first love (Rev. 2:4)

2095—pater ho en tois ouranois—Father in heaven

2098—phos to alethinon—the true light (John 1:9)

2120—photismos—enlightening

2141—psephos leukes—white stone (Rev. 2:17)

2161—Pyanopsion—the 4th month

2182—Ego eimi he hodos kai he aletheia kai he zoe—"I am the way and the truth and the life" (John 14:6)

2191—apolytrosis—redemption

2232—Sophia Achamoth

2241—Autophytos—self-begtting—the fifth aeon of the decad

2277—rhododactylos Eos—rosy-fingered dawn

2288—stephanos asteron (st = 6)—a crown of stars

2290—Ioannes ho Baptistes—John the Baptist

2299—theos phos esti—God is light (I John 1:5)

2308—Poseideon deuteros—Second Poseideon, the intercalary month

2310—psychopompos—psychopomp

2368—Iesous Christos (Jesus Christ)

2409—pantos psyche—Soul of the All, World Soul

2440—phosphoros—bringing light, morning star

2486—Oros ton Elaion—Mount of Olives

2605—pater mou ho en tois ouranois—my Father in heaven

2617—polymetis Odysseus—Odysseus of many counsels

2655—chaire kecharitomene—"Hail, one full of grace" (Luke 1:28); pater humon ho en tois ouranois—your Father in heaven

2764—he meter ton pornon—the mother of harlots (Babylon)

2782—stephanos asteron—a crown of stars

2880—basileia ton ouranon—kingdom of heaven

2888—he basileia ton ouranon—the kingdom of heaven

2941—eulogemenos ho karpos tes koilias sou—"Blessed is the fruit of thy womb" (Luke 1:42)

2960—huios tou anthropou—Son of Man

3023—phos tes zoes—light of life (John 8:12)

3070—phos tou kosmou—light of the world (John 8:12)

3151—bdelugma tes eremoseos—abomination of desolation; kleidos tou hadou kai tou thanatou—keys of hell and death

3162—hai kleides tou hadou kai tou thanatou—the keys of hell and death (Rev. 1:18)

3410—to phos en te skotia phainei—"the light shineth in darkness" (John 1:5)

3659—Oudeis erchetai pros ton Patera ei me di emou—"No one cometh unto the Father, but by me" (John 14:6)

4451—ego tas kleis tou hadou kai tou thanatou—"I hold the keys of hell and death" (Rev. 1:18)

Bibliography

Andrews, Ted. *Imagick: The Magick of Images, Paths and Dance*. St. Paul, MN: Llewellyn Publications, 1989.

Ashcroft–Nowicki, Dolores. *The Ritual Magic Workbook*. Wellingborough, Northamptonshire, UK: The Aquarian Press, 1986.

Ashcroft–Nowicki, Dolores. *First Steps in Ritual*. Wellingborough, Northamptonshire, UK: The Aquarian Press, 1990.

Asimov, Isaac. *Asimov's Guide to the Bible—Volume Two: The New Testament*. New York: Avon Books, 1971, copyright 1969.

Barrett, Francis. *The Magus*. Secaucus, NJ: The Citadel Press, 1967 (original pub. in 1801).

Blavatsky, H. P. *Isis Unveiled*. Pasadena, CA: Theosophical University Press, 1976, 2 volumes (original pub. in 1877).

Bulfinch, Thomas. *Bulfinch's Mythology*. New York: The Modern Library, no date.

Burkert, Walter. *Greek Religion*. Cambridge, MA: Harvard University Press, 1985.

Burt, Kathleen. *Archetypes of the Zodiac*. At. Paul, MN: Llewellyn Publications, 1988.

Campbell, Joseph. *The Masks of God: Occidental Mythology*. New York: The Viking Press, 1964.

Campbell, Joseph. *The Hero with a Thousand Faces*. Princeton, NJ: Princeton University Press, 2nd edition, 1968.

Campbell, Joseph, editor. *The Mysteries: Papers from the Eranos Yearbooks*. Princeton, NJ: Princeton University Press, 1978, copyright 1955.

Copleston, Frederick. *A History of Philosophy: Book One*. New York: Doubleday and Co., Inc., 1985.

Crowley, Aleister. *777 and Other Qabalistic Writings of Aleister Crowley*. ed. Israel Regardie. York Beach, ME: Samuel Weiser, Inc., 1973.

Crowley, Aleister. *Magick*. ed. John Symonds and Kenneth Grant. York Beach, ME: Samuel Weiser, Inc., 1974.

Cumont, Franz. *Astrology and Religion Among the Greeks and Romans*. New York: Dover Publications, Inc., 1960 (reprint of 1912 edition).

de Camp, L. Sprague. *Lovecraft: A Biography*. New York: Doubleday and Co., Inc., 1975.

Denning, Melita, and Phillips, Osborne. *Mysteria Magica*. St. Paul, MN: Llewellyn Publications, 1986.

Denning, Melita, and Phillips, Osborne. *The Sword and the Serpent*. St. Paul, MN: Llewellyn Publications, 1988.

Denning and Phillips. *Planetary Magick*. St. Paul, MN: Llewellyn Publications, 1989.

Denning, Melita, and Phillips, Osborne. *The Foundations of High Magick*. St. Paul, MN: Llewellyn Publications, 1991.

Dodds, E. R. *The Greeks and the Irrational*. Berkeley, CA: University of California Press, 1956.

Fideler, David R. "The Passion of Sophia," *Gnosis Magazine* #1, Fall/Winter 1985, pp. 16-22.

Flowers, S. Edred. *Fire & Ice: Magical Teachings of Germany's Greatest Secret Occult Order*. St. Paul, MN: Llewellyn Publications, 1990

Frazer, Sir James George. *The Golden Bough: A Study in Magic and Religion*. I Volume Abridged Edition. New York: The Macmillan Company, 1958, copyright 1922.

Godolphin, F. R. B., editor. *Great Classical Myths*. New York: The Modern Library, 1964.

Goodrich, Norma Lorre. *Priestesses*. New York: Franklin Watts, 1989

Graves, Robert. *The Greek Myths*. New York: George Braziller, Inc., 1959.

Graves, Robert. *The White Goddess*. New York: Farrar, Straus and Giroux, 1966.

Green, Jay P., Sr., ed. & trans. *The Interlinear Bible: Greek/ English – Volume IV: The New Testament*. Grand Rapids, MI: Baker Book House, 1980.

Grimal, Pierre. *The Concise Dictionary of Classical Mythology.* ed. Stephen Kershaw. trans. A. R. Maxwell-Hyslop. Oxford, U.K.: Basil Blackwell Ltd., 1990.

Grimal, Pierre. "Greece: Myth and Logic," in *Larousse World Mythology.* Pierre Grimal, editor. New York: Excalibur Books, 1965.

Guthrie, Kenneth Sylvan. *The Pythagorean Sourcebook and Library.* Grand Rapids, MI: Phanes Press, 1987.

Guthrie, W. K. C. *The Greeks and Their Gods.* Boston, MA: Beacon Press, 1950.

Guthrie, W. K. C. *Orpheus and Greek Religion.* New York: W. W. Norton & Company, Inc., 1966.

Hall, Manly P. *The Secret Teachings of All Ages.* Los Angeles, CA: The Philosophical Research Society, Inc., 1977.

Hamilton, Edith. *Mythology: Timeless Tales of Gods and Heroes.* New York: New American Library, 1989, copyright 1940, 1942.

Hamilton, Edith, and Huntington Cairns, editors. *The Collected Dialogues of Plato Including the Letters.* Princeton, NJ: Princeton University Press, 1964.

Hesiod. *The Homeric Hymns and Homerica.* trans. Hugh G. Evelyn-White. Cambridge, MA: Harvard University Press, 1914, 1982.

Homer. *The Iliad.* trans. A. T. Murray. Cambridge, MA: Harvard University Press, 1976, 2 volumes.

Homer. *The Odyssey.* trans. A. T. Murray. Cambridge, MA: Harvard University Press, 1966, 2 volumes.

The Homeric Hymns. trans. Charles Boer. Dallas, TX: Spring Publications, Inc., 1970.

Hope, Murry. *Practical Greek Magic.* Wellingborough, Northamptonshire, UK: The Aquarian Press, 1985.

Iamblichus. *On the Mysteries.* trans. Thomas Taylor. San Diego, CA: Wizards Bookshelf, 1984.

Idries Shah. *The Sufis.* New York: Anchor Books (Doubleday & Company, Inc.), 1971.

James, Geoffrey, ed. & trans. *The Enochian Evocation of Dr. John Dee.* Gillette, NJ: Heptangle Books, 1988.

Jaynes, Julian. *The Origin of Consciousness in the Breakdown of the Bicameral Mind.* Boston, MA: Houghton Mifflin Company, 1976.

Jonas, Hans. *The Gnostic Religion: The Message of the Alien God and the Beginnings of Christianity.* Boston, MA: Beacon Press, revised second edition, 1963.

Kane, J. P. "Greece," in *An Illustrated Encyclopedia of Mythology.* Richard Cavendish, editor. New York: Crescent Books, 1980.

Kerenyi, Karl. *Athene: Virgin and Mother in Greek Religion.* trans. Murray Stein. Dallas, TX: Spring Publications, Inc., 1978.

Kerenyi, Karl. *Goddesses of Sun and Moon.* trans. Murray Stein. Dallas, TX: Spring Publications, Inc., 1978.

King, C. W. *The Gnostics and Their Remains.* San Diego, CA: Wizards Bookshelf, 1982 (reprint of 1887 edition).

Knight, Gareth. *The Rose Cross and the Goddess.* New York: Destiny Books, 1985.

Kraig, Donald Michael. *Modern Magick.* St. Paul, MN: Llewellyn Publications, 1988.

Liddell, Henry George, and Scott, Robert. *A Greek–English Lexicon, with 1968 supplement.* Oxford, UK: Oxford at the Clarendon Press, 1989 (orig. 1843).

Lovecraft, H. P. *Juvenilia: 1895–1905.* ed. S. T. Joshi. West Warwick, RI: Necronomicon Press, 1984.

Lovecraft, H. P. *Dagon and Other Macabre Tales.* Sauk City, WI: Arkham House Publishers, Inc., corrected fifth printing, 1987 (includes "Poetry and the Gods").

Luck, Georg. *Arcana Mundi: Magic and the Occult in the Greek and Roman Worlds.* Baltimore, MD: The Johns Hopkins University Press, 1985.

Marinus of Samaria. *The Life of Proclus; or, Concerning Happiness (Proklos e peri eudaimonias).* trans. Kenneth S. Guthrie. Grand Rapids, MI: Phanes Press, 1986.

Mathers, S. Liddell MacGregor, trans. & ed. *The Key of Solomon the King (Clavicula Solomonis).* York Beach, ME: Samuel Weiser, Inc., 1984 (first published 1888).

McLean, Adam. *The Triple Goddess: An Exploration of the Archetypal Feminine.* Grand Rapids, MI: Phanes Press, 1989.

Mead, G. R. S. *Fragments of a Faith Forgotten.* New Hyde Park, NY: University Books, 1960.

New Larousse Encyclopedia of Mythology. intro. Robert Graves. New York: Crescent Books, 1989, 1968 edition.

Olson, Carl, editor. *The Book of the Goddess: Past and Present.* New York: The Crossroad Publishing Company, 1983.

Pagels, Elaine. *The Gnostic Gospels.* New York: Vintage Books, 1981, copyright 1979.

Paris, Ginette. *Pagan Grace: Dionysos, Hermes, and Goddess Memory in Daily Life.* trans. Joanna Mott. Dallas, TX: Spring Publications, Inc., 1990.

Plotinus. trans. A. H. Armstrong. Cambridge, MA: Harvard University Press, 1988, 7 volumes.

Pomeroy, Sarah B. *Women in Hellenistic Egypt: From Alexander to Cleopatra.* Detroit, MI: Wayne State University Press, 1990.

Porphyry's Launching Points to the Realm of Mind: An Introduction to the Neoplatonic Philosophy of Plotinus (Pros ta noeta aphorismoi). trans. Kenneth Guthrie. Grand Rapids, MI: Phanes Press, 1988.

Regardie, Israel. *The Golden Dawn.* St. Paul, MN: Llewellyn Publications, 6th edition, 1989.

Regardie, Israel. *Ceremonial Magic.* Wellingborough, Northampton-shire, UK: Aquarian Press, 1980.

Richardson, N. J. "Eleusis," in *Man, Myth & Magic: An Illustrated Encylopedia of the Supernatural.* Volume 6. Richard Cavendish, editor. New York: Marshall Cavendish Corporation, 1970.

Robinson, James M., editor. *The Nag Hammadi Library.* San Francisco, CA: Harper & Row, Publishers, 1988.

Sharman–Burke, Juliet, and Greene, Liz. *The Mythic Tarot.* New York: Simon & Schuster, Inc. (A Fireside Book), 1986.

Smith, F. Kinchin, and Melluish, T. W. *Greek.* Sevenoaks, Kent, UK: Hodder and Stoughton (Teach Yourself Books), 1968.

Steinbrecher, Edwin C. *The Inner Guide Meditation.* York Beach, ME: Samuel Weiser, Inc., 1988.

Stone, Merlin. *When God Was a Woman.* San Diego, CA: Harcourt Brace Jovanovich, 1976.

Taylor, Thomas. *The Hymns of Orpheus.* Los Angeles, CA: The Philosophical Research Society, Inc., 1981 (facsimile reprint of 1792 edition).

Tyrrell, Wm. Blake. *Amazons: A Study in Athenian Mythmaking.* Baltimore, MD: The Johns Hopkins University Press, 1989.

Waite, Arthur Edward. *A New Encyclopaedia of Freemasonry.* New York: Weathervane Books, no date, copyright 1970.

Wallis, R. T. *Neoplatonism,* London, UK: Gerald Duckworth & Company Limited, 1972.

Wilson, Robert Anton. *The New Inquisition: Irrational Rationalism and the Citadel of Science.* Phoenix, AZ: Falcon Press, 1987.

Wolfe, Gene. *Soldier of the Mist.* New York: Tom Doherty Associates (TOR), 1986.

Wolfe, Gene. *Soldier of Arete.* New York: Tom Doherty Associates (TOR), 1989.

Zeller, Eduard. *Outlines of the History of Greek Philosophy.* revised by Wilhelm Nestle, trans. L. R. Palmer. New York: Dover Publications, Inc., 1980 (reprint of 1931 edition).

STAY IN TOUCH

On the following pages you will find listed, with their current prices, some of the books now available on related subjects. Your book dealer stocks most of these, and will stock new titles in the Llewellyn series as they become available. We urge your patronage.

However, to obtain our full catalog, to keep informed of new titles as they are released and to benefit from informative articles and helpful news, you are invited to write for our bi-monthly news magazine/catalog. A sample copy is free, and it will continue coming to you at no cost as long as you are an active mail customer. Or you may keep it coming for a full year with a donation of just $5.00 in U.S.A. & Canada ($20.00 overseas, first class mail). Many bookstores also have *The Llewellyn New Times* available to their customers. Ask for it.

Stay in touch! In *The Llewellyn New Times'* pages you will find news and reviews of new books, tapes and services, announcements of meetings and seminars, articles helpful to our readers, news of authors, advertising of products and services, special money-making opportunities, and much more.

The Llewellyn New Times
P.O. Box 64383-Dept. 285, St. Paul, MN 55164-0383, U.S.A.
• • •

TO ORDER BOOKS AND TAPES

If your book dealer does not have the books described on the following pages readily available, you may order them direct from the publisher by sending full price in U.S. funds, plus $1.50 for postage and handling for orders *under* $10.00; $3.00 for orders *over* $10.00. There are no postage and handling charges for orders over $50. UPS Delivery: We ship UPS whenever possible. Delivery guaranteed. Provide your street address as UPS does not deliver to P.O. Boxes. UPS to Canada requires a $50 minimum order. Allow 4–6 weeks for delivery. Orders outside the U.S.A. and Canada: Airmail—add retail price of book; add $5 for each non-book item (tapes, etc.); add $1 per item for surface mail.

FOR GROUP STUDY AND PURCHASE

Because there is a great deal of interest in group discussion and study of the subject matter of this book, we feel that we should encourage the adoption and use of this particular book by such groups by offering a special "quantity" price to group leaders or "agents."

Our Special Quantity Price for a minimum order of five copies of *Light in Extension* is $38.85 cash-with-order. This price includes postage and handling within the United States. Minnesota residents must add 6.5% sales tax. For additional quantities, please order in multiples of five. For Canadian and foreign orders, add postage and handling charges as above. Credit card (VISA, Master Card, American Express) orders are accepted. Charge card orders only may be phoned free ($15.00 minimum order) within the U.S.A. or Canada by dialing 1-800-THE-MOON. Customer service calls dial 1-612-291-1970. Mail Orders to:

LLEWELLYN PUBLICATIONS
P.O. Box 64383-Dept. 285 / St. Paul, MN 55164-0383, U.S.A.

GODWIN'S CABALISTIC ENCYCLOPEDIA
by David Godwin

This is the most complete correlation of Hebrew and English ideas ever offered. It is a dictionary of Cabalism arranged, with definitions, alphabetically, alphabetically in Hebrew, and numerically. With this book the practicing Cabalist or student no longer needs access to a large number of books on mysticism, magic and the occult in order to trace down the basic meanings, Hebrew spellings, and enumerations of the hundreds of terms, words, and names that are included in this book.

This book includes: all of the two–letter root words found in Biblical Hebrew, the many names of God, the Planets, the Astrological Signs, Numerous Angels, the Shem ha-Mephorash, the Spirits of the *Goetia*, the correspondences of the 32 Paths, a comparison of the Tarot and the Cabala, a guide to Hebrew Pronunciation, and a complete edition of Aleister Crowley's valuable book *Sepher Sephiroth*.

Here is a book that is a must for the shelf of all Magicians, Cabalists, Astrologers, Tarot students, Thelemites, and those with any interest at all in the spiritual aspects of our universe.

0–87542–292–6, 500 pgs., 6 x 9, softcover $15.00

THE GOLDEN DAWN
by Israel Regardie

The Original Account of the Teachings, Rites and Ceremonies of the Hermetic Order of the Golden Dawn as revealed by Israel Regardie, with further revision, expansion, and additional notes by Regardie, Cris Monnastre, and others. Expanded with an index of more than 100 pages!

Originally published in four bulky volumes of some 1200 pages, this 6th Revised and Enlarged Edition has been entirely reset in modern, less space-consuming type, in half the pages (while retaining the original pagination in marginal notation for reference) for greater ease and use.

Also included are Initiation Ceremonies, important rituals for consecration and invocation, methods of meditation and magical working based on the Enochian Tablets, studies in the Tarot, and the system of Qabalistic Correspondences that unite the World's religions and magical traditions into a comprehensive and practical whole.

This volume is designed as a study and practice curriculum suited to both group and private practice. Meditation upon, and following with the Active Imagination, the Initiation Ceremonies is fully experiential without need of participation in group or lodge. A very complete reference encyclopedia of Western Magick.

0–87542–663–8, 803 pgs., 6 x 9, illus. $19.95

PLANETARY MAGICK
by Denning & Phillips

This book is filled with guidelines and rites for powerful magical action. There are rites for the individual magician, rites for the magical group. The rites herein are given *in full,* and are revealed for the first time. *Planetary Magick* provides a full grasp of the root system of Western Magick, a system which evolved in Babylonia and became a principal factor in the development of Qabalah.

By what means do the planetary powers produce change in people's moods, actions, circumstances? As the ancient script has it: "As above, so below." "The powers which exist in the cosmos have their focal points also in you. The directing force of Mind which operates in and beyond the cosmos is the very source of your inner being. By directing the planetary powers as they exist within your psyche—in the Deep Mind—you can achieve inner harmony, happiness, prosperity, love. You can help others. You can win your heart's desire.

The rites of Planetary Magick will powerfully open up level after level of the psyche, balancing and strengthening its perceptions and powers.
0-87542-193-8, 400 pgs., 6 x 9, color plates $19.95

MODERN MAGICK
by Donald Michael Kraig

Modern Magick is the most comprehensive step-by-step introduction to the art of ceremonial magic ever offered. The eleven lessons in this book will guide you from the easiest of rituals and the construction of your magickal tools through the highest forms of magick: designing your own rituals and doing pathworking. Along the way you will learn the secrets of the Kabalah in a clear and easy-to-understand manner. You will also discover the true secrets of invocation (channeling) and evocation, and the missing information that will finally make the ancient *grimoires,* such as the **Keys of Solomon**, not only comprehensible, but usable.

Modern Magick is designed so anyone can use it, and is the perfect guidebook for students and classes. It will also help to round out the knowledge of long-time practitioners of the magickal arts.
0-87542-324-8, 608 pgs., 6 x 9, illus. $14.95

ABOUT THE AUTHOR

Emese "Meshi" Parker is a registered nurse, board-certified women's health nurse practitioner (NP), and certified perinatal mental health specialist. After completing bachelor of science degrees in exercise science and nursing, Parker earned her master of science in nursing from Boston College, and master of public health from Johns Hopkins Bloomberg School of Public Health.

Parker has over twenty years of experience in healthcare, specializing in women's health since 2008. She has partnered with women of all ages in various Ob-Gyn settings, advocating for them as they navigate their distinct journeys through life. In her current role as women's health NP, Parker strives to promote health and wellness through compassionate, holistic care, while empowering women to make informed decisions about their bodies. Her devotion to improving care for the underserved has fueled her involvement in public health leadership positions with organizations like the University of California San Francisco and the U.S. Health Resources and Services Administration's Health Disparities Collaborative.

Parker lives in California, where she is a wife and mother to three mischievous children. She enjoys spending time with her family and friends, road-biking, getting outdoors, playing piano, and traveling.

tocarrywonder.com